Ethnicity and the Persistence of Inequality: The Case of Peru

Conflict, Inequality and Ethnicity
Series Editor: Frances Stewart, Professor of Development Economics and Director, CRISE, University of Oxford, UK

The series focuses on the relationships between inequality, human security and ethnicity emanating from the work of the Centre for Research on Inequality, Human Security and Ethnicity (CRISE), UK. Some books cover general issues such as mobilization, affirmative action, the role and management of natural resources, and post-conflict policies; others are rooted in the experience of different regions, for example South East Asia, West Africa and Latin America.

The series is unique since it is united by interest in an unusual perspective – that of exploring these issues in relation to horizontal inequalities or inequalities among groups. While each book stands alone, they also have unity of approach and share some basic ideas. The publications from the *Conflict, Inequality and Ethnicity* series will be highly relevant to students, academics and policy-makers working on questions of contemporary conflict.

Titles include:

Frances Stewart (*editor*)
HORIZONTAL INEQUALITIES AND CONFLICT
Understanding Group Violence in Multiethnic Societies

Rosemary Thorp and Maritza Paredes
ETHNICITY AND THE PERSISTENCE OF INEQUALITY
The Case of Peru

Forthcoming:

Graham Brown, Arnim Langer and Frances Stewart (*editors*)
DEBATING AFFIRMATIVE ACTION
International and Interdisciplinary Perspectives

Yvan Guichaoua (*editor*)
UNDERSTANDING COLLECTIVE POLITICAL VIOLENCE

Arnim Langer, Frances Stewart and Rajesh Venugopal (*editors*)
POST-CONFLICT RESOLUTION AND HORIZONTAL INEQUALITIES

Conflict, Inequality and Ethnicity
Series Standing Order ISBNs 978–0–230–24608–9 (hardback) and 978–0–230–24708–6 (paperback)
(*outside North America only*)

You can receive future titles in this series as they are published by placing a standing order. Please contact your bookseller or, in case of difficulty, write to us at the address below with your name and address, the title of the series and one of the ISBNs quoted above.

Customer Services Department, Macmillan Distribution Ltd, Houndmills, Basingstoke, Hampshire RG21 6XS, England, UK

Ethnicity and the Persistence of Inequality

The Case of Peru

Rosemary Thorp
and
Maritza Paredes

palgrave
macmillan

First published 2010 by
PALGRAVE MACMILLAN

Palgrave Macmillan in the UK is an imprint of Macmillan Publishers Limited, registered in England, company number 785998, of Houndmills, Basingstoke, Hampshire RG21 6XS.

Palgrave Macmillan in the US is a division of St Martin's Press LLC, 175 Fifth Avenue, New York, NY 10010.

Palgrave Macmillan is the global academic imprint of the above companies and has companies and representatives throughout the world.

Palgrave® and Macmillan® are registered trademarks in the United States, the United Kingdom, Europe and other countries.

ISBN 978–0–230–28000–7

This book is printed on paper suitable for recycling and made from fully managed and sustained forest sources. Logging, pulping and manufacturing processes are expected to conform to the environmental regulations of the country of origin.

A catalogue record for this book is available from the British Library.

Library of Congress Cataloging-in-Publication Data
Thorp, Rosemary.
Ethnicity and the persistence of inequality : the case of Peru / Rosemary Thorp and Maritza Paredes.
p. cm. — (Conflict, inequality and ethnicity)
ISBN 978–0–230–28000–7 (hardback)
1. Group identity—Peru—History. 2. Ethnicity—Peru—History. 3. Equality—Peru—History. 4. Social conflict—Peru—History. I. Paredes, Maritza. II. Title.
HN 350.Z9S675 2010
305.898'085—dc22 2010027568

10 9 8 7 6 5 4 3 2 1
19 18 17 16 15 14 13 12 11 10

Printed and bound in Great Britain by
CPI Antony Rowe, Chippenham and Eastbourne

For Tim and José Carlos

Contents

List of Tables

List of Figures, Map and Box

Figures

Map

Box

Preface

This book is about inequality and in particular the inequalities suffered by the Andean indigenous population. It focuses on the explanation of the persistence and depth of that inequality by exploring the dynamics of the interrelations between politics, economics, geography and culture, over several centuries.

The book is the realization of a dream in the head of one of the authors for a long time. When the writing of an economic history of Peru since 1890 was under way, in the 1970s (Thorp and Bertram 1978), it took much time and creativity to trace out the analysis of the modern export economy, its domination by the international market, and the difficult birth and youth of industrialization, and as young scholars the authors had neither the contacts nor the audacity to embark on a major interdisciplinary effort. The result was a book essentially focused on the modern economy and its international economic relations, with very little space for the interrelations between economics and politics and for the institutions that rule the lives of ordinary people, in particular indigenous people of the Sierra and Selva. The present book is an attempt to complement the earlier book. Its elaboration has demanded a challenging but fruitful equal interdisciplinary dialogue between both authors, a creative effort to learn from people's accounts of their lives, archives, surveys and the process of tracing the history. All this new enterprise has required extensive collaboration to make it possible.

As a result we owe many debts. First, we owe a special debt to two close collaborators in Peru who became co-authors of four important chapters. Carlos Contreras worked with us in the writing of the chapters on the Colony and Independence up to 1960, and his deep knowledge of the literature and considerable wisdom gave us confidence in the rich field of early Peruvian political economy. Adolfo Figueroa was the creator of the empirical measurements used to estimate group inequalities, and elaborated the conceptual framework used in Chapter 4. He also was our constant inspiration, believing in our project from the first conversation.

Other close collaborators in Peru included Ismael Muñoz, who took over from Adolfo the organization of the Peruvian group of researchers working with us at the Catholic University in Lima, and we worked together in the collective action studies which have been written up separately but also give depth and life to Chapter 8. David Sulmont carried out the survey of perceptions of identity which provided rich primary material for Chapters 2 and 3, and he is the author of the methodological appendix to Chapter 2. His own contribution can be found on the CRISE website. Manuel Barrón worked with Adolfo Figueroa on group inequalities and later with us on the analysis of the gender dimension of the data. Andrea Portugal wrote a paper on the origins of Sendero which has contributed greatly to the analysis of Chapter 7. Gisela Cánepa provided a working paper with an insightful analysis of the subtleties of ethnicity in Peru. Juan Ansión wrote a useful paper on education and Manuel Piqueras wrote another on ethnicity in the army and police. Javier Jimenez, Paola Lazarte and Denisse Rodríguez carried out research assistance. In Oxford, Tony Jack worked patiently and perseveringly on the bibliography. Nigel James of the Bodleian assisted us with the map of Peru.

Second, the book has been written as part of a wider team effort at thinking about ethnicity, inequality and the relation to insecurity. This has taken place in the context of a Research Centre funded by DFID, the overseas aid arm of the British government, whose financial support we warmly acknowledge. The Centre is CRISE, the Centre for Research on Inequality, Security and Ethnicity, based in Oxford University and led until 2010 by Dr Frances Stewart. The theoretical and comparative work carried out by the Centre is reflected in its website and very well in Stewart (2008). The driving concept has been inequalities between groups, or 'horizontal' inequalities, to distinguish the concept from the orthodox 'vertical' inequality – that between individuals. Most importantly it refers to all dimensions of inequality, not merely economic. We have used this framework, though we tend to prefer the label of 'group' inequality, since in Latin America the overlap of ethnic and class inequality is such that there is nothing intuitively 'horizontal' about the resulting inequality. We are grateful to all our colleagues in CRISE for support and good company, to Nicola Shepard and Jo Boyce for administrative support, and in particular we thank Frances Stewart and Corinne Caumartin for invaluable comments.

Other colleagues in the wider community have played their role. We acknowledge important and helpful comments from Brooke Larson at Stony Brook on Chapter 5, from Gonzalo Portocarrero at the Catholic University and from an anonymous reader for Palgrave Macmillan. A very large number of Peruvians – scholars, policy-makers, peasants, leaders and social promoters – patiently talked to us on many occasions. The Catholic University gave us facilities and the space for workshops.

Then we each owe a debt to the other. We have each learnt enormously from each other in the demanding work of trying to think in an interdisciplinary manner. And finally, our families tolerated our obsession and our absences, and gave all sorts of practical help. To them we dedicate the result.

ROSEMARY THORP
MARITZA PAREDES

List of Abbreviations

AEMET	Asociación Gremial de Empresarios Metalmecánicos (Metalworking Businessmen's Association)
AP	Acción Popular (Popular Action)
APRA	Alianza Popular Revolucionaria Americana (American Popular and Revolutionary Alliance)
BHP	Broken Hill Proprietary
CAA	Community Aid Abroad
CAN	Comunidad Andina de Naciones (Andean Community of Nations)
CAPs	Cooperativas Agrarias del Perú (Agricultural Cooperatives of Peru)
CCP	Confederación Campesina el Perú (Peasant Confederation of Peru)
CODELCO	Corporación Nacional del Cobre de Chile (National Corporation of Copper of Chile)
CONACAMI	Confederación Nacional de Comunidades de Perú Afectadas por la Minería (National Confederation of Communities in Peru Affected by Mining)
CORECAMI	Coordinadora Regional de Comunidades del Perú Afectadas por la Minería (Regional Coordinator of Communities in Peru Affected by Mining)
CP	Comedor Popular (People's Kitchens)
CVR	Comisión de la Verdad y la Reconciliación (Truth and Reconciliation Commission)
FONCODES	Fondo de Cooperación para el Desarrollo del Peru (Cooperation Fund for the Development of Peru)
FOVIDA	Fomento de la Vida ONG (Fostering Life NGO)
FUCAE	Federación Unificada de Campesinos de Espinar (Unified Peasant Federation of Espinar)
GDP	Gross Domestic Product
Ha	Hectare
HIs	Horizontal Inequalities

INDECOPI	Instituto Nacional de Defensa de la Competencia y de la Protección de la Propiedad Intelectual (National Institute of Defence of Competition and of Protection of Intellectual Property)
INTI	Movimiento Independiente Regional Inti
IU	Izquierda Unida (United Left)
JNE	Jurado Nacional de Elecciones (National Electal Jury)
MINCAP	Movimiento Independiente de Campesinos y Profesionales (Independent Movement of Peasants and Professionals)
N	Number
NGO	Non-Governmental Organization
PEMTEC	Pequeña Empresa Tecnología y Sociedad (Small Business, Technology and Society)
PRONAA	Programa Nacional de Asistencia Alimentaria (National Program of Food Assistance)
PYME	Pequeñas y Medianas Empresas (Small and Medium Businesses)
SAIS	Sociedades Agrarias de Interés Social (Agricultural Societies of Social Interest)
SEA	Servicios Educativos del Agustino (Agustino Educational Services)
SERCOTEC	Servicio de Cooperación Tecnica de Chile (Chile's Technical Cooperation Service)
SUNAD	Superintendencia Nacional de Aduanas (National Customs Superintendency)
SUNAT	Superintendencia Nacional de Administracion Tributaria (National Superintendency of Tax Administration)
UNCP	Universidad Nacional del Centro del Perú (National University of the Centre of Peru)
UNI	Universidad Nacional de Ingeniería (National University of Engineering)
UNMSM	Universidad Nacional Mayor de San Marcos (Major National University of San Marcos)
UNSCH	Universidad Nacional de San Cristobal de Huamanga (National University of San Cristobal of Huamanga)
VR	Vanguardia Revolucionaria (Revolutionary Vanguard)

1
Introduction

As we were planning the outline of this book, the popular Lima 'Café del Mar' was closed by the authorities on the grounds of ethnic discrimination in its clientele: an emblematic event to signal that in Peru the issue of ethnicity is on the table in a new way since 2000. This and other such examples suggest a wind of change, which did indeed begin to blow in Peru with the new century. In 2000 the *de facto* dictatorship of Alberto Fujimori came to a surprising end in a welter of exposure of corruption, some of it caught on tape and played on television for all to see. The new atmosphere was embodied in the transition government of Paniagua, mandated to take the country through to elections. As part of the desire for a new beginning, it became possible to look at issues of inequality and even their ethnic component. The government showed an unprecedented zeal for human rights, and within that, a deep concern with the injustices wrought through twelve years of war. Paniagua appointed a Truth and Reconciliation Commission, led by Dr Salomon Lerner, which worked for two years, took numerous testimonies, and produced a magnificent and challenging report in 8000 pages. What is more, by the time the Commission reported, the country had elected its first self-proclaimed *cholo* President, Alejandro Toledo, who chose to hold his inauguration ceremony in Machu Picchu, as a symbolic identification with Peru's Inca past and indigenous present. In the 2006 presidential campaign, the *mestizo* candidate Ollanta Humala based his campaign on the need to assert Peru's indigenous roots (the 'copper peoples' as he said repeatedly), arousing much fear and strong support.[1] He eventually lost.

The story of this book is about the embeddedness of the inequalities thus challenged. It is our strong opinion that only by engaging with the depth of that embeddedness can policies and political support be built that will enable change. We will demonstrate that the embeddedness and extreme nature of overall inequality has much to do with the depth and embeddedness of ethnic inequality. The book also considers the consequences of not so engaging, which include the awful bloodshed and injustices which the Commission was to review. The phenomenon of Sendero Luminoso, the movement which initiated civil war in the early 1980s in the Central Highlands, eventually engulfed one third of the country and finally spread to Lima itself, in some of the worst years of the city's history. We do not view Sendero as 'an ethnic movement', but one which fed on deep ethnic inequalities and injustices, and with terrible consequences for indigenous people. It is not by chance that of the 72,000 people killed in the course of the violence, 74 per cent were of indigenous origin.

The issue of inequality in Latin America between indigenous and non-indigenous is striking, because of its persistence over time in most of the continent (Hall and Patrinos 2006). But indigenous peoples have not been passive. Their mobilization in recent decades around particular issues has given rise to a rich literature. In this literature, Peru is typically presented as an outlier, because, while presenting the persistent ethnic inequality of other cases, ethnicity has not been a salient factor for politicization or mobilization (Van Cott 2005, Yashar 2005).

Concepts, Methods and Literature: 'Group' or 'Horizontal' Inequalities, and a Historical Approach

We consider that a detailed case study is essential to define the role of ethnic inequality in the Peruvian case, since it is significantly different from other Latin American cases but the inequality is no less persistent. Such a case study comprises our basic methodology, using qualitative and quantitative techniques and an interdisciplinary approach. We find a multifaceted approach to be important for our work: the answers are found in the interplay over time of the economic, social, political and geographical aspects of group inequality.

In terms of concepts, to take our analysis forward we use the concept of 'group inequalities', or 'horizontal inequalities' (HIs). This refers to the inequalities between groups of people, rather than simply between individuals, the concept behind most discussions of inequality, sometimes called vertical inequality, hence the adjective 'horizontal' to emphasize the distinction. In the literature from which we are drawing (Stewart 2008), groups are defined, for the purpose of such discussions, by whatever is the salient group identity. The 'salient' identity is that which 'leaps out' – in this case as predominant in awareness and most likely to shape attitudes and behaviour. Usually the salient identity is ethnicity or religion or class, but it may also be that the key inequality is one of gender, age or region, or some blend of more than one. Which identity, or mix, is salient, may be affected by the context and/or shaped by political leaders.

We use both terms, group and horizontal, interchangeably in what follows. We realize that the word 'horizontal' may ring strangely to observers of Peru, since the most relevant group differentiation, by ethnicity, overlaps heavily with class and has no intuitive 'horizontal' characteristic. We would ask the reader to bear in mind that the literature is using the phrase to emphasize the group dimension.

Why use groups as a framework? The discussion above already begins to make this clear. In summary, in the case of Peru, groups help us to think about the persistence of inequality for three principal reasons:

1. Discrimination and prejudice are always in relation to groups. Such attitudes shape institutions over time, shape how identities are perceived and used, and affect distribution through factor markets, through social relations and through politics at every level and in all its forms. All these elements will be important components of our analysis.
2. Thinking in terms of groups draws attention to space. Groups often have a spatial dimension – in Peru this is crucial since the indigenous population has historically been centred in the Highlands, the white-*mestizo* population in the Coast. The interplay between groups and geography and policies reinforcing and building geographical inequality is a key theme explaining the embedding of inequality. Space matters because of the distribution of resources – where natural resources occur and where political resources are concentrated. In Peru migration changes the spatial aspect with time, but it will be a central part of our argument that the interaction between migration and discrimination and prejudice gradually shapes new forms of ethnic identity that are highly significant for the durability of inequality.
3. Groups are central to political behaviour. People typically mobilize or are mobilized in groups. Political inequalities are central to the possibility of mobilizing. Whether a group finds a way to fight its corner, or not, and what instruments get chosen, will have a great deal to do with the evolution of group inequalities, and thus of inequality over time. Recourse to violence, mobilization, or contentious politics

followed by repression may set back the fortunes of the group. In Peru the absence of vigorous indigenous politics appears to be part of the explanation of the persistence of inequality.

Does an 'ethnic' group identity 'matter' in Peru? This is an extremely relevant question for us. The significance that people give to different aspects of their identity varies according to context and time, and they may differentiate themselves – or perceive they are differentiated by others – according to regional, racial, cultural or physical characteristics and so on. However only those divisions that have or may acquire strong social significance – that is, such connotation for their members and for others in society that they influence conduct and welfare in a significant way – are likely to trigger and awaken the consciousness of a group, whether politicized or not. Whether ethnicity is strongly perceived as being socially significant for Peruvians – both by those who may claim themselves 'indigenous' and by those who do not – and how it is significant, has to be part of what we try to answer in the coming chapters.

Interpreting ethnicity: the literature

Social scientists have differed sharply on how to approach the study of ethnicity. Traditionally, the debate has been between primordialists on the one hand and instrumentalists on the other. The primordialist approach has been much discussed (Geertz 1973, Isaacs 1975, and Van de Berghe 1981). Although Geertz and Isaac acknowledge some transformation and fluidity of ethnic identity, they were surprised by the power of ethnic 'endowments' received through birth and childhood and their resilience. The 'overpowering coerciveness' of the group (Geertz 1973: 259) or the 'genuine security' offered by endowed characteristics, and the 'urge to belong' of the individual psyche (Isaacs 1975: 35) are offered as explanations. Most of these approaches were developed in the 1970s. Without doubt primary bonds are powerful and deeply felt, but these approaches do not help us understand why some bonds have become more powerful than others, why new identities are created and bonds reproduced, and how people face these changes. For example, in the Andes of Peru new *mestizo* and *cholo* identities have been created (see De la Cadena 2000 for a brilliant analysis and documentation), but these identities are likely to have different meanings in, for instance, Peru and Bolivia.

Instrumentalists, in contrast, affirm that ethnic identities are strategically chosen and manipulated, and even reconstructed by individuals and ethnic entrepreneurs on the basis of self-interest (Brass 1997: 26), and generally in order to obtain desired patronage goods from the state, land, jobs, or markets (Bates 1971, Bates et al. 1998). These approaches have been mainly used to explain the politicization of ethnic identity and the emergence of ethnic violence. But while these approaches are sometimes useful to explain how ethnic groups mobilize and sustain their campaigns (Laitin 1986, Cohen 1985), they do not answer questions such as why some ethnic ties become more important than others, and how they become the basis for political action at one time rather than another, or why people occasionally act in ways that appear detrimental to their material interests. Moreover they tend to assume that people within the group share preferences and that the boundaries are well established. All of these are very problematic assumptions in Latin America where ethnicity is fluid and changeable over time.

An intermediate perspective is that of social constructivists. This view does not deny that there is a need for some felt differences in conduct, customs, ideology or religion to make it possible for ethnic or other consciousness to develop. In contrast to the extreme instrumentalist view, the fundamental emphasis is on the making and remaking of ethnic boundaries. Benedict Anderson with his 'imagined communities' – an influential and deep historical study of the formation of nationalism – has pushed forward the research on constructive processes. He argues that these political communities are 'imagined because the members of even the smallest nation will never know most of their fellow-members, meet them or even hear of them, yet in the minds of each lives the image of their communion' (p.6). His work, with that of many others who have followed him, has advanced an agenda of careful analysis on how cultural and political communities have come into historical existence, in what forms their meanings have changed over time and why today they have such profound strength (Anderson 1983). Studying this process, some scholars have put more emphasis on processes that have reframed the identity of people – for example, modernization processes (Gellner 1983).

However, there is more than one way of seeing ourselves and the groups to which we belong. We are simultaneously part of a variety of categories, a fact which helps us in our everyday social life. The question is why and how some identities have been stressed over time and have interacted with our capacity to express our identity in one way or another. In Latin America, a rich literature has put emphasis on the development of significant framing institutions around ethnic identity, such as the colonial state, authoritarian corporatist regimes or education policy. De la Cadena (2000), Garcia (2005), Mallon (1995) and Yashar (2005) are substantial and comprehensive examples of this type of study for Latin America, and we draw heavily on these sources.

Although within this view, it seems that identity is a matter of discovery, of our belonging to one or other and often more than one identity, choices and the formation of a collective identity are limited by feasibility. 'The constraints may be especially strict in defining the extent to which we can persuade *others* to take us to be different from (or more than) what they insist on taking us to be' (Sen 2006: 31). In this line, one of the most influential and early contributions to the constructivist approach was that of Barth (1969). He stressed the significance of group interaction for the construction of boundaries. Group identities arise partly from individuals' *own* perceptions of membership of and identity with a particular group – that is, the self-perceptions of those *in* the group – but they are also determined by the perceptions of *those outside the group* about others. At one extreme, where categorization by others is the source of group boundaries, what people themselves feel about their own identities may not be important at all: what matters is what others think they are.

In summary, in almost every case, there is some fluidity and uncertainty about precise group boundaries, which evolve over time in response to circumstances. Moreover, while people can choose which identities are important to them, for the more enduring aspects of their identity they are not free to choose any identity, as it were, 'off the shelf', shifting to whatever seems most convenient at a given moment. Thus, while someone can readily choose to change their social club or abandon it altogether, one's ethnicity cannot be so easily managed. In any particular case, history, the context and the power of institutions shaping and ruling lives will determine the possibilities. In Peru today, someone who is of indigenous origin can choose to define themselves as *mestizo* but they still cannot choose to avoid all racism. It is where there is limited freedom to switch groups that group boundaries are particularly important in terms of creating potential group grievances, and hence in terms of political mobilization. Where people can shift groups in an instantaneous and costless way, then group distinctions and boundaries matter much less.

Ethnicity in Peru

In Peru racial and ethnic mixing has occurred on a significant scale since colonial times, and a majority of the population in certain regions, mainly in the Coast, is of mixed ethnicity. However, this '*mestizaje*', or mixing, has not eliminated the perception of distinctive and hierarchically organized cultural and racial traits by Peruvians; nor has it prevented discriminatory practices based on these traits. The idea that migration, access to education, and the learning of Spanish have created a homogeneous 'mestizo' culture, particularly in the cities, and only regional and class differences remain, is usually associated with another misguided notion: 'indigenous' people only exist in small and dispersed numbers in the hinterlands of the Sierra or in the Amazon, 'frozen in time'. Van Cott (1994) argues that this vision is false. No indigenous people live exactly as their ancestors did 500 years ago, nor have their multiple cultures stayed static in time and place. Indigenous people in Peru have transformed themselves according to the opportunities and constraints they have met, incorporating customs, technologies and ideas from a white-*mestizo*-dominated society. We argue that the idea that when indigenous people enter into contact with 'civilization' they are no longer indigenous is at the heart of the type of discrimination that has created the cultural and psychological barriers preventing indigenous people from organizing politically along ethnic lines. This prejudice is a mechanism that has been historically constructed, reproduced and consolidated in Peru over the years by the institutions built around it. 'Indigenous' is a community identity in the Highlands, and has changed in the cities, just as people from all cultures change. In line with a strong vein of writing in Peruvian social science, we understand the formation of identity as a social construction which happens in time and space, and therefore has a history (Cánepa 2008, 1998; De la Cadena 2000; García 2005).[2]

The embeddedness of group inequality

To explain the embeddedness of groups' inequality this book takes a simple but often forgotten observation: the mechanisms of reproduction of inequalities, the norms and values that sustain particular inequalities across groups, as well as the opportunities for organization and the construction of political identities to challenge these inequalities, have been historically defined, reproduced and consolidated over the years by the institutions built around them. We distinguish institutions from organizations (North 1990). A bank, say, would seem to be an institution in ordinary speech, but for North and much academic literature the bank is an organization; 'banking practices' or 'the banking sector' would comprise an institution. North also emphasized the role of norms, beliefs and customs – informal institutions – as perhaps more significant and harder to change than formal institutions such as 'the banking sector'. We find institutions, formal and informal, to be central to our understanding of the persistence of inequality, often what embodies the 'embedding'. What we find underdeveloped in many economists' preoccupation with institutions is how they change or do not change, and the politics behind that evolution. We find we need to explore this latter dimension, to understand the phenomenon of persistent group inequality. In this we diverge from the new institutional economics, in which institutional origins are largely explained in functional terms.[3]

Another theme of importance is that this embeddedness occurs in time and space. In this regard particular institutions become deeply embedded over significant periods of time, by a particular sequence of events and subject to some kind of repetition in moments of change, producing what some scholars have called an 'institutional layering process' (Thelen 2003) . Moreover, these institutions became part of the infrastructure upon which other less foundational institutions, such as major public policies, were constructed. These policies represent very substantial extensions of political authority that further alter the incentives and resources of political actors (Pierson 2004), and therefore the embeddedness of inequality or the likelihood of its challenge. Our historical approach has the aim of making the development of the embeddedness over time as clear as possible. In a parallel way, this embeddedness is shaped by the relation between the national and the local, with the regional as the intermediate level. We use the concepts of 'micro, meso, macro', where micro is the level of the family or the community, macro is the national, and meso refers to what lies in between. In political terms this may be the municipal or the regional government. In economic terms, this may be, say, a development agency based at the regional or municipal level, or a policy for a sector rather than a national policy.

In what follows, we assess how this inequality has been challenged, both from the top-down and from the bottom-up. We face the fact that ethnicity has not been a salient factor for mobilization and change in spite of the admitted grievances and sense of alienation as a group. Our approach to these issues is again an emphasis on the process, and how the politicization of ethnic identity is bounded in the history of the country. There is an increasing consensus that neither long-lasting ethnic cleavages, nor the emergence of ethnic entrepreneurs able to manipulate these deep feelings, are enough to explain the mobilization of ethnic groups. To understand properly the politicization of indigenous peoples we need to consider carefully in what ways indigenous peoples' identities and their meanings have changed during the process of contention and the particular features of the unfolding mobilization process. The literature of indigenous movements in Latin America (Van Cott 2000, 2005; Yashar 2005) has emphasized that favourable changes in the structure of political opportunities are generally required, to facilitate mobilization. This literature has further emphasized the construction of networks and grassroots organizations that can generate and sustain collective action. Mobilization resources promote an 'interlocking network of groups' that provides the stimulus for the movement and for collective action, which Olson saw as highly unlikely (Tarrow 1994).[4] Yet, identity, and particularly ethnic identity, can be transformed and sharpened during the process of mobilization and because of it. This endogenous character of ethnic identity and its politicization and mobilization have given researchers a complex task. Understanding mobilization triggered by ethnic identity requires attention to collective processes of interpretation accessible to indigenous peoples in a particular context, and the framing and reframing of identity in a field in which indigenous leaders act together with others, both allies and opponents (Bedford and Snow 2000; Gamson 1992).

Violence and mobilization of indigenous people is not only a result of challengers' collective action. Groups because of their characteristics can end up on the receiving end of violence. Ethnic traits can be obvious enough for others to target groups directly or indirectly, with drastic consequences for them. Ethnic identities may or may not be politically salient; they may be kept in the sphere of 'private' life, but with little or no repercussions in the public arena in terms of patterns of collective action, organization, political choice and mobilization. However, ethnic violence is still not necessarily prevented: of the five countries with substantial indigenous populations in Latin America (Bolivia, Peru, Ecuador, Guatemala and Mexico), armed conflict and a disproportionate number of casualties with people of indigenous origin have occurred in the three countries with the least politicized ethnic identities. And Peru is an emblematic case of this group.

Our Work: The Plan of the Book

Our methodology is mainly historical, with a strong emphasis on institutions. Only through a careful historical account of the evolution of institutions can we show how the three dimensions of groups – discrimination, space and identity – interact and evolve over time, interacting with each other and also with all the more familiar elements of Peru's development story – the interaction with the international market, dependence on foreign capital, the weakness of the state (Thorp and Bertram 1978).

But first, we have three important scene setting chapters, where we include our efforts at measurement. There is no way we can converse about group inequalities in Peru without an initial consideration of ethnicity – its fluidity, complexity, salience and the prejudice it evokes. This is the topic of Chapter 2. In Chapter 3 we attempt to demonstrate the quantitative importance of HIs, exploring their degree in socioeconomic and political terms. We devote Chapter 4 to the same topic but we develop the theme more deeply for the specific area of education, which plays a key role in our analysis of the embedding of inequalities. Our analysis shows why: education is as much part of the problem as it is part of the solution. This has much to do with all three aspects of groups – discrimination, space and identity – and education enters and compounds the vicious circles.

The empirical backbone of Chapters 2–4 comprises measurement work using household surveys and census data, a survey of perceptions of identity which we carried out in 2005, with follow-up interviews for a sample of those surveyed, and community case studies carried out in three of the survey sites. The methodology of the survey is explained in the appendix to Chapter 2. Where we report the views of private individuals, names have been changed where appropriate, to protect privacy. People interviewed because of their role or representative position are identified by name and position. The community case studies are drawn on throughout the text, but most fully described in Chapter 8.

The following chapters develop the analysis of how horizontal inequalities get built up over time and 'embedded'. We trace the process chronologically. In Chapter 5 we see how already in the colony, institutions of discrimination and prejudice and the role of the indigenous Highland population as a supply of cheap labour were deeply embedded and complementary. We explain the particular forms by which oppression in Peru had taken its toll by decimating the leadership, with implications for political development. The ambiguities of the relations between indigenous-*cholo* and white-*mestizo* were already signalling the complexity of the clientelist culture that took on more force with time. With Independence, the focus of the economy gradually shifted from the Sierra to the Coast, in response to the dictates of the international market. The political dominance of Lima grew, and the interaction of economics and politics operated to cause an embedding of inequality between Coast and Sierra, with consequences in ethnic terms.

One consequence of the shift of economic and political focus was that traditional institutional structures in the Sierra could continue: in the course of the nineteenth century the institution of '*gamonalismo*' – domination by *mestizo* power brokers with their roots in land[5] – inherited the traditions of the colony in terms of domination, exploitation and clientelism. Forces of contention were not lacking but indigenous organizational capacity was limited and the reaction to indigenous revolts was punitive. The indigenous were now subject to a 'double inequality': the local power structure and the subordination of the region to Lima and the Coast.

In Chapter 6 we show how this double inequality became deeper as the last elements of prosperity of the Sierra died away. We explore the fashionable solution of the time to 'the ethnic problem' – education and hygiene – and show how education in particular remained as much the problem as the solution. We trace the ebb and flow of centralism, the evolving interaction between ethnic and regional inequalities, and the implications of migration in this context. At this point regional differentiation became more significant, making it more difficult to provide a coherent national account.

Chapter 7 deals with the discontinuity of the radical military regime led by Velasco following the coup of 1968, and the missed opportunities of the next two decades. We show how Velasco's time in government opened opportunities for political mobilization and for representation, but land reform perversely created conflict and helped to open the door for Sendero. The role of political parties, particularly from the Left, became key in the building of alliances and organization, arousing great hopes as democracy gave an important place to these parties. We explain how the characteristics of these parties limited the potential of these organizations, and of democracy itself, as a peaceful channel for change. We trace the interactions of horizontal inequalities, political violence, repression, political mobilization and economic mismanagement.

In Chapter 8 we explore the interaction of the Fujimori regime with neo-liberalism, political repression, and the mining boom, taking group inequalities to a new level, weakening not only the political parties but social movements as a whole and creating new exclusions. Chapter 9 resumes and concludes, reflecting on why the process produced so little contestation of group inequalities through effective collective action.

We have chosen to end our detailed analysis with the end of the Fujimori regime. That seemed to us to represent a point of discontinuity, and hopefully of change: what has happened since 2000 has had elements of hope, as we have signalled, but also strong elements of continuity and failure to face the depth of action needed for change. We felt that more time needed to pass before the story of 'after Fujimori' could be clearly told. But the reader needs to be aware that our local-level fieldwork took place in 2005: had we found surprising and new elements of change at the local level, that might well have invalidated our decision to stop the wider analysis at the earlier date. We would have needed to explore the source of the surprise. Sadly, we did not: although at the local level we find a very large number of apparently new dynamics, we also find depressing amounts of continuity with the previous decade.

Our Apologia: What the Book is Not

We feel deep regret that given the already massive scope of the book, we could not include the Amazonian indigenous peoples in our analysis. Similarly, environmental issues are only touched on in passing, rather than given the weight they deserve. And we find gender to be important in interpreting inequalities between groups and their persistence, but we did not design our research to focus on this aspect in the way which in retrospect appears desirable. These are three areas for further research on the genesis and persistence of inequality that we wish to acknowledge and place firmly on the table.

Appendix to Chapter 1: Background on Peru

Since we hope there will be motivated readers who as yet are not acquainted with Peru, we here present a minimum of information to allow you to follow the text. Geography features largely in our analysis: we are considering a country comprised of three zones, each very different. The basic geography is shown in Figure A1. The narrow strip of Coastal land is fertile but only with irrigation. The Andes, or Sierra, run in three great ridges down the length of the country, rising to well over 20,000 feet. Some 40 per cent of the population live there, many in inhospitable if very beautiful territory. The mineral deposits of the Sierra are enormous and diverse; the agriculture is largely livestock and the key bottleneck is transportation. Sixty-one per cent of the territory of Peru is to the east, the beginning of the Amazon basin, tropical and with a small population – some 9 per cent of the total. The Amazon has oil, gas and timber, and its indigenous population is much under threat.

In terms of basic political structure, Peru is a unitary state. Initially on Independence (1826) the republic was divided into eight departments but it fragmented into 18 in less than half of a century and today there

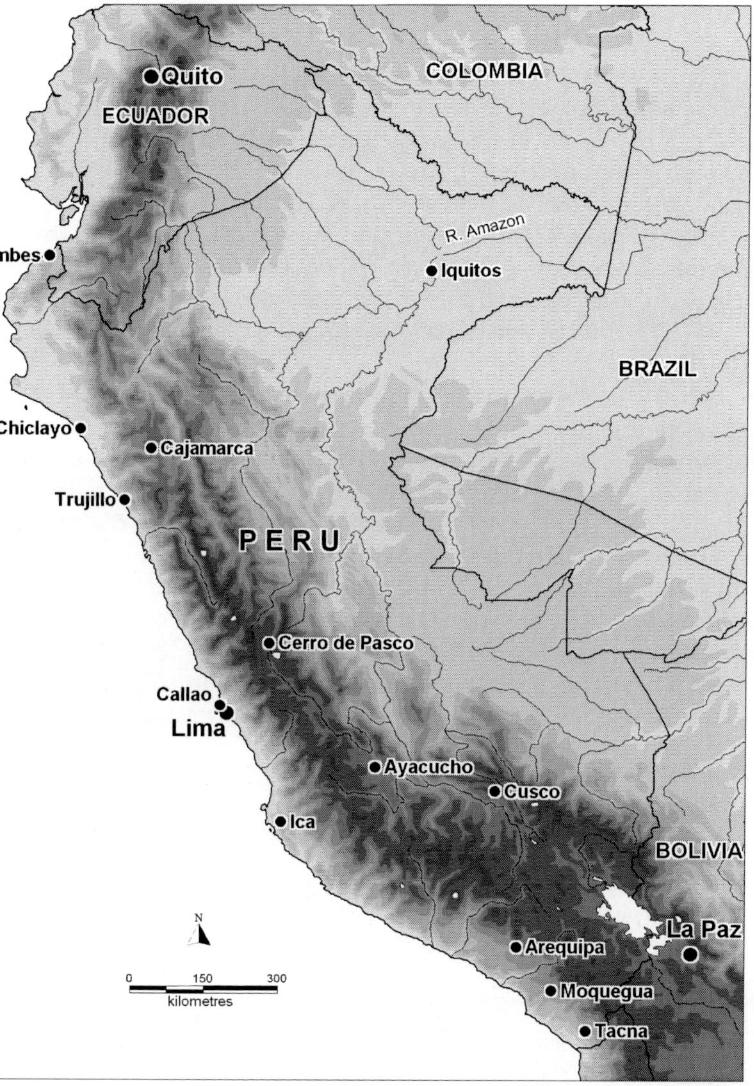

Figure A1 Map of Peru
Source: Collins Bartholomew Maps, with permission.

are 25 units. The provinces followed the same tendency, rising from 50 to 100 units, and close to 200 today (Contreras and Cueto 1999). On several occasions, there was an effort at solving this proliferation of territorial units with the creation of larger regions but the attempt failed, for the very reason that probably led to fragmentation – the desire at the local level to be in the political and administrative hierarchy in order to share the centre's resources. Thus, by 2002 25 'regions' had been created using the boundaries of the previous departments. The former 25 departments are still the commonly used way of describing regional aspects of Peru. In much of our discussion in subsequent chapters, we refer to 'the Southern Highlands', meaning the area that concentrates the largest indigenous population and contains the regions of Apurimac, Ayacucho, Cusco, Huancavelica and Puno, including the Highlands of Arequipa and Moquegua. We also refer to the 'Central Highlands', meaning Huánuco, Pasco and Junín; and 'the Northern Highlands', meaning Ancash, Cajamarca, Amazonas, including the Highland areas of Piura and La Libertad.

Since Independence, Peru has been formally a democracy, but with several periods of unlawful rule; the most notable of these regimes were the 11-year rule (1919–30) of Augusto Leguía, the 8-year rule of the General Odria and the 12-year dictatorship that ended in 1980, following the military coup led by General Velasco in 1969. The ten year period from 1980 was characterized by the democratization of political institutions, universal suffrage, open competition and the flourishing of the political party system, but also the beginning of political violence that led the country to many years of state of siete, and close to 70,000 deaths. In 1992, the elected government of Alberto Fujimori suspended Congress and the period is frequently referred to as a dictatorship.

Notes

1. We discuss the meanings of different ethnic categories and concepts fully in Chapter 2. For now, the reader should note that in the indigenous-white context, *mestizo* in its literal sense refers to all of mixed race, but in Peru, commonly those who perceive themselves as close to their indigenous roots, may prefer the word *cholo*. *Cholo* is also used as a term of disparagement or affection, depending on the context.
2. In understanding that history we have been able to draw on a rich historical literature on Peru: Deere 1990; Degregori 1990; Flores Galindo 1986, 1976; Larson 2004; Mallon 1995, 1992, 1983; Manrique 2002, 1988, 1981; Montoya 1998, 1992, 1989; and Stern 1998, 1993, 1987 among others.
3. For a brilliant exposition of the three versions of the 'new institutionalism', see Hall and Taylor 1996. They distinguish historical, rational choice and sociological institutionalism, and see contributions as being made through all three perspectives.
4. This literature is strongly influenced by the approach emphasizing political structures of opportunity for mobilization; see McAdam, Tarrow and Tilly 2001; Tarrow 1983.
5. We define and explore this concept fully in Chapter 5.

2
The Complexity and Salience of Ethnic Identity in Peru

The first challenge in reflecting on identity, and in particular ethnic identity, is that every one of us has multiple dimensions to our identity. As Amartya Sen says, 'The same person can, for example, be a British citizen, of Malaysian origin, with Chinese racial characteristics, a stockbroker, a nonvegetarian, an asthmatic, a linguist, a bodybuilder' (Sen 2006: 24). And which identity is most important will often depend on the person's history and context. There may also be a variation between that identity I feel within me, that ascribed to me by others, and that I am prepared to present to the outside world. Identities evolve, and our use of our own or others' identity can be highly instrumental. Society's attitudes and prejudices may affect both how we see ourselves and how we try to be seen by others. Discrimination and prejudice are realities, the more difficult to analyse and evaluate because they are often denied.

In this chapter we first present our findings on identity and ethnicity. Our focus is on the individual's perception of his or her identity and the role ethnicity plays in that. Secondly we explore discrimination and prejudice.

Identity and Ethnicity

Although a key cross-country interest of this comparative research programme is in culturally defined – and in particular ethnic – inequality, we could not assume that in the case of Peru, ethnic identity was the mover and shaker. To shed light on this issue, as well as to provide a basis for comparison with other studies in the project, we undertook a survey of how people saw themselves, their ethnicity and the significance of ethnicity in general in the country. We carried out the survey in three sites, surveying some 200 informants in each site. The methodology is described in detail in the appendix to this chapter. The two sites in the Sierra were places with different experiences of indigenous identity: Huanta in Ayacucho and Bambamarca in Cajamarca.[1] In both places we carried out interviews in urban and rural areas. We chose a third site, a Lima barrio, made up of migrants and displaced people from Ayacucho (Huanta Uno and Huanta Dos in San Juan de Lurigancho). We were not attempting any kind of national-level representativeness.[2] We focused on learning to understand how Peruvians see their identity, ethnicity and life experiences of communities in varying degrees of peripheral status, and did not attempt to cover the full range of the Peruvian population. Since we did not aspire to national representativeness with the survey, our findings can only be taken as suggestive at anything beyond the local level we study.

We had no easy way of solving the problems posed by the complexity of our topic. We know that given discrimination and a history of oppression, how people speak about their identity, and in particular ethnic identity, is never straightforward, and a questionnaire format has severe limitations as a result. What we did do, however, which proved very rewarding, was to conduct in-depth follow-up interviews with a sample (5 per cent) of the surveyed population. We present below the main results we wish to highlight here: fuller discussions are available as working papers (Paredes 2007, Sulmont 2006). As explained in the previous chapter, we have changed the names of private individuals interviewed, though public officials and others with semi-official or representative roles are named and their posts identified.

First, we asked all informants to tell us which three of a list of characteristics were most important in defining 'their identity as a person'. The results are shown in Table 2.1. Overwhelmingly, people rated 'ser hombre/mujer' (being male or female) and their occupation as the most important. But it is clear that ethnicity is there: the three overlapping ethnic markers in the list – place of birth, mother tongue and racial origin – accumulated between them one third of the places, more than any other, and if place of residence is included, practically as many as gender and occupation together. We felt confident from this that people's ethnicity does feature strongly among the multiple dimensions of their identity. This was confirmed in the follow up interviews, where in more open-ended conversation, a regional/ethnic identity was always important. For those born in the Highlands, 'Andino' or 'Serrano' *and* indigenous were common forms of expression.

The survey then asked about identity in terms of ethnic origin, using racial or cultural origin as a proxy for ethnicity.[3] The result of such

Table 2.1 Significance of various elements in informants' identity[a] (percentage mentioning each element)

	Total survey	Huanta (Ayacucho)	Bambamarca (Cajamarca)	San Juan de Lurigancho (Lima)
Gender	69.4	65.7	72.1	70.6
Work or occupation	52.4	38.5	62.7	56.7
Place of birth	39.3	53.5	31.3	32.3
Mother tongue	36.1	49.8	26.4	31.3
Religion	32.7	30.5	36.8	30.8
Racial origins	21.3	25.8	15.9	21.9
Place of residence	18.0	18.3	19.9	15.9
Political ideas	13.7	11.3	10.9	18.9
Belonging to an organization	6.3	1.4	10.4	7.5
Other	1.3	0.0	2.0	2.0
Not available	4.6	3.3	4.0	6.5

[a] Informants were asked to list the *three* most important to them.
Source: Sulmont (2010) using the CRISE Perception Survey (Peru).

self-identification was: 18 per cent indigenous/Andean (N = 108); 9 per cent white (N = 54); 18 per cent *cholo* (N = 108), and 54 per cent *mestizo* (N = 330).[4] We do not include in this analysis the tiny proportion of people who self-identified as black, Chinese/Japanese and Amazonian (N = 15).[5] We remind the reader that these proportions are only applicable to our own sample and cannot be extrapolated to the country as a whole.

An analysis of self-classification across our cases (localities) shows the differences we would expect. Huanta in Ayacucho and San Juan de Lurigancho in Lima show more ethnic differentiation than Bambamarca in Cajamarca. Figure 2.1 shows the distribution of each salient ethnic group in the three cases. Those who self-identify as white are a small group, even in Bambamarca; and the category *cholo* was chosen in a larger proportion in the migrant neighbourhood of San Juan de Lurigancho. In Bambamarca self perception is largely *mestizo*; Huanta and San Juan de Lurigancho are more differentiated.

An analysis of language shows that about half our sample speaks Quechua. On average, whites have the lowest percentage of Quechua speakers (28 per cent), followed by *mestizos* (38 per cent), *cholos* (53 per cent) and indigenous (76 per cent). What is revealing is the presence of Quechua speakers across all self-defined ethnic categories in Ayacucho and Lima. Quechua is not spoken in Bambamarca. A large majority in Huanta (96 per cent) said they spoke Quechua, including

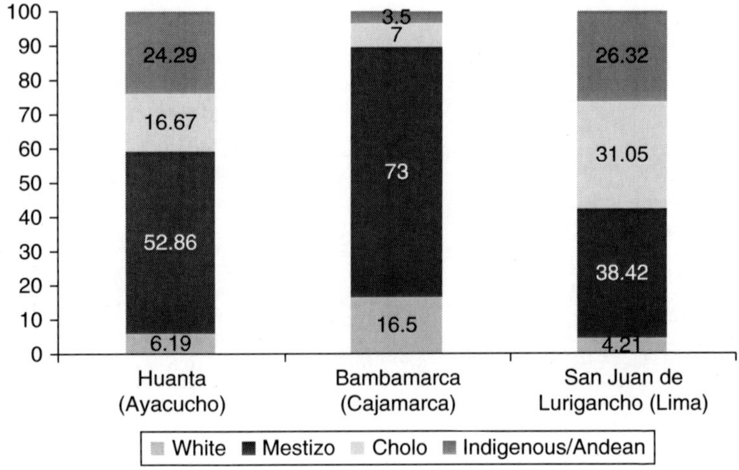

Figure 2.1 Distribution of each salient ethnic group in the three localities (percentages)
Source: Own elaboration using CRISE Perception Survey (Peru).

those who self-defined as white or *mestizo* (100 per cent and 95 per cent respectively). In the case of San Juan de Lurigancho in Lima, our more heterogeneous case, 41 per cent speak Quechua, and although the percentage of whites and *mestizos* speaking the language (25 per cent and 28 per cent respectively) is significantly smaller than the percentage of *cholos* and indigenous (41 per cent and 62 per cent respectively), Quechua speakers are found across all categories.[6] Language does not therefore seem useful for distinguishing power relations and subsequent socioeconomic inequalities among different ethnic groups, for instance *mestizos* and indigenous. It is important to remember that as recently as 35 years ago, and for several centuries before that, the use of both languages (Spanish and Quechua/Aymara) was an important source of power for *gamonales*[7] *(mestizos* or whites), as few indigenous people spoke Spanish. The use of both languages enabled Sierra landlords to become the main intermediaries between marginalized indigenous groups and the central authorities (Bourricaud 1970, Cotler 1970, De la Cadena 2000).

This information helps us to understand why in the survey it is more likely that a person who speaks Quechua and lives in San Juan de Lurigancho in Lima will report him or herself as *cholo* or indigenous than that a Quechua speaker in Huanta in Ayacucho will do so

(71 per cent vs. 41 per cent). This difference is quite considerable and it increases slightly if we narrow the analysis to those who reported Quechua as their first language (80 per cent vs. 46 per cent). Knowledge of Quechua may be an ethnic trait in Lima, but not in Ayacucho.

We argue below that place of birth gives us the best, though still imperfect, ethnic marker at the national level. At the level of our own survey, we cannot very well compare, since we have deliberately chosen sites in the Sierra and one urban site with a high migrant population.

However, we do get an interesting insight from the survey for the issue of measurement. Our cases show that people born in 'peripheral' small towns (outside Lima and the capital cities of the regions) tend to self-define themselves differently across localities. Among people born in the 'periphery', those now living in Lima are more likely to perceive themselves as *cholo* or indigenous (63 per cent) than those living today in Ayacucho (43 per cent). Almost none of those in Cajamarca perceive themselves in this way (only 9 per cent).

Thus we are already seeing how important the experience of migration seems to be in people's self-definition. This is reinforced when we explore the significance of colour of skin. We used a scale from 1 to 7, where 1 is indigenous colour ('*cobrizo*')[8] and 7 is white.[9] On average, whites see themselves as lighter compared with *mestizos* (5.4 vs. 3.7). *Cholos* feel almost identical to *mestizos* with respect to their skin colour (3.6); but they feel lighter skinned than indigenous (2.6). And perceptions about skin colour vary among ethnic groups according to where they currently live. Whites living in San Juan de Lurigancho in Lima are likely to feel darker than whites living in Bambamarca and Huanta. In contrast, indigenous and *cholos* who currently live in Huanta are likely to feel darker than indigenous and *cholos* in Lima. The exceptions are the *cholos* and indigenous in Bambamarca. *Mestizos* do not reveal differences: they believe themselves to be in the middle of the skin-colour scale in the three places (Table 2.2).

In assessing these variables of language, skin colour and place of birth, our first conclusion is that moving to or living in Lima raises self-awareness of ethnic traits. This is confirmed in our interviews: people living in Lima or 'cosmopolitan' Peruvians,[10] described how new and recreated markers and traits emerge in the capital city. For instance, Simon, a 35-year-old man from Bambamarca, who sees himself as *cholo,* is a good example. He told us that he never thought of himself as a '*cholo*' when he was young. When he first arrived in Lima, in San Juan de Lurigancho, at the age of 15, he heard people calling him *cholo* or *Serrano*. He also learned from observing in public buses how people

Table 2.2 Average of perception of skin colour across the three localities (*cobrizo* = 1; white = 7)

Ethnic Identity	**Huanta (Ayacucho)**	**Bambamarca (Cajamarca)**	**San Juan de Lurigancho (Lima)**
White[a]	5.3	5.6	4.9
Mestizo[a]	3.4	4.0	3.9
Cholo[a]	2.8	4.1	4.1
Indigenous/Andean	2.1	3.9	3.0
Total	210	200	190

[a] Differences are significant at 95 per cent level.
Source: CRISE Perception Survey (Peru).

rejected a woman in traditional indigenous dress, calling her *'serrana'* and *'chola'* and 'complaining about her smelling of llama'.[11]

Another interesting example shows us that middle-class Lima may represent a higher degree of 'whiteness' even for white or *mestizo* people living in the migrant community of San Juan de Lurigancho in Lima. Florencia, a woman who considers herself white, lives in a neighbourhood that is mostly *cholo* in Lima but works in the well-off residential district of San Isidro. She observed differences between her 'whiteness' and that of her colleagues in San Isidro: when talking about her place of work, she sees herself 'only *clara*' (light-skinned) instead of 'white' (the word she was using when comparing herself with her neighbours), while her colleagues are 'white'; she described her boss's characteristics as 'tall, white and fair-haired'.[12] It is reasonable that in a largely differentiated society, where most of the whites (the rich and more educated) live, the deeper the contrast, the stronger the awareness of people of their ethnic traits and of the way they are seen by others.

Just as the experience of migration to Lima becomes a key experience to recreate and renew perceptions of ethnic traits, the interviews also help deepen our understanding of how geography and skin colour play a major role in the redefinition of ethnic identity, more so than elements such as language. The 'Sierra' becomes the common 'place of origin' in which both indigenous and *cholos* find the roots of their ethnic identity: 'we came from the Sierra'. Some see the categories, indigenous, 'serrano' and *cholo,* as the same, precisely because they share this 'geographical origin'. However some indigenous people prefer to stress differences, suggesting a degree of superiority of the *serrano* over the *cholo*. While 'Serrano' is also used to humiliate and insult as we will see later in the chapter, *cholos* seem to be more aware of their ethnic traits and of being the subject of disdain because of them. However, they tend to express a special pride in having overcome these humiliations, particularly if they have lived a long time in Lima and have achieved some education.

With very few exceptions[13], *mestizos* and whites did not mention their *serrano* origin in the interviews and most explained their self-defined categories by referring to the colour of their skin (mixed or '*morenito(a)*'). Planas and Valdivia (2007) who have carried out a significant number of focus groups in Lima and in Cusco have found similar results. *Mestizo* denotes the mixing of races, mainly white and indigenous (p.77). In Cusco, *mestizo* tend to be associated with '*criollo*' as its cultural expression (p.78).

All these cultural and racial categories are complex 'social constructions' and the survey and interviews oblige us to confront their subjective and context-specific nature. Long-term processes, such as *mestizaje* and migration, as well as a history of discrimination, have had a profound impact on the convoluted way that ethnic identity was constructed, contested and reconstructed, and as a result, it has become not only fluid, but ambivalent and difficult to capture. This echoes the outstanding work on this subject by Marisol de la Cadena. Although she studied only a limited region of the Sierra of Cusco, her results resonate with all we have found in our various contexts. She encounters the key phrase '*en proceso*' – in process. By urbanizing, people move on the spectrum indigenous–*cholo*–*mestizo*, and significantly, she finds, women move more slowly than men. In her community of Chitapampa, she reports, when she asks a Chitapampino about the ethnic status of one or another villager, a common response is 'he is neither one nor the other; he is "in process"' (2000). The history behind this is taken up in Chapters 5 and 6 below.

Given these findings, it does not seem useful to try to force connections between people's current ethnic identities and their 'ancient origins'. Nor does it seem correct to believe that the only result of *mestizaje* has been ethnic homogenization and the dilution of ethnic traits in a 'melting pot' where only class differences matter. It seems even more erroneous to believe that people no longer perceive ethnic differences and do not create new ethnic divisions. Motivated by these conclusions and by the rich testimonies that we gathered in our three cases, we attempt in the next section to explore how ethnic identity is expressed in our cases. In particular we want to understand what role prejudice plays in the way people make ethnic differentiations or feel they are classified by others. Group identities arise partly from individuals' *own* perceptions of membership of and identity with a particular group – that is, the self-perceptions of those *in* the group – but they are also determined by the perceptions of *those outside the group* about others. Sometimes categorization by others can turn out to be the main source of group boundaries, and in an extreme, what people themselves feel about their own identities may not be important at all: what matters is what others think they are.

Prejudice against cholos and indigenous

As we have said before, the theory of self-categorization underlines the importance of the interethnic interaction and of perceptions of others in the construction of the *in-group* identity and, most importantly, how the relation that an individual can establish with the outside world is determined, in part, by the individual's assessment of how others see him or her (Barth 1969).[14] Many of the case studies looking at the phenomenon of ethnic identity in Latin America and Peru have come to the same conclusion.[15] For these reasons, we believe it is particularly important to study how ethnic prejudice operates in Peru, while reminding ourselves and the reader repeatedly that our material is in no way representative of Peru. In particular, our sample of whites is small and limited to a relatively less well-off part of the country. We have not explored 'white' attitudes in Lima.

Prejudice is defined as a hostile attitude toward a group predicated on false, simplistic, over-generalized, or unconscious beliefs. It may be felt or expressed, may be directed toward a group as a whole or toward an individual because he or she is a member of that group (Allport 1954). According to this definition, prejudice has two essential ingredients. First, there must be an attitude (of favour or disfavour) in respect of the characteristics of a group. Second, prejudice must be related to an over-generalized belief about the group itself. A good illustration of these two concepts is given in some of the survey's results. The 45 per cent of people who would neither accept their daughter or sister marrying a *cholo* or indigenous, nor vote for a *cholo* or indigenous running for Congress, illustrate the attitudinal factor. The 48 per cent that placed *cholo* and indigenous groups on the lowest level of a violent(1) – peaceful(7) scale are illustrating the belief factor.

We tend to make many over-generalizations or form misconceptions in our everyday lives, but not all these simplifications turn into prejudices. For instance, we avoid insects that are unfamiliar to us, but after a proper explanation, we are capable of distinguishing which are still dangerous. Prejudices, however, exist when we are not capable of rectifying our judgement in the light of new information and our beliefs resist all contrary evidence (Allport 1954). Such prejudices have the power to organize our feelings and sentiments (Balibar 1991).[16] Florencia told us that her mother is against her relationship with a man she considers *cholo*: her mother tells her that '*cholos* are bad men, they abuse women, and they are drunk'. The young woman, who has painfully maintained her relationship for about four years, has introduced her boyfriend to her mother so 'she can see that he is not a *cholo*, he is a good person and wants the best for me', she says, 'but my mother does not change her opinion about him, she just does not like him'.[17]

In the subsequent parts of this section, we will analyse prejudice against *cholos* and indigenous drawing on both the survey and the interviews. First, we will present the results of the survey and second, we will turn to the interviews to explain how people become aware of being the subject of prejudice, particularly in Lima; how strong the prejudice against Highlanders and indigenous peasants appears to be in Huanta and Bambamarca; and how people respond to prejudice.

Evidence of prejudice from the survey

The results of the survey are interesting in terms of attitudes toward *cholo* and indigenous people. We use three questions from the survey to analyse prejudice: (1) would you agree with your daughter or sister marrying a *cholo* or indigenous, (2) would you vote for a *cholo* or indigenous running for Congress and (3) how would you rank *cholos* and indigenous on a violent(1) – peaceful(7) scale?

The first question contains an ambiguity, since an indigenous parent might seek upward mobility for their daughter and so disagree, but not from prejudice. For that reason we give particular attention to the responses of whites and *mestizo*s in the three localities studied.[18] For them, it comprises a very strong statement and we expected people would overwhelmingly answer in a 'politically correct' way, but still we found that one fifth of whites and *mestizo*s in our sample would disagree with a marriage between their daughter or sister and a *cholo* or indigenous (16 per cent). The percentage of those who disagree is still close to 10 per cent among indigenous and *cholos,* possibly reflecting social aspirations. Education does not make a difference, but age and gender do. The percentage of women who disagree is twice that of men (20 per cent vs. 10 per cent) and disagreement increases with age: 10 per cent in the 18 to 25 age group, 15 per cent in the 26 to 40 age group; and 20 per cent in the 40 to 70 age group.

Greater prejudice is manifested in the second question. Around one in three individuals in the sample would not vote for a *cholo* or indigenous running for Congress (38 per cent). The percentage of whites and *mestizos* who would not so vote is the largest (43 per cent), but the percentage of *cholos* and indigenous who feel the same is also significant (29 per cent). Opposition decreases slightly with education: 50 per cent of those with less than secondary education would not so vote, and 31 per cent of those with more than this level would not so vote. Opposition decreases as well among those living in San Juan de Lurigancho-Lima (47 per cent in Huanta and 45 per cent in Bambamarca vs. 19 per cent in San Juan de Lurigancho, Lima). There are no differences of opinion between women and men, but willingness to vote for indigenous and *cholos* decreases among older respondents.

If we consider both questions together to analyse prejudice, 46 per cent of the individuals in our sample have some type of prejudice against *cholos* and indigenous. Whites (54 per cent) and *mestizos* (52 per cent) in these three localities tend to be more prejudiced than indigenous (39 per cent) and *cholos* (30 per cent). Note that the attitudes of whites and *mestizos* are rather close. Among *cholos* and indigenous, the latter tend to be more prejudiced about the first than vice versa (30 per cent vs. 22 per cent). Indigenous and *cholos* express prejudice against their own group in identical proportions (17 per cent). The proportion of people with an overall prejudice against *mestizos* and whites is much lower (25 per cent).

Prejudice is also clearly manifested in the third question related to associations between being *cholo* and indigenous and violence. The proportion of people who think that indigenous and *cholos* are violent is 48 per cent. Whites (62 per cent) and *mestizos* (53 per cent) tend to be more prejudiced than *cholos* (38 per cent) and indigenous (37 per cent) on this subject. Education and gender do not make a difference, but age does: prejudice is greater among older people.

Table 2.3 shows the profile of those who expressed prejudice against *cholos* and indigenous in at least one of the three questions: marriage, vote and violence. The percentage of prejudiced people is larger in Bambamarca and Huanta than in Lima and prejudice is also more predominant among older people than among the young, and among women rather than men. Surprisingly, education does not make a significant difference, a point we will pick up later.

Being on the receiving end

We asked in the interviews about why people would not agree to their daughter or sister marrying a *cholo* or indigenous, and why they would not vote for somebody belonging to either of these groups. People

Table 2.3 Prejudice against indigenous and *cholos* by important characteristics (percentages)

	Expressing prejudice	**Claiming no prejudice**	**Total, absolute numbers**
Locality*			
Huanta (Ayacucho)	28.0	72.0	210
Bambamarca (Cajamarca)	23.0	77.0	200
San Juan de Lurigancho (Lima)	42.0	58.0	190
Age group			
- between 18-25	38.0	62.1	195
- between 26-40	30.4	69.6	207
- between 40-70	24.8	75.2	198
Gender *			
- male	33.9	66.1	317
- female	28.4	71.6	283
Education*			
- no formal education	33.3	66.7	36
- primary completed	23.2	76.8	164
- secondary completed	35.2	64.8	239
- post secondary qualification	32.3	67.7	161
Ethnicity*			
- white	14.8	85.2	54
- *mestizo*	24.8	75.2	330
- *cholo*	47.2	52.8	108
- indigenous	41.7	58.3	108
Skin colour			
Mean of scale: 1 (indigenous)-7(white)	3.0	4.0	

* Differences are significant at 95 per cent level.
Source: Own elaboration using CRISE Perception Survey (Peru).

did not seem comfortable addressing this type of question. Only Elvira Macedo, a 27-year-old *mestiza* woman, who told us that her grandfather had advised her never to allow anybody to put her down because she is a *mestiza* and that she should eat 'red meat' to make her cheeks rosier, was willing to explain. She is married to a *cholo* who is 'a good man'; but she would like somebody 'better' for her daughter, a "*limeñito*", she said. We asked about the difference between a *limeño* and a *cholo*, and she explained to us that a *limeño* is a mix between skin colour and place of origin.[19]

While we cannot address these questions directly from our interviews, we can see that our respondents seem to be very aware of negative beliefs associated with the categories *cholo* and *serrano*. It is clear from their responses that this awareness comes from negative experiences, either directly experienced or witnessed.[20] On some occasions, they have been excluded from certain circles. Marco from Bambamarca, who travelled to Lima to study, told us: 'the children *de bien* never joined the groups of provincials, *serranos* or *cholos* ... there was a hidden behaviour going on ... people from the Sierra look more aggressive, but it is because they are defensive, they do not remain silent. I think it is because they feel rejected. They do not say it, but a *serrano* feels it.'[21] Harold, from Huanta and studying in Lima, said: 'there is in the Conservatory a group of friends that are always together, they are from Lima and the majority are white and fair-haired, they have studied together in school ... they do not join the rest and are given preferential treatment in the Conservatory ... my friends are mostly from the provinces'.[22] Finally, we can identify an awareness of 'being visible'. Julio, 48, a *cholo* living in Lima, told us that when he walks in the street in residential places such as Miraflores or San Isidro he feels that people look at him. When asked how, he replied 'as a *cholo*'.[23] Soledad, a 38-year-old teacher from Huanta, told us that she went to work in Lima for one year as a maid when she was 17 years old. She was well treated by the family, but she felt that people looked at her as *serrana* with contempt or disdain.[24] Elvira told us of her experiences in residential areas in Lima where she worked as a maid. When she arrived in La Molina she 'felt fearful, embarrassed, different, observed, and intimidated'. She could never talk in a relaxed way with her employer, even when it was necessary to explain her non-attendance at work to keep her job. Her silence prompted anger on the part of her female boss, who pulled her hair and fired her without pay. On another occasion, she tried to sell some goods in the streets of Miraflores and felt the same: 'embarrassed, observed, without words'. Now, she prefers to take her daughter for entertainment to other places, such as the Park of Huachipa and the *Parque de las Leyendas* (zoo),[25] places packed with migrants during the weekends. Whether the rejection is intended in ethnic terms or not, the way in which people receive it has a strong ethnic component. While it is hard to generalize from our interviews, the most painful experiences were related by women: Elvira lost the ability to speak, so strong was the disempowering effect of the prejudice experienced.

However, not all those interviewed felt the same. Some were completely unaware of any type of negative perception. This group has two characteristics. First, they are mainly women from Cajamarca (and to a lesser extent from Huanta) with little experience of travelling to the Coastal cities or Lima. We never encountered this unawareness in our conversations with men from Cajamarca. When such women did travel, they visited their families and were not looking for jobs. Second, they are the type of *cajamarquino* with lighter skin, which probably minimizes the visible traits that tend to serve as the 'condensing rod' for prejudice.[26] Lilian, a 35-year-old woman from Bambamarca, described herself as 'fairly white, fair and with brown eyes'. Two years ago she had visited her cousin in Lima for the second time. In her memory, he used to live in a small house with straw-mat walls, but now both the house and neighbourhood were prettier. She had been treated with affection in Lima, but she had not left the house very often, only with her cousin to the centre of Lima or to Huachipa (her brother had advised her to avoid going out alone because she might lose her way). She had felt comfortable in Lima and, if Lima offered jobs, she would like to move there with her family.[27] Another example is Judith, a *mestizo* woman who said that her father was a little bit darker but her mother was white with red hair. She said she had visited not only Lima, but also cities such as Cajamarca and Trujillo (always visiting relatives). In all the places, she had felt comfortable and had not felt any discrimination. She said she would not like to move to Lima because there are too many cars and life is different, although her children study there and she misses them.[28] A third example of this group is Gladys, a white woman from Bambamarca, who told us that she was 'in love with Lima'. She travels with her husband and daughter every year for a vacation and stays for months in the house of her sister in Chorrillos. She goes out with people there, loves 'the green places and the parks'. Gladys thinks that people in Lima are calm; however, she stresses that she only walks in the central areas (Surco and San Borja); she does not like the suburbs.[29]

Prejudice against indians[30]

An important element of prejudice emerged in the interviews which we had missed in the survey. While it is mild in Bambamarca and very strong in Huanta, prejudice against indians (or *chutos* as they are called in Huanta) was reported by people from all three cases. Unfortunately, the survey missed this population; the sample included surrounding rural towns, but Highland communities were not reached[31]. Harold, an indigenous 23-year-old student, explained to us what a *chuto* is: 'the word '*chuto*' is used to identify a peasant or an indian offensively'. For him, *cholo* is different; it is the same as indigenous. 'In Lima everybody is a *cholo*', he emphasizes.[32] Jacinta, a 23-year-old indigenous woman in Huanta, who considers herself *blancona* (as a way of saying she is fairly white), expressed it with more clarity: 'there is not much difference between indigenous and *cholos*, we both speak Quechua; but *chutos* or indians are different. They are those who live in the Highlands, in the mountains.'[33] For Margarita, a 55-year-old woman in Huanta, being *chola* means being *serrana*: 'We Peruvians, we are all *cholos*'. The *chutos* are different, she affirms. 'They don't talk Spanish, don't know how to read and write, and have a special character: they are stubborn.'[34]

Bertha, a young primary school teacher, told us that children who come from the Highlands are called *chutos* or 'the stinking ones', because they do not know how to speak Spanish very well, have an accent, or because of their different appearance or odour. She has listened to her colleagues, especially 'those coming from the city', calling them 'those of the Highlands', 'the *chutos*'. She adds that 'it is easy to identify them because they wear their *hojotas* (traditional sandals)'.[35] Marco tells us that in Bambamarca people from the city treat peasants in a similar way: 'often they insult them, call them ignorant ones, dirty ones'. He mainly witnesses these situations on the buses to Cajamarca, since there are no special, or luxury, buses: 'people avoid sitting with them, touching them, and peasants realize'.[36]

What Harold and Jacinta made clear for us is that being indigenous or *cholo* is not the same as being indian. Indians, *chutos* or peasants (in the case of Bambamarca) tend to be seen by *serranos* as a specific category different from them, in which ethnic elements are present. Eliana, a young white teacher from Huanta, told us that *chutito (*little *chuto*) is someone who comes from the Highlands, with *cobrizo* (copper) or darker skin, trousers of *bayeta* (a cloth material), socks of sheep wool and *hojotas* (typical sandals). She added that these children speak only Quechua and do not understand Spanish very well. The other children, who do not want to learn Quechua, laugh at them and complain to her: 'teacher, they do not understand', 'they are donkeys'.[37] Beatriz, a *mestizo* teacher in Huanta, described the situation of a 6-year-old girl insulting an indian boy, calling him *chuto* and foolish (*bruto*), and making him cry. She said such situations are always happening.[38]

We do not know how these so-called indians would self-define. Probably they would not use the word 'indian', and would consider themselves *cholos*, *mestizos*, or even whites. However, for the *serrano* people living in the towns, or closer to them, this group does exist, as an imagined solid category with specific visible traits. They can be easily identified and a series of negative, oversimplified characteristics are associated with them. This serves to justify practices (insults, rejection, intolerance, humiliation and shame) and discourses (ignorant, dirty, bad smelling). These practices and discourses around the stereotype of 'indianness' not only organize the feelings and emotions of those who exercise the prejudice, but also of those who are its victims (Balibar 1991, Kaufman 2001). Beatriz emphasizes that 'people come to hate Quechua and make their children feel ashamed of their language'.[39] Marco from Bambamarca agrees with her. He said that 'when people discriminate against peasants and laugh at their traditions, the result is loss of self-esteem, of their own culture. The young feel shame and start looking for other accepted forms, alienated ones'.[40]

While we cannot say exactly how people feel about or process these situations, or to what degree they happen, we find significant evidence here of the existence of prejudice, discriminatory mechanisms and degrees of acceptability of them in Peruvian society. In order to avoid being laughed at in school, it is necessary to stop speaking Quechua. Poor peasant parents, who know the suffering produced by the stigma, will not jeopardize their children's learning of Spanish. Consequently, they oppose bilingual education (we return to this in Chapter 4). Traditional clothing and traditions are visible traits of the stigma. It is not the breaking of the rules that matters, or whether the clothing is in fact clean or not: what matters is that the other children laugh at them. A level of rupture with one's own community and a desire to leave behind the despised ethnic traits become unavoidable.

Prejudice in a Lima *barrio*

We have seen how prejudice is present in Huanta and Bambamarca against the indigenous peasants. Urban-based indigenous call them 'indians, *chutos*' and consider them 'ignorant', 'dirty', 'stubborn'. In the provinces, in the interior of Andean society, differences between urban serranos and indians (as they call indigenous peasants) are clear. In Lima, prejudice is directed at *cholos* and *serranos*. Differences between 'chutos' and 'urban' serranos are not obvious in the Lima context. Eliana complained: 'in Lima they call the *serrano* people *cholos* because they are from the Sierra and in Lima they see the Sierra as backward, but it is not like that. *Cholo* is a negative expression and the *serrano* says, yes, I am *cholo*, just to shut their mouths.'[41]

According to our interviews, whether a migrant is a 'so-called indian' or not, he or she will try to speak Spanish and dress in an urban way; if not, without a doubt, someone would quickly appear – very likely another *serrano* – to call them '*cholo*' or '*serrano*'. This is in order to remind them that they are exposing those markers nobody wants to be identified with (Nugent 1992). While some of these traits can be removed, others cannot. Unfortunately, we did not ask about how a *serrano* can be recognized in Lima (what are the visible traits?). Within a community, however, it is enough to know the neighbours' place of origin. Julio, a 48-year-old *cholo,* living in San Juan de Lurigancho, told us that he does not like to be called *serrano* or *cholo* because in the neighbourhood most people come from the Sierra: 'why do people only call some of them *cholos*?' He told us that during parties there are fights and people, when drunk, insult each other as *'cholo de mierda'* and '*serrano*'.[42] He was specific that the *norteños* (from the North Coast) are not insulted as *cholos*. The young do not like to be called *cholo*. On the contrary, they want to be seen as *limeños*.[43]

Outside the migrant community, in the traditional or residential areas of Lima, the contrast between *serranos* and others can become more pronounced, and other traits become significant. We do not have information from our data to describe those traits; interviews with people living in more residential areas would be needed. Yet, according to those we interviewed in Huanta Uno and Huanta Dos in San Juan de Lurigancho, traits such as accent, colour of skin and features become more important, particularly when looking for jobs. Hilario has not completed secondary school and says there is no discrimination by race or ethnicity in his field of work, construction: 'we are all *provincianos* but it is different if you want to work in a bank'.[44] While those coming from the Sierra bear the heaviest stigma, discrimination based on the colour of the skin and physical phenotype seems to be experienced independently of the region of origin. Karen from Chiclayo experienced discrimination when she went to look for a job in the centre of the city. She claimed that those selected were 'whiter'.[45] Fhara also reported a similar situation as happening to her darker friend when looking for job in a supermarket.[46] Planas and Valdivia (2007) in a recent study based in focus groups found similar results: 'race, colour of skin or physical appearance emerge as the most important motive of discrimination in Lima' (p.68).

However, discrimination in Lima – based on race or appearance – can be downplayed through using opportunities to change one's appearance, obtain education or possess some level of wealth – markers of modernity. We are not dealing here with a predominant discourse based on the superiority of the biological heredities of certain groups; external traits such as skin colour, clothes, and other visible characteristic are often used to 'identify' and 'direct' discriminatory practices against a group, but mainly based on prejudices against their culture, their 'tastes', conducts and lifestyles. Eliana gave us a clue: 'they think the Sierra is backwardness' and Fatima's mother thinks that *cholo*s are 'violent and drunk'.[47] Sometimes this prejudice has unconsciously shaped a person's aesthetic criteria to the extent that 'white' and 'beautiful' are not distinguishable in the same phrase.[48] Portocarrero (2004) provides us with a larger frame to understand this. For him 'physical' and 'cultural' differences have been used historically in Peru to classify people into different 'ranks': at one end, the 'indigenous' is the completely undesirable; and at the other end, the 'occidental' is the desirable model (p.286).[49] This discourse suggests that there is nothing wrong with the Sierra or the *serrano* or *cholo* people 'in their nature', but that it is necessary for them to overcome the 'backwardness', 'the irrational', 'the authoritarian' aspects of their culture to become compatible with the modern Peru, with the culture of progress. According to Balibar (1991) in this type of system of discrimination 'culture criteria' tend to replace 'race criteria' to justify the emergence of a new set of prejudices and stereotypes against particular groups, and physical features remain important because they are visible traits that enable these identifications to be made.[50] We shall pursue the history of this notion in Chapters 5 and 6 below.

Reactions to prejudice

How people react to this prejudice is a much more complex question. People's reactions may vary according to the different contexts and circumstances in which they live. However, our interviews allow us to offer some insights that can serve as a useful foundation for further research. The emotion of shame, and the consequences it has for those who feel it, is important in our cases. For instance, as the school teachers Beatriz and Marco pointed out, the humiliation of indian children in school may result in a loss of self-esteem, embarrassment at their own culture, and dropping out of school.[51]

To our knowledge, no scholar has studied the consequences of emotions in politics more comprehensively than John Elster. His study of multiple circumstances in which a 'culture of shame' develops induced by the disapproving stare of others has led him to recognize its significance. 'Shame is not only a support for the enforcement of social norms, but *the* support' (Elster 1999: 145). He argues that shame is unique among other emotions because it is so intensely unpleasant that the pressure to avoid it can undermine rational self-interest (ibid: 148). The immediate impulse is to hide, to run away, to shrink, but other reactions to shame are always possible. Reconstruction or improving of oneself may be attempted. Sometimes, shame can induce aggression, not only as a reaction to shaming, but as a mechanism of differentiation, 'by putting another down, one may attempt defensively to repair and in comparison raise up one's shattered sense of self-worth' (ibid: 153). All these complex reactions were encountered in our interviews.

We have seen how prejudice is present in Huanta and Bambamarca against the indigenous peasants. But in Lima, the differences between '*chutos*' and the rest of the *serranos,* which may be very visible in the province, are no longer clearly identifiable. All *serranos* may fall into the same category. In these circumstances, denial of group membership to avoid the shame may be the response. They want to suppress their identity when they arrive in Lima and discover that those characteristics that are ascribed to peasants, or '*chutos*' in their words, tend to be attached to all *serranos*. As Elvira and Julio illustrate, 'I am *cholo,* but I don't want to be called *cholo*.'[52] Another important response is to make clear the differences between these 'indians' and themselves: here education becomes a central strategy. Agustin Carrasco, a 52-year-old mechanic in Volkswagen Lima, told us that 'the *raza cobriza* [copper race] is the race with capacities'. He added that if you are professional, it is difficult for others to treat you badly: 'they speak to you with more respect, nobody can *cholear* you [call you *cholo* offensively]'. For him, '*cholear*' is the same as 'to humiliate'.[53] However, facing the pressure of colleagues, he felt the need to distinguish himself, an educated *cholo,* from 'indians': 'non-educated', 'still dressed in their traditional clothes'. He described to us how a couple of *serranos* came to the Volkswagen store to buy a car and his colleagues mocked him, saying: 'you go and help your *paisanos* [those from the same place of origin]'. He made clear to us that these two were a different type of *cholo* from him: 'they were dressed in their typical clothing with a sack in their hand'. In order to demonstrate this to his colleagues, he sold the car to the couple for a much higher price. 'I bought a car with the commission', he told us proudly.[54]

The interviews show us how the construction of ethnic identity is an ambivalent and painful process, more openly expressed in Lima than in the provinces, by the youth than by the old, by the men than by the women. It is contradictory and ambivalent for both those *cholos* or indigenous who are looking for their 'ethnic roots' and those looking for a *mestizo* identity who sometimes cannot avoid discrimination and cannot change the identity others assign to them. For *cholos* and indigenous, the construction of identity is a process of affirmation and negation at the same time, shaped by a context that imposes degrees of differentiation in order to avoid discrimination. For instance, Soledad, Marco, and others who self-define as *cholos* and refuse to feel shame,[55] behave in a different way to Agustin, the car mechanic who takes pride in how he cheats his peasant customers, to prove to his friends that he is not one of those 'paisanos'. For Soledad and Marco, the awareness of being the subject of prejudice has led them to a new appreciation of their own identity. Soledad was driven to hide her language, but now she is teaching Quechua to her daughter, taking advantage of the new opportunities that are appearing in the Huanta labour market: 'the State and NGOs are hiring people with knowledge of Quechua'.[56] Marco, a teacher from Bambamarca, is proud of being the son of a peasant. He told us he still in his spare time works with his father using the *yunta*, an agricultural tool inherited from pre-Spanish cultures. He argues that his trips to Lima and new experiences have helped him to accept his identity, whereas when he was young, he used to feel shame.

An important number of our cases, mainly self-defined as *cholos*, acknowledge that the word *'cholo'* is used to humiliate and insult by the wider world, but their response is not shame but pride, a deliberate affirmation against the insult others are offering to them: 'I am *cholo*, and so what?' This retort we heard as vigorously from *chola* women as from men. In the survey, *cholo/as* emerge as a special group. They have above average education, are concentrated in Lima, and are more likely to have positive views of indigenous than of *mestizos*. Nonetheless, pressure for differentiation is a reality in the society and can even lead to those who feel proud of being *cholo*s reproducing discriminatory practices against those 'less literate' and 'less urban' than themselves, as we have illustrated with the case of Agustin. We want to highlight that the problem with this vicious circle of discrimination is that an important number of those indigenous who 'succeed' tend to reproduce ethnic 'discrimination', making 'differentiation' and 'distinction' the root of their own identity.

Conclusions

Our initial hypothesis was that a strong prejudice against *cholo*s and indigenous people, mainly in Lima, and against indians in the Sierra, was a significant explanation of the fluidity of identity in Peru. It was presumed that people would try to escape this negative stereotype and hide those traits that allowed others to associate them with it. What the data and the interviews reveal, however, is more complex. We find that being subject to ethnic prejudice has not only resulted in passivity, denial of the group or alienation, but also, in other instances, in a new appreciation of an individual's own identity. However, it is clear that, coming from an environment that is very prejudiced against indigenous peasants ('indians' or '*chutos*' as they are known in the Sierra), *serrano* people are horrified when they arrive in Lima and discover they are being put in the same category, one that they themselves regard with such contempt. In this context, we can understand better the need for denial or suppression of identity, or the creation of clear differences between uneducated *cholo*s and indigenous (*indios, chutos*), and educated *serranos*. The imperative of this differentiation can include harm to an individual's own group.

We find evidence of a strong sense of ethnic identity, strongest among those who self-identify as *cholos*. In the interviews, the category of indigenous/Andean heavily overlaps with the *cholo* category: both emphasize their common place of origin, the Sierra, but it is among indigenous that we have identified the need for differentiation from the *cholo*s. There is also evidence of the importance of skin colour for some groups, particularly whites and *mestizo*s, whether as an important marker in itself or as the most easily comprehensible element when struggling with an understanding of identity (this seems to be particularly the case for poor women in Cajamarca).

Our interviews also show how migration is a key 'catalyser' in the process of construction of ethnic identity and how powerful the process has been in rearranging the 'spatial' configuration of ethnicity in the country, as well as the mechanisms through which boundaries are made. Before the waves of migration transformed the demography of the country – from Sierra to Coast and from rural to urban – ethnic boundaries, while still not completely clear-cut, were easier to understand. The Census of 1940 declared that there were 53 per cent whites and *mestizo*s and 46 per cent indians.[57] Most indians lived in their communities far from urban areas and only exceptionally visited the largest cities (even less Lima). The *mestizo*s lived in the largest cities including Lima, but many of them lived in the small towns in the periphery surrounded by indian communities. The whites lived mostly in the main cities, highly concentrated in Lima. Migration broke up this landscape and the whole structure of ethnic boundaries was transformed into the very complicated setting we have today.

The progressive migration of *mestizo*s from the small provinces of the Sierra to Lima and to larger cities made the 'traditional' urban setting more racially and culturally diverse, but it was the migration of the 'indians' that dislocated ethnic boundaries. Quijano (1980) was a visionary in regard to this process and saw from a very early date the emergence of a *cholo* identity such as the one we have registered in our survey and interviews. While *mestizo*s tended to integrate, more or less, into the *mestizo-criollo* ('urban-occidental') society,[58] the indians, sons and daughters of indigenous peasants arriving in Lima, tended to take another route. From the literature we have learnt that indigenous peasants adopted new behaviours, new tastes and lifestyles, and reconstructed their identity in multiple forms, which incorporated '*mestizo/criollo*' elements that are identified with the city and the *mestizo* population. Yet, at the same time, we have learnt from our interviews that they kept an important attachment to the culture and the practices of their places of 'origin': an attachment that often has been passed to their children.[59]

These multiple and diverse local cultures – sometimes only with reference to a tiny community – are characterized not only by pre-hispanic traditions, but by elements that were incorporated in the course of five hundred years of subordination, first in the colony and later in the republic.[60] As Karen told us, this attachment is not only to traditions, such as special fiestas, but to practices, such as the use of language, the admiration of the landscape, the way of living,[61] music,[62] and values.[63] People coming from the Sierra find in the Andes a common place of reference, but the Sierra has also been a common source of 'stigma'. In spite of these contradictory forces, the Sierra has become the main 'substance' of the emerging *cholo* and indigenous identity we find in our interviews. In the provinces, this takes the form of a different *mestizaje*, the indigenous *mestizo*.[64] But as Julio told us in describing his neighbourhood, people from different parts of the country (including people from the Coast and the Selva) have met in the migrant neighbourhoods. And today, all those once considered members of 'less urban', 'less occidental', or 'less modern' cultures are reconstructing and remaking their identity: a 'more urban', 'more occidental' or 'more modern' one, but different from the *criollo-mestizo* identity, different from the one that predominates in the centre and traditional areas of Lima.

With this understanding we find that geography and history are the best proxies to understand ethnic boundaries in Peru today when self-identification is not available. Most whites and a significant part of *mestizo*s have been born and live in the traditional and residential areas of Lima. Most of the *mestizo*s and a significant number of *cholo*s have been born and live in the migrant and peripheral neighbourhoods together with the largest cities of the departments. In the rest of the country, in the countryside and in the small towns, *mestizo*s, *cholo*s, but mainly indigenous peasants (the so-called 'indians') have been born and still live.

Appendix to Chapter 2

The methodology of the CRISE Perception Survey: the questionnaire and the sample

David Sulmont

The 2005 CRISE Perception Survey questionnaire was intended to measure perceptions on identity, ethnicity, religion and collective and political action among respondents of samples in the different countries of the regions where the CRISE project is working (Latin America, Africa and Asia). The draft versions of the questionnaire were discussed in a CRISE workshop in Oxford in February 2005. The original English questionnaire was translated into Spanish by David Sulmont to be used as a template in the Latin American countries (Bolivia, Guatemala and Peru). Further modifications were made by the researchers responsible for each country's survey in order to adapt the questionnaire to their specific realities.

In the Peruvian case, the questionnaire was extensively tested and modified in order to accommodate to local terminology and social, ethnic and racial identity issues. A draft version of the questionnaire was first tested in January 2005 in peasant communities and villages in the region of Cusco, as an input for the Oxford workshop in February. Later, in July 2005, a first version of the post-workshop questionnaire was tested with 40 respondents in some locations of Huanta, Ayacucho. After the final modifications, the survey fieldwork was conducted in late August and September 2005.

Regarding the measurement of ethnic or racial categories, we adopted four types of indicators:

- Respondent's mother tongue.
- *'Ethnic / racial self-identification'*: respondent's single self identification with one of the following categories: White; *Mestizo*; Andean Indigenous; Amazon Indigenous; *Cholo*; Black / *Zambo*;[65] Chinese / Japanese.[66]
- *'Ethnic scale self-location'*: respondent's self location in a 7 point 'chromatic scale', ranging from White (=1), through Indigenous (=7).[67]
- *Ancestry*: respondent's categorization of her or his parents in the 'ethnic / racial' categories described above.

We also asked the respondents to identify the two main groups in their communities or neighbourhoods using the 'ethnic / racial' categories and to locate them in the '7 point ethnic scale'.

According to agreements reached in the CRISE workshop, in order to carry out an exploratory analysis on the relationships between horizontal inequalities and social conflict, the sample design was intended to represent different contexts of cultural identification and categorization, and different levels of social conflict or violence. In the light of the resources that could be allocated to the surveys in each country, the average sample size was set around 600 interviews.

In Peru, this sample design led to the definition of three different types of cases, each one represented by a specific location. In order to maximize the possibility of examining the cases using different methodological perspectives, these locations were the same as those studied by Ismael Muñoz, Maritza Paredes and Rosemary Thorp during 2004 and 2005 in the context of the CRISE project (Muñoz *et al.* 2006).

The cases were defined with the aim of testing differences based on region, cultural heterogeneity, urban and rural settings, and areas or people affected by the internal armed conflict in the 1980s and 1990s. In some locations, we made a subdivision intended to represent different levels of social integration and exclusion. It is important to bear in mind that the sample does not represent the whole Peruvian society; therefore, country-level generalizations are not possible. Instead, the sample is intended to represent a variety of social settings where we can observe different configurations of horizontal inequalities, perceptions of identity, politics and collective action.

The selected locations were the Highland provinces of Bambamarca in Cajamarca and Huanta in Ayacucho, and two neighbourhoods in the district of San Juan de Lurigancho in the capital city of Lima.[68]

San Juan de Lurigancho is the most populated district of the city of Lima, and incidentally, the most populated district of the country. According to the 2005 census, it has 812,656 inhabitants; most of them are migrants who came to the city during the mid-1980s and the 1990s. In this location we selected two neighbourhoods: 'Huanta I' and 'Huanta II'. The inhabitants of those neighbourhoods come mostly from the province of Huanta, in the department of Ayacucho. They left their region of origin because of the political violence they experienced during the 1980s and 1990s. According to the Peruvian Truth and Reconciliation Commission, Huanta in Ayacucho was the province most affected by the internal armed conflict.

The people who founded 'Huanta I' in San Juan de Lurigancho came primarily from the urban areas of their original province; they have higher educational levels and socioeconomic status than their fellow countrymen. In contrast, inhabitants of 'Huanta II' came from poorer

Table 2A.1 CRISE survey: respondents' principal characteristics by location of residence

Variables	Categories	Total %	Location of residence		
			Huanta	Bambamarca	SJL – Lima
Gender	Female	**52.7**	50.2	50.7	57.2
	Male	**47.3**	49.8	49.3	42.8
Age group	18 to 24	**29.9**	32.9	23.4	33.3
	25 to 34	**22.1**	18.8	26.4	21.4
	35 to 44	**24.1**	23.0	27.4	21.9
	45 to 54	**13.3**	13.1	10.4	16.4
	55 plus	**10.6**	12.2	12.4	7.0
Occupational status	**Occupied**	***57.1***	*49.2*	*67.7*	*54.9*
	Peasant	**10.6**	19.7	11.4	0.0
	Self employed, unqualified	**23.1**	12.7	34.3	22.9
	Employed in small size enterprises (< 10 employees)	**1.8**	0.9	0.5	4.0
	Employed in big / medium size enterprises (> 10 employees)	**4.1**	0.9	2.0	9.5
	Public servant	**8.8**	11.7	8.5	6.0
	Small business owner (< 10 employees)	**5.0**	1.9	5.0	8.5
	Self employed, professional	**2.9**	1.4	5.0	2.5
	Big / medium business owner	**0.8**	0.0	1.0	1.5

	Not occupied	***42.9***	*50.7*	*32.4*	*45.3*
	Housewife / housekeeper	**23.4**	26.8	19.9	23.4
	Student	**15.6**	22.5	9.0	14.9
	Temporarily unemployed, do not work	**2.9**	0.5	3.0	5.5
	Retired	**1.0**	0.9	0.5	1.5
Educational level	None	**6.0**	2.3	15.4	0.5
	Some secondary or primary school	**43.1**	47.9	51.8	29.4
	Secondary school	**34.2**	32.4	18.4	52.3
	Post secondary other than university	**7.6**	6.1	7.0	10.0
	University degree	**8.9**	11.3	7.5	8.0
Racial / ethnic self identification	*Mestizo*	**53.7**	52.1	72.6	36.3
	Indigenous / Andean	**18.7**	25.3	3.5	26.9
	Cholo	**17.6**	16.4	7.0	29.4
	White	**8.8**	6.1	16.4	4.0
	Other / none / not known	**1.3**	0.0	0.5	3.5
Number of cases		**615**	**213**	**201**	**201**

areas of the province and arrived in the city in the early 90s. 'Huanta II' is more heterogeneous than 'Huanta I', since some people came also from other provinces of Peru.

Huanta is the second most important province of the department of Ayacucho, located in the Central Highlands of the country. The 2005 census found 85,559 inhabitants in this province. During almost 15 years, political violence in Huanta was extremely intense, causing several thousands of deaths.[69] In this region we selected two locations to be surveyed: the city of Huanta and the district of Luricocha. The first one is an urban area (population 40 thousand) and the second one is a rural district (population 5.7 thousand). The majority of the inhabitants of the province of Huanta has Quechua as their mother tongue and come from a peasant background.

The district of Bambamarca, capital of the province of Hualcayoc, is located in the department of Cajamarca, in the Northern Highlands of Peru. In 2005 Bambamarca had 74,513 inhabitants. It is a rural district; many of its inhabitants are employed in agriculture-related activities, as peasants, artisans or in the commercial sector. The most important organizations in the region are the 'rondas campesinas', a form of rural autonomous police and community justice organization. In terms of cultural characteristics, Bambamarca is more homogeneous than Huanta and San Juan de Lurigancho.

In each of the locations the respondents were selected using an area-clustered multi-stage random sample design. In order to be selected, respondents had to be between 18 and 70 years old. In total, 615 questionnaires were completed, evenly distributed among the three locations. The fieldwork teams were organized and trained by the staff of the Public Opinion Institute of the Catholic University of Peru, under the supervision of David Sulmont and Vania Martínez.

In Table 2A.1, we can see the main characteristics of the respondents in the three surveyed locations. The distributions of the categories in the socioeconomic variables (occupational status, educational level) are consistent with the different social contexts that the cases were supposed to represent. If we had to put the three locations in a socioeconomic scale, creating an index which combines occupation status and education, the order of the three locations will be (from less to more): Bambamarca, Huanta and San Juan de Lurigancho.

Notes

1. As explained in the Appendix, the experience of violence was also a criterion, a dimension we return to in Chapter 7.

2. Studies which attempt to estimate the proportion of indigenous people in Peru are: Carrión and Zárate (2006), Trivelli (2005) and UNDP (2005). The three use different ethnic markers and arrive at different estimations. See Chapter 3 for a fuller discussion of the issue of estimation.
3. As in Peruvian society the concepts of ethnicity and race have been and continue to be very much suppressed, a card offering options was used. The question was phrased as follows: many people think that the racial or cultural groups living in Peru are the following: (1) indigenous/Andean, (2) Amazonian, (3) black or *Zambos*, (4) whites, (5) *cholos*, (6) *mestizos*, (7) Chinese or Japanese and (8) others. Using this list, if you had to define which of these groups you belong to, which would it be?
4. In the course of the analysis we will call these four groups white, *mestizo*, *cholo* and indigenous for simplicity.
5. This small proportion was to be expected given the sites that the CRISE survey sample targeted.
6. This supports our earlier claim, that language is not a good ethnic marker in Peru. In order to examine this result further we analysed the National Household Survey of 2001 (ENAHO) which asks for ethnic identity and we found that in regions where an indigenous language predominates, it will be spoken by both those who self-define as indigenous and those who do not.
7. Exploitative landlord, generally from the Sierra.
8. '*Cobrizo*' is a common term referring to the colour of skin of indigenous people. Literally it means 'copper-coloured'.
9. This question was based on the methodology used in Ñopo *et al.* (2004).
10. The word 'cosmopolitan' generally describes an environment where many cultures from around the world coexist, or a person whose cultural and identity baggage comes from many different cultures. Its sense overlaps to some extent with citizen of the world, implying identification with a world community rather than with a particular nation or people. In Peru, the term 'cosmopolitan' refers to an individual who identifies with different spaces and cultures in Peru. She or he will have travelled to other regions for work, including Lima; will have interacted with people from other regions, and moved from his or her little province to the largest cities, or returned to his or her town of birth.
11. Interview with Simon Barreto, Bambamarca, Cajamarca (22 June 2006).
12. Interview with Fátima Aguirre, San Juan de Lurigancho, Lima (17 June 2006).
13. Interview with Beatriz Calderon, Huanta, Ayacucho (27 June 2006).
14. The imposition or pressure from outside in the self-definition or self-categorization of social identity has been much studied in social psychology, as has been noted previously. See extensive work by Hogg, particularly with McGarty (1990) and with Abrams (1988). These studies have rarely interacted with macro-political explanations of ethnicity. Efforts in this direction have been made by Green and Seher (2003) and Brubaker, Loveman and Stamatov (2004).
15. In Peru, De la Cadena (2000), Mendez (1996) and Portocarrero (1993) have done interesting work in this direction.
16. Prejudices are understood as cognitive structures that contain knowledge, beliefs and expectations about social groups that are deeply rooted in an

ordinary cognitive process of the individuals and the groups. Therefore their content is highly variable across cultural settings, over time, and across groups. For an overview of social psychological literature on stereotypes, see Hamilton and Sherman (1994).

17. Interview with Fátima Aguirre, San Juan de Lurigancho, Lima (17 June 2006).
18. We need to remember that the proportion of white in the sample is very small; therefore we present the results combining whites with *mestizos* for the three provinces.
19. Interview with Elvira Macedo, San Juan de Lurigancho, Lima (15 June 2006).
20. Interviews with Marco Balbín, Bambamarca (20 June 2006), Pablo Cavero, Bambamarca (21 June 2006), Simon Barreto, Bambamarca (22 June 2006), Jorge Pajuelo, Bambamarca (22 June 2006), Beatriz Calderón, Huanta (27 June 2006), Eliana Cabrera, Huanta (28 June 2006), Soledad Tello, Huanta (28 June 2006), Jacinta Cáceres, Huanta (27 June 2006), Julio Aguilar, SJL (15 June 2006), Agustin Carrasco, SJL (17 June 2006) and Hildebrando Vargas, SJL (19 June 2006).
21. Interview with Marco Balvin, Bambamarca, Cajamarca (20 June 2006).
22. Interview with Harold Ramos, Huanta, Ayacucho (28 June 2006).
23. Interview with Julio Aguilar, San Juan de Lurigancho, Lima (15 June 2006).
24. Interview with Soledad Tello, Huanta, Ayacucho (28 June 2006).
25. Interview with Elvira, San Juan de Lurigancho, Lima (16 June 2006).
26. Allport (1954) underlines that a genuine physical difference comes to be regarded as a total (categorical) difference in *kind*. Whether real, such as skin colour, or imaginary, as generally other 'sensory' qualities such as odour are, they become a central symbol, a 'condensing rod', which enables us to think about another group as a solid unit and attach specific qualities to them. In different cultures or historical times, women were not only thought of as different in appearance, but also in biological nature, less intelligent, less rational and – in some cultures – without a soul.
27. Interview with Liliam Benicio, Bambamarca, Cajamarca (20 June 2006).
28. Interview with Judith Valera, Bambamarca, Cajamarca (21 June 2006).
29. Interview with Gertudris Valverde, Bambamarca, Cajamarca (22 June 2006).
30. Although the word *indio* is not commonly used any more in public and academic literature, it is still used, and with a very well-defined meaning, among the people we interviewed.
31. In order to reach these communities, special transportation is needed. Infrastructure is extremely limited and inadequate.
32. Interview with Harold Ramos, Huanta, Ayacucho (28 June 2006).
33. Interview with Jacinta Cáceres, Huanta, Ayacucho (27 June 2006).
34. Interview with Margarita Cardenas, Huanta, Ayacucho (28 June 2006).
35. Interview with Beatriz Calderon, Huanta, Ayacucho (27 June 2006).
36. Interview with Marco Balvín, Bambamarca, Cajamarca (20 June 2006).
37. Interview with Jacinta Cáceres, Huanta, Ayacucho (27 June 2006).
38. Interview with Beatriz Calderon, Huanta, Ayacucho (27 June 2006).
39. Interview with Beatriz Calderon, Huanta, Ayacucho (27 June 2006).
40. Interview with Marco Balvín, Bambamarca, Cajamarca (20 June 2006).
41. Interview with Eliana Cabrera, Huanta, Ayacucho (28 June 2006).

42. This is a recurrent theme in the testimony. For example, see interviews in Lima: Julio Aguilar, SJL (15 June 2006), Elvira Macedo, SJL (15 June 2006) and Carlos Zambrano (16 June 2006).
43. Interview with Julio Aguilar, SJL, Lima (15 June 2006).
44. Interview with Hildebrando Vargas, SJL, Lima (19 June 2006).
45. Interview with Karen Valcazar, SJL, Lima (15 June 2006).
46. Interview with Fátima Aguirre, SJL, Lima (17 June 2006).
47. Interview with Fátima Aguirre, SJL, Lima (17 June 2006).
48. We found significant evidence of this on our interviews, especially from women. Planas and Valdivia (2007) found similar testimonies (see pp.43–54).
49. Another hypothesis to explore in a future study is how 'rapid changes' are seen. Becoming an accepted, assimilated *mestizo* takes time. Migrants coming back from Miami and Paterson, New Jersey, holding the appearance 'card', such as modern clothing and some relative wealth, constitute another, different group, which is not necessarily well accepted.
50. The recent elections in the country have revived all these stereotypes and prejudices in the Highlands, and the highest authorities in the country have felt free to make prejudiced comments. In 2006 the then prime minister told the press that it was the lack of oxygen that prevented people from the Sierra making a good and rational decision, referring to the high support enjoyed by candidate Ollanta Humala in these areas. Cited by Degregori 'Inclusión vs. Racismo in Peru' (http://peru21.pe/impresa/noticia/inclusion-vs-racismo/2006-07-15/5423), and no doubt meant as a joke, but a nation's jokes reveal a great deal.
51. Interviews with Marco Balvín, Bambamarca, Cajamarca (20 June 2006) and Beatriz Calderon, Huanta, Ayacucho (27 June 2006).
52. Interviews with Elvira Macedo, SJL, Lima (15 June 2006) and Julio Aguilar, SJL, Lima (15 June 2006).
53. Interview with Agustin Carrasco, SJL, Lima (17 June 2006).
54. Interview with Agustin Carrasco, SJL, Lima (17 June 2006).
55. Interviews with Soledad Tello, Huanta, Ayacucho (28 June 2006) and with Marco Balvín, Bambamarca, Cajamarca (20 June 2006).
56. Interview with Soledad Tello, Huanta, Ayacucho (28 June 2006).
57. White and *mestizo*s were reported together but the categories were written as different ones. Others groups were seen as minorities.
58. See: Sinesio López (1997), Gonzalo Portocarrero (1993) and Quijano (1980).
59. See: Degregori et al. (1986), Carlos Franco (1991) and Golte and Adams (1990).
60. An example of this is the practice of using the coca leaf. It is true that it was used in pre-hispanic time to celebrate in traditional ceremonies, but during the colony it acquired different uses and meanings in the context of exploitation of the mines and the plantations. Its overall importance has not lost meaning; it has just changed.
61. Interview with Karen Valcazar, SJL, Lima (15 June 2006).
62. Interview with Harold Ramos, Huanta, Ayacucho (28 June 2006).
63. Interview with Marco Balvín, Bambamarca, Cajamarca (20 June 2006).
64. Contrary to the idea of *mestizo* who disappear into a national, gradually homogenizing culture, De la Cadena (2000) show how there are indigenous *mestizo*s, at least in Cusco, who distance themselves from the 'indian' stigma,

but at the same time promote different ways of doing this de-indianization and promote non-stereotypical characteristics of the culture.

65. In Peru, '*Zambo*' is a word which designates someone of black African origins.
66. The question wording was: 'If you have to define which group in this card you belong to, which one it would be?'
67. This question was inspired by the methodology used in Ñopo *et al.* (2004). The question wording was: 'Many people think that the contemporary Peruvian's identity is mainly the product of the encounter between the Spanish of white race and the native inhabitants of Peruvian territory of indigenous race. Using this scale, where 1 means "white" and 7 means "indigenous" in which point would you locate yourself? Remember that you can choose any point between 1 and 7.'
68. For a deeper description of the social context of those locations, see Muñoz et al. (2006).
69. Based on the CVR information and using the Multiple Systems Estimation methodology (CVR 2003: Appendix 3), we figure that 6.5 thousand people died in Huanta during the conflict, almost 8.5 per cent of the overall population of the province enumerated by the 1981 census at the beginning of the conflict.

3
Measuring Group Inequalities*

The previous chapter has been devoted to making two points. First, in Peru ethnic identities are complex and fluid, with divergences between subjective and objective perceptions. Second, they *matter.* They matter, because people find that they matter, as part of identity, but also as a source of disparate life experiences. Prejudice and discrimination are unpopular realities to admit to in Peru, but they do exist.

With this depth of understanding we now need to evaluate the degree of group, or 'horizontal', inequality and its forms. It will be clear that to do this in a clean straightforward statistical sense is impossible. But we need to try to give a quantitative sense, and this is the task of this chapter, where we abstract from the complexities we have developed rather fully, to investigate the best proxies we can find for group-ethnic identity in Peru. First, we comment more deeply on the problem of ethnic markers. Second, we present our evidence on socioeconomic and political horizontal inequalities. Then we explore people's *perceptions* of horizontal inequalities, drawing again on the results of our survey and the follow up interviews. Finally we conclude. We show that despite the ambiguities of measurement and the degree of fluidity, felt grievances of an ethnic nature clearly exist.

The effort of measurement is important, despite its difficulty. This is not only because it can reinforce our case on the salience of ethnicity, but also because, based on that case, one clear policy implication of our analysis will be that inequalities between groups need to be monitored as part of a responsible development policy, and targeted with specific actions. Such a policy needs data to implement it, and simply improving such data may need to be part of the policy recommendation.

---

*As explained in the Preface, Adolfo Figueroa is co-author of this chapter.

Ethnic Markers

After the discussion of Chapter 2, it will be evident that it is difficult to produce adequate ethnic markers, given the fluidities and ambiguities we have described and the way people's views of their own and others' ethnicity varies, over time and in different contexts. Even the language of markers becomes part of the problem: one might think, for example, that 'white' had a clear meaning, but in Peru the word contains a mixture of racial and cultural elements. Thus someone who by his or her parentage and skin colour and features would appear to be *mestizo*, might well be called, and call him or herself, 'white', based on cultural characteristics.

The usual candidates for ethnic markers include race, language, religion and place of origin. In the case of Peru, data on race are mostly unavailable or unreliable. The usual way to measure race is to use self-identification of the individual. In our survey, reported in the previous chapter, we used self-identification, precisely because we were interested in people's *perceptions* of identity. But as an objective measure, this method has proved to be unreliable in a hierarchical society, because people tend to hide the stigma of not belonging to the dominant group, in our case being 'non-white'. It is possible to circumvent this problem with sophisticated methods, as shown in the case of Brazil (Lovell 1999, Silva 1992); however, these methods have not been used in Peru when data on race have been collected, as in the 1940 Census or the 2001 National Household Survey (ENAHO).

We have seen that language is only a partial marker of ethnicity in Peru, despite the fact that it is the most commonly used marker. As discussed in Chapter 2 above, indigenous languages are spoken by a subset of descendants of indigenous populations. Spanish is the common language even in regions where well-developed pre-colonial civilizations existed, such as the Chimu in the north. Today, not all indigenous populations speak indigenous languages. In addition, other minority ethnic groups, such as Africans, Asians and Europeans, all speak Spanish. Hence, language is a poor ethnic marker in Peru. Further, religion cannot be used as a social marker in a country that is largely Catholic (about 95 per cent of the population), and in which Catholicism cuts across almost all ethnic groups.

We are thus left with place of origin, for which we think a good case can be made.[1] In Chapter 5 below we describe the historical process that led to a physical separation of indigenous and white/*mestizo*: today, migration has enormously confused the issue, but by using place of birth, not residence, we can at least partially compensate. Further, the same segregation has tended to reproduce itself in Lima. Acknowledging fully the arbitrariness of the process, we have distinguished seven geographical categories for place of birth. The city of Lima-Callao is separated into two areas: 'Lima-core', the residential districts of Lima where those born are mostly white, and 'Lima-periphery', where the children of migrants are born. Then we have a grouping of the residential districts of the capital cities of the regions, mainly white and *mestizo* regions, which we call 'local core'. The rest of the population of the Andean region outside the regional capitals is divided into Southern Andes, with Quechua and Aymara as the predominant languages, and Central and Northern Andes, where Spanish dominates over Quechua. The 'rest' of the Coast and the 'rest' of the Amazonian region complete the seven categories.

As an abstraction and to attempt a synthetic presentation in the text, we group our seven regions of place of birth into three principal divisions. The first group, principally indigenous/*cholo*, is defined as those born in the provinces of the Andes, Amazon and Coast, but excluding the residential districts of the regional capitals. This group for shorthand purposes we call 'indigenous' in the text, but the reader needs to note the inverted commas. The next group comprises those born in provincial capitals or the barriadas of Lima, and is principally *mestizo*, with many who self-identify as '*cholo*'. For shorthand purposes we call this group '*mestizo*', and again the inverted commas are important. The remaining group comprises those born in the 11 most residential districts of Lima (Barranco, Jesús María, La Molina, Lince, Magdalena, Miraflores, Pueblo Libre, San Borja, San Isidro, San Miguel, and Surco), and is principally white with a large *mestizo* but not *cholo* element. The shorthand will be 'white'.

For the adult population (aged 25 or over), the estimates are as follows: 'white' 3.5 per cent, '*mestizo*' 27.5 per cent, and 'indigenous' 69 per cent. This definition of indigenous is wide, including as it does those born in the rural areas and small towns of the Coast, Amazon and Central and Northern Sierra. A much narrower definition might include only those born in the Southern Sierra, without its capital cities. That gives a figure of 21 per cent. We consider that such a definition is far too narrow, even while our own is arguably too broad, but neither solves the real problem: that place of birth is the best proxy for ethnic origin but still imperfect. However, sensitivity analysis for different definitions did not lead us to qualify the results we report below.

Most other studies have calculated indigenous populations based on language, which yields a much lower figure. An important recent work is that of Carolina Trivelli (2005). In a careful statistical analysis using the 2001 ENAHO survey, she shows that combining self-identification and use of an indigenous language, the most embracing definition gives a figure of 45 per cent. We have explained above our concern over the language criterion and even self-identification: no calculation is exempt from error. Our measure for instance assumes that all those born in non-capital regional districts in Peru are indigenous, which is obviously far from true, and explains why we have such a high percentage of indigenous – even higher than in Bolivia.

Using the proposed classification, *pace* its problems, we can develop measures of social, economic and political group inequalities. The evaluation of political inequalities requires, however, some further ingenuity, since we want to explore political representation of distinct groups at various levels of the political and judicial system. For this, place of birth was unavailable, and the best objective measure we could apply was to use surnames as a proxy. Using surnames is extremely problematic in Latin America because of the process of *mestizaje* in some regions. Also, we can only evaluate the *tendency,* as we do not know the proportion of people with indigenous surnames in the country. Another problem that we cannot resolve is that indigenous people may have lost their ethnically-rooted second surname in the process of *mestizaje.* An illustrative example is the case of Maximo San Roman, who was Vice-President during the first government of Alberto Fujimori (1990–1992). He has lost the last names with Quechua roots from his mother, Natividad Cáceres Chuchullo, and his father, Julio San Román de Pomacanchis. Because of situations like this one, we are very probably underestimating the participation of indigenous people and the trend we observe is only valid if this underestimation occurs in the same proportion in each period. Nevertheless, we find we can gain some insights, and we present the results below.

Measures of Group Inequalities

Group inequalities in income and poverty

From the 2003 household survey, Figueroa has estimated inequality of labour incomes (Figueroa 2008). We need to stress that use of this source underestimates group inequalities, since it is a well-known limitation of household surveys that they do not capture well non-labour income, and that this is where much of the inequality tends to lie. The income distribution is shown in Table 3.1. It can be seen that our proxy for the 'white' population has only 9 per cent in the four lowest deciles of the national ranking, and 39 per cent in the top decile, while for

Table 3.1 The distribution of income within each group[a] (percentages)

	'Indigenous'	'Mestizo'	'White'
Poorest 40 per cent of the national income levels	49	22	9
Middle 50 per cent of the distribution	45	62	52
Richest national income levels (top 10 per cent)	6	16	39
All income recipients	100	100	100

[a] Principally labour income from data from the ENAHO (year 2003).
Source: Figueroa (2008).

'indigenous', the percentages are more than reversed: 49 per cent in the bottom group and only 6 per cent in the top decile.

Horizontal inequalities contribute significantly to the high degree of vertical inequality in Peru. Figueroa estimates that if horizontal inequalities were eliminated, Peru's Gini coefficient of nearly 0.60 would fall to around 0.40. This is the figure shown by Latin American countries with insignificant shares of indigenous people, such as Argentina and Costa Rica (Figueroa 2001a, Table 1: 37).

Poverty incidence can be calculated from the household surveys. As Table 3.2 shows, 24 per cent of the 'indigenous' population are identified as 'extremely poor' in the survey, compared with 6 per cent of '*mestizo*s' and very few of the 'white' population.[2]

Trivelli, in her study using the ENAHO survey of 2001, finds a higher percentage of the indigenous population to be poor than we do. This is consistent with our different choices for classification: it is probable that the population she excludes and we include is somewhat better off than the average of her 'indigenous' group. However, what is striking about both studies is that we *agree* on the size of the gap: the absolute gap of some twenty percentage points is similar in both studies (Trivelli 2005).[3]

From the Trivelli study we can take further insights: she explores distribution *within* each group, and finds that the non-indigenous group on her definition is significantly more unequal than the indigenous, though there is still significant inequality within the indigenous population. She also highlights the significance of residence: the *rural* population is poorer than the urban population, indigenous and non-indigenous alike. But '[a]mong rural households, those who are indigenous and only speak an indigenous language are those with the most unfavourable indicators' (Trivelli 2005: 23). These are the 'chutos' of the

Table 3.2 Share of households by poverty status[a] and by social group of the household head (percentages)

	'Indigenous'	'Mestizos'	'White'	Total
Extremely poor	24.1	5.8	1.8	19.5
Poor (non extreme)	29.3	22.2	7.2	27.3
Non poor	46.6	72.0	91.0	53.2
Total	100.0	100.0	100.0	100.0

[a] According to household expenditure per capita.
Source: Barrón (2008) and data supplied by Barrón.

previous chapter, carrying their multiple burdens of poverty, inequality and discrimination.

Human development indicators

Next we turn to human development indicators. The most illuminating, education, is one that is hugely important for our study, so much so that we reserve its full discussion to a special chapter (Chapter 4). Table 3.3 presents the summary results for our three groups on years of schooling. What Chapter 4 will demonstrate at length is that the measure 'years of schooling' significantly underestimates the true human capital inequality, since what a person learns with years in school will vary widely depending on ethnic variables, and on average the outcome variables show that being indigenous is a disadvantage. So again, we have here an underestimate. Table 3.3 shows lower levels of education for groups born in predominantly indigenous regions. Illiteracy rates are higher for those groups. Only 43 per cent of indigenous attained a secondary qualification or more, *no matter where they lived*. At the other extreme, this share is 93 per cent for the group born in Lima-core. Chapter 4 will also discuss the gender dimension of the figures, which demonstrates a further horizontal inequality within groups as well as between, though diminishing over the generations.

Health indicators are unsatisfactory, since all we have from the survey is medical attention and health insurance: we have no outcome data in this source, whereas at least for education we have literacy data. The data in Table 3.4, on percentage figures for medical attention and health insurance, show little difference in the per cent attaining attention, but we have no information on need. The insurance data show the '*mestizo*' and 'white' groups with higher percentage of insurance: 65 per cent of the 'indigenous' group have no insurance compared with 40 per cent of those born in Lima core. In this case there is no gender difference.

Table 3.3 Level of education by social group and gender[a] (percentages)

Level of education	'Indigenous'			'Mestizos'			'Whites'		
	Male	**Female**	**Total**	**Male**	**Female**	**Total**	**Male**	**Female**	**Total**
None	6.2	21.4	14.1	1.0	5.0	3.1	0.0	0.6	0.3
Primary	43.0	63.4	63.1	16.4	19.8	18.3	4.1	8.2	6.4
Secondary or higher	50.8	35.2	42.8	82.6	75.2	78.6	95.9	91.2	93.3
Total	**100**	**100**	**100**	**100**	**100**	**100**	**100**	**100**	**100**
per cent literate 15+	91.7	75.6	83.5	98.2	95.1	96.6	99.1	99.5	99.3

[a] Population aged 25 or older.
Source: Barrón (2008) and data supplied by Barrón.

Table 3.4 Medical attention and health insurance, by ethnic group[a] (per cent of population in each group and subgroup)

	'Indigenous'			'Mestizo'			'White'		
	Male	**Female**	**Total**	**Male**	**Female**	**Total**	**Male**	**Female**	**Total**
Medical attention									
Public	31.3	33.6	32.6	35.0	35.7	35.4	24.4	28.9	27.0
Private	3.4	4.1	3.8	6.2	8.2	7.3	9.5	11.6	10.7
None	65.3	62.2	63.6	58.8	56.1	57.3	66.1	59.5	62.3
Total	100.0	100.0	100.0	100.0	100.0	100.0	100.0	100.0	100.0
Health insurance									
Public	34.6	34.6	34.6	40.4	41.9	41.2	41.6	45.9	43.8
Private	0.9	0.8	0.9	3.3	3.4	3.4	18.2	14.8	16.4
None	64.5	64.6	64.5	56.3	54.7	55.5	40.3	39.3	39.8
Total	100.0	100.0	100.0	100.0	100.0	100.0	100.0	100.0	100.0

[a] Data from ENAHO (2002).
Source: Barrón (2008) and data supplied by Barrón.

We can however get somewhat more help from a different source, the regular surveys of maternal and child health carried out by *Cuanto*[4] in collaboration with the World Bank, the so-called Living Standards Measurement Surveys. Unfortunately these surveys do not provide data which allow us to do a classification comparable with our other data. The early surveys ask about language spoken in the home, yielding some 10 per cent of Quechua or Aymara speaking.[5] Those for 2000 and 2004 do not ask that question, but do invite people to name their ethnic origin. As we have explained, this leads to a distinct under-representation as people conceal their identity: the figure is still around some 10 per cent. Table 3.5 shows HIs in child mortality on this basis: they are significant. We cannot tell how the different classification affects the results without begging the very questions we want to answer: we can only record significant inequalities under this measure.

Another set of indicators is provided by housing quality and access to services for the household. As Table 3.6 shows, access to running water, sewerage and phone is progressively less across the groups, and housing is more primitive. Only 40 per cent of 'indigenous' households are connected to a sewerage system, where 93 per cent of 'whites' are, and 95 per cent of the latter have running water compared to 57 per cent of the 'indigenous' group.

Access to wage employment

Our third source of insight is equality or the lack of it in access to wage employment. This is fully analysed by Figueroa and Barrón (2005) and by Figueroa (2008), whose work we draw on here. An important source of exclusion from the labour market is unequal educational opportunities, which we have already discussed. A further avenue to explore is whether the indigenous population is over-represented in the category of un- and under-employed, *controlling* for levels of education. Figueroa (2008)

Table 3.5 Horizontal inequality in child mortality according to LSMS[a] (indigenous/white-*mestizo* ratio)

Year	HI indigenous/white-mestizo
1996	1.76
2000	1.85
2004	1.93

[a] Classification by language spoken in the home.
Source: ENNIV surveys.

Table 3.6 Households' services and housing characteristics by social groups (percentages)

	'Indigenous'	'Mestizos'	'White'	Peru
Running water[a]	57.4	82.4	95.0	63.9
Sewerage[b]	39.8	76.5	92.8	49.2
Phone[c]	17.3	46.6	80.7	25.2
Walls[d]	81.3	86.6	96.0	82.7
Floor[e]	44.4	80.0	96.7	53.4
Roof[f]	40.3	63.1	88.8	46.3
Mean rooms per capita	0.8	1.0	1.4	0.9
Cooking fuel[g]	26.9	60.2	89.4	35.7

[a] Running water connection in the dwelling.
[b] Household connected to sewerage system (not septic tanks, etc.).
[c] There is at least one landline or mobile phone in the household.
[d] Walls: 1: brick, cement, stone, adobe; 0: *quincha*, mud, wood, mat, other.
[e] Flooring other than dirt floor.
[f] Roof: 1: concrete, wood, shingles; 0: cane, mat, hay, palm tree leaves, other.
[g] The household uses electricity or gas as cooking fuel.
Source: Barrón (2008) and data supplied by the author.

develops a methodology to control for education: he takes as 'underemployed' all those self-employed whose income is lower than the average wage for their ethnic category.[6] Exclusion from the labour market, over and above the effect of differential human capital, is then the sum of unemployment and underemployment thus measured, controlling for education. Table 3.7 presents the results for the three ethnic group proxies. It will be seen that taking the economically-active population (EAP) aged 25 or older,[7] for the 'indigenous/*cholo*' group, the proportion of unemployed plus self-employed is nearly two-thirds, whereas for those born in Lima-core, it is less than a third.

Political group inequalities

If we take the standard measures of political rights, then the position is good in Peru by the end of the twentieth century. Table 3.8 shows voting rights by our seven regions. The total number of citizens with voting rights doubled between 1963 and 1980, from around 45 per cent to 80 per cent. As Table 3.8 shows, the increase was greatest in the areas most heavily populated by indigenous people. Identity documents also are widely possessed, even by women. The usual inequalities of ethnicity and gender are observed, but the inequalities are not great. Of those still excluded, however, the vast majority are indigenous women from the Highlands or the Amazon.

Table 3.7 Excess labour supply,[a] 2003 (percentages)

	'Indigenous'	'Mestizo'	'White'	Total
Underemployment	59.0	36.4	25.1	51.4
Unemployment	6.6	8.1	6.4	7.0
Total excess labour	65.6	44.5	31.5	58.4

[a] Includes unemployment and underemployment.
Source: Based on ENAHO (2003).

Table 3.8 Percentage of people registered to vote in different regions[a]

Regions	1963	1980	1998	2001
Non-indigenous Lima (Core)	100	100	100	100
Indigenous Lima (Periphery)	69	77	86	88
Non-indigenous (Regional Cores)	45	70	94	98
Indigenous coast (Periphery)	54	76	97	100
Indigenous Amazon (Periphery)	39	53	75	84
Indigenous Central & Northern Andes (Periphery)	36	64	84	85
Indigenous Southern Andes (Periphery)	19	61	82	83

[a] Percentage of people registered to vote as a proportion of the total of voting age.
Source: Own elaboration from data taken from Tuesta (1994); ONPE (electoral list 1998, 2001) and Population Census – INEI (1961, 1993).

However, despite the gains, the chapters which follow show how the political system still contrives to disenfranchise people. So we need an 'output' measure. In principle, it would be reasonable to assume that greater electoral participation would generate a greater percentage of indigenous people in the government, able to advocate on behalf of marginal people, and it is this that we would like to measure for an objective view of political group equality. However, we face a serious problem of lack of information, as explained above, as we only have surnames to use as proxy. We have to remind the reader that we can only evaluate the *tendency,* as we do not know the proportion of people with indigenous surnames in the country and we cannot solve for the problem that indigenous people may have lost their ethnically-rooted second surname in the process of *mestizaje*.

Having recognized these problems, we see that the trend of participation of indigenous people in the Congress has been positive, but moderate. Figure 3.1 shows the results for the Congress and we can see a clear increment of participation since 1995.[8] For the period 2001–2006 in which the proportion of indigenous candidates was the highest, it is interesting to see indigenous candidates' distribution among parties.

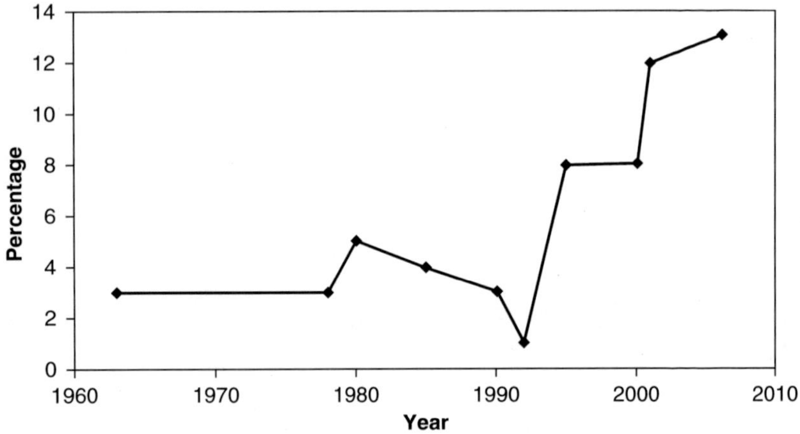

Figure 3.1 Numbers of members of the Congress with indigenous names, 1963–2006

Note: 1. points correspond to the years of the elections; 2. no Congress elections between 1960 and 1978.

Source: Own elaboration from data taken from Tuesta (1994) and the website of the National Congress of Peru.

Renacimiento Andino had 24 per cent of candidates with indigenous names and Toledo's party, *Peru Posible*, 21 per cent. The second in 2001 positioned 38 per cent of its candidates with indigenous names in the Congress (ten of the 26). These ten elected members represented the majority of those in Congress with indigenous names; no other group put forward a significant number of candidates with indigenous names. The right wing parties presented the lowest percentage of candidates with indigenous names: *Accion Popular* (AP) and *Unidad Nacional* had 9 per cent and 8 per cent respectively. Only one candidate with an indigenous name from *Unidad Nacional* was elected. In 2006, the distribution was different. Most of the candidates with indigenous names were in small new parties, which obtained less than 1 per cent. The distribution in the national parties was as follows: 6 per cent APRA, 17 per cent *El Frente de Centro*, led by Valentin Paniagua, and 13 per cent in the party of Ollanta Humala.

The tendency of participation in provincial municipalities as mayors is similar to that for Congress, positive but moderate (Figure 3.2).[9] Elections for municipalities have been officially performed in Peru since 1963, but they were interrupted in 1968 by the military coup and were not resumed until 1980. As the database of names was organized by provinces, we were able to see the trend for the different geographical groups. Table 3.9 shows the results. It is important to realize that these

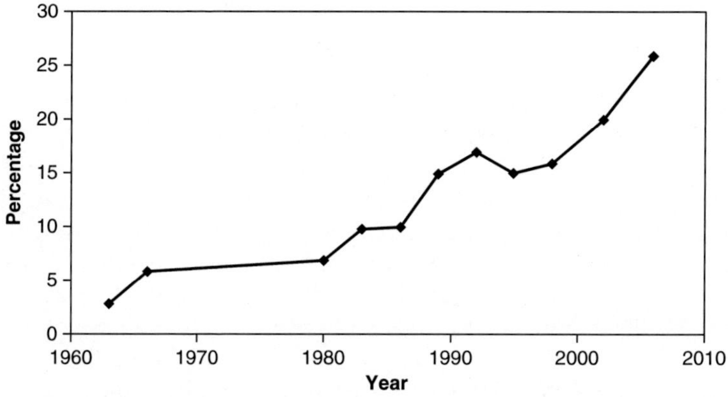

Figure 3.2 Numbers of Mayors with indigenous last names, 1964–2006
Notes: 1. points correspond to the years of the elections; 2. no municipal elections between 1966 and 1980.
Source: Own elaboration from data taken from Tuesta (1994) and information from the National Congress of Peru and the Electoral National Jury (JNE).

Table 3.9 Provincial mayors with indigenous last names, 1963–2003 (percentages)

	1963	1980	1983	1986	1989	1993	1995	1998	2003
Local core	0	0	8	8	4	8	13	4	17
Rest coast	10	0	5	5	10	0	10	5	15
Rest Amazonian	0	0	11	6	17	22	17	11	22
Rest central and north	1	1	3	6	5	9	8	8	9
Rest southern Andes	2	18	16	15	27	29	27	33	38

Sources: Own elaboration with data from Tuesta (1994) and Electoral National Jury (JNE).

percentages cannot be read across the groups for comparison purposes because each region may have a different proportion of people with indigenous names. However, we can see the trend in each region. In particular, it is clear that the trend is positive for most of the groups, but the tendency for indigenous mayors is consistently positive in the Southern Highlands. The situation changed from almost no provincial mayors with indigenous last names in 1963 to close to 40 per cent in 2003.

The cabinet in Peru is composed of 16 members who are appointed by the President.[10] In a review of a complete list of ministries since 1968, we only found six ministers with indigenous names in seven periods (one per cent). We also looked at the position of vice-ministries, but almost no organized data was found. Putting together information coming from official records and interviews with former officers, we found that almost no vice-ministries in education (since 1986), agriculture (1983) and interior (1992) had an indigenous last name. The two exceptional cases were in agriculture and interior.

The selection of judges and prosecutors has improved recently,[11] incorporating fewer elements of subjectivity, though it is still not ideal according to the specialists. These new methods put more weight on exams than personal interviews, for instance. However, from a data base of 2,412 judges and prosecutors selected in the period 1995–2004, we found no clear tendency towards an increase in the number of judges and prosecutors with indigenous names. Part of the problem is our limited data, which start in 1995, when first-instance judges were not selected. Table 3.10 shows the results for judges and prosecutors with indigenous names. However, what is interesting is the distribution of judges and prosecutors in the hierarchy of the system. Judges with indigenous names are concentrated in the lower ranks of the pyramids (peace and first instance) and we find fewer cases in the Supreme Court.

We can draw some conclusions from this analysis. It suggests, with the data available, that indigenous people were the most disenfranchised before the reforms and that the electoral reforms significantly helped the inclusion of indigenous in the electoral system. However, although indigenous people can today vote massively and run for elected and appointed positions, it seems that the achievement has not been significant, particularly at the central level. The state remains largely white and *mestizo* upper-middle-class led. Moreover, the participation of indigenous people – the Ayaipomas, the Carhuaricras, the Sucaris – has been part of a fragile process of indigenous political

Table 3.10 Judges and prosecutors with indigenous last names by period of selection and position in the hierarchy (percentages)

Year of selection	**Supreme Court**	**Superior Court**	**First Instance**	**Peace**	**Per cent of total named**	**Total named**
1995–1996	0	12			**10**	226
2000	0	13	15	14	**15**	708
2001–2003	8	10	19	13	**15**	650
2004	0	12	16	18	**16**	828

Source: Own elaboration with data from the Consejo Nacional de la Magistratura (1995–2004).[12]

inclusion. The way that democracy has developed in Peru, largely lacking a system of political parties and social organizations, has opened up opportunities for politicians to use ethnic symbols, demands and candidates to attract indigenous voters (see Madrid (forthcoming) for a detailed account).Yet the use of ethnicity has been occurring in the absence of an effective indigenous organization, and therefore has not resulted in the development of institutional channels of political representation to articulate, discuss and arrive at solutions to indigenous people's demands. We explore the weak politicization of ethnic grievances in Chapters 7 and 8 below.

In addition, throughout we have found very few instances of indigenous women. Given problems of sample size and the difficulty of identification through surnames, we hesitate to draw firm conclusions, but the data 'suggest' the participation of indigenous women is even more difficult than that of indigenous men.

Thus, with important exceptions,[13] it has not been possible for an indigenous identity or political agenda to emerge through indigenous political actors, a fact which signals a serious group political inequality.

Perceptions of Inequalities between Groups

The survey of perceptions we explained and drew on in Chapter 2 also gave information on inequality, though we must repeat that we were deliberately surveying relatively marginal communities, so the views of white middle- and upper-class Peruvians are significantly under-represented. Questions were asked specifically about the effects of ethnicity on people's chances of getting employment, and public services, and more broadly about group domination in ethnic terms and government favouritism and discrimination. We also used our interviews to explore these areas more intimately. These are the types of perceptions we address in this section.

The interviews reveal that in such marginal communities, people are highly attuned to the consequences of ethnicity for group inequality. This is also apparent in the survey: 52 per cent consider that the importance of racial and cultural characteristics for accessing opportunities for success has not changed or has become even more important over time in the country. This awareness is not significantly different across ethnic groups, but it is different across localities (47 per cent in Huanta, 47 per cent in Bambamarca and 62 per cent in Lima). Lima, as we have seen in the previous section, forces people to confront their ethnicity as a problem – and/or a source of pride.

Perceptions as to the effect of ethnicity on employment

At least half of all respondents perceive that ethnic background affects a person's chance of obtaining jobs, whether in the government or in the private sector (53 per cent and 56 per cent respectively). The impact of ethnicity on getting access to contracts with the state is slightly smaller (47 per cent). Differences between the perceptions of (self-identified) *cholos*-indigenous and white-*mestizos* are statistically significant (the question asked generally about the system, not about personal experience). A higher proportion of the first group perceive the effects of ethnicity than of the latter: 61 per cent vs. 49 per cent respectively for public jobs and 67 per cent vs. 50 per cent respectively for private jobs.

Differences across localities are significant. More than 70 per cent in our case of San Juan de Lurigancho in Lima believe that ethnic characteristics affect one's chances of getting jobs both in the public and private sector; in Huanta, 52 per cent believe this is true for public jobs and 66 per cent for private jobs; and in Bambamarca, the percentage of people who believe the same is much smaller (38 per cent for public jobs and 35 per cent for private jobs). We have learnt from the interviews that *serranos* migrating to Lima are likely to feel more discrimination

Table 3.11 'Ethnic background affects access to...'[a] (per cent saying yes)

		Public sector jobs	**Private sector formal jobs**
Huanta (Ayacucho)	Subtotal	100	100
	White	7.3	4.7
	Mestizo	52.7	52.8
	Cholo	15.4	18.9
	Indigenous	24.6	23.6
Bambamarca (Cajamarca)	Subtotal	100	100
	White	21.0	18.3
	Mestizo	68.4	67.6
	Cholo	7.9	9.9
	Indigenous	2.6	4.2
San Juan de Lurigancho (Lima)	Subtotal	100	100
	White	3.0	5.0
	Mestizo	38.1	37.1
	Cholo	33.6	31.4
	Indigenous	25.4	26.4

[a] Since we are dealing with perceptions, recorded in informal interviews, here we classify according to people's self-identification.
Source: CRISE Perception Survey (Peru).

than those who have not migrated. These results seem to capture that idea as our case in Lima is composed largely of migrants.

The interviews allow us to deepen our understanding of the form and manner in which this discrimination is experienced, and why discrimination is perceived more in the private sector than in the public sector. According to the interviews, 'preparation' and 'qualifications' are seen as important, but '*buena presencia*' ('good appearance') seems to be the key.[14] Eliana from Huanta told us 'yes, there is discrimination when looking for jobs. They request people with good presence. It does not mean that you have a nice dress or you know how to express yourself, but a person who is good looking, pretty; if you are unattractive, darker, they say, *ay no*!'[15] Those who self-identify as whites are particularly aware of this mechanism. Florencia, living in Lima, added that in companies in Lima the first thing they look at is if girls are thin, tall, have a good manner and a pretty face. 'The colour is also a criterion', she added. Florencia had a friend who told her that a supermarket chain was hiring. When they went there, a man separated her friend from the queue, despite her friend having the same qualifications as she did. She believes it happened because her friend was darker.[16]

The perception of discrimination based on 'physical appearance', whether it is purely aesthetic or ethnic, is more widely perceived in the search for jobs in the private sector than in the government. Discrimination is perceived in the government as well, but more linked to party membership and contacts. Gertudris from Bambamarca said that personal interviews are convenient because they not only evaluate your oral performance, but 'your *pinta*' (physical appearance); however, for finding a job in the government, 'qualifications are not important, but whether or not you are affiliated to the party in power'.[17] Soledad from Huanta said that the Regional Government of Ayacucho only offers jobs to people affiliated to its party: 'relationships with the ruling party are needed in order to access a job in the government'.[18] While interview responses downplay ethnicity compared to party affiliation, this is an insight that comes from an open question, compared with the questionnaire's closed question. The emphasis on party affiliation does not mean an ethnic element is not there.

Perceptions as to the effects of ethnicity on political power

Another set of questions in the questionnaire aimed to explore perceptions about whether or not an ethnic group has power in four institutions of the state (local government, central government, top ranks of the police and the army) and two in the private sector (large private firms and the media). This was a closed question, and interviewees were asked to indicate in which institutions each ethnic group had power. The identification of power in the hands of whites was significant across the different institutions, with the exception of local government, where *mestizos* were perceived to have more power (see Figure 3.3). In the case of central government, the percentage of people who believe *mestizos* have power comes closer to the percentage affirming that whites do, but is still significantly different. An important, though still small, percentage of people think *cholos* hold the power in central government[19]. The proportion of people affirming that whites have power in the private sector and the media is by far the greatest.

We find several significant differences across our cases when we assess the perception of power across public institutions. Power in local and central government is perceived significantly differently in SJL-Lima compared with Huanta and Bambamarca. For most people living in Lima, power in both local and central government is in the hands of whites, while for most people living in Huanta and Bambamarca, power in local government is in the hands of *mestizos* while in central government it is shared between whites and *mestizos*.

When asking about power in the top ranks of the police and army, a higher percentage of people both in Huanta and San Juan de Lurigancho consider whites to be the dominant group (for the police the percentages are 46 per cent and 53 per cent respectively and for the army 47 per cent and 55 per cent respectively). In contrast, in Bambamarca,

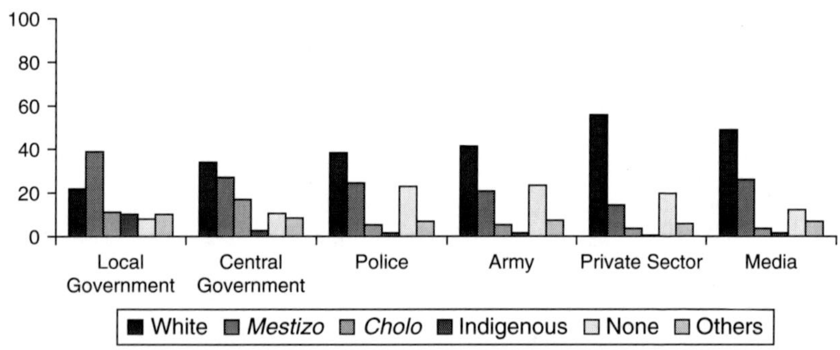

Figure 3.3 Which ethnic groups do you believe have power in the following institutions? (percentages)
Notes: Total = 600.
Source: Own elaboration with data from CRISE perception Survey (Peru).

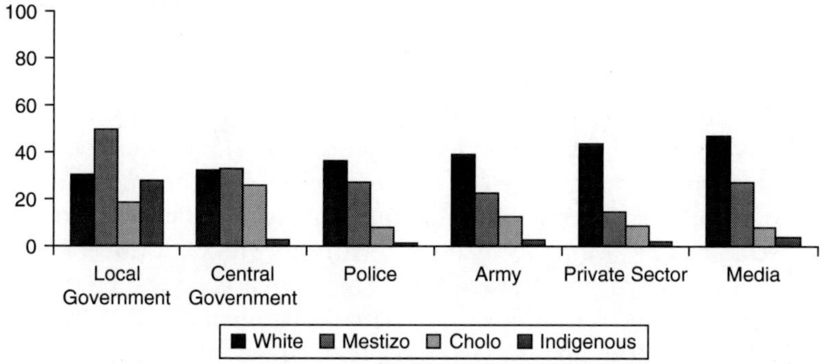

Figure 3.4 People who think that the ethnic group they subscribe to has power (per cent saying yes, by institution)
Notes: Total = 600; White = 54, *Mestizos* = 330, *Cholo* = 108 and Indigenous/Andean = 108.
Source: Own elaboration with data from CRISE perception Survey (Peru).

the most widely held view is that no ethnic group dominates the police (43 per cent) or the army (40 per cent).

In the case of the big private firms and the media, results are definitely more clear-cut across all localities. However, differences between Huanta and San Juan de Lurigancho, and Bambamarca are significant. In San Juan de Lurigancho and Huanta, 71 per cent and 61 per cent, respectively, think that the power in big private firms is in the hands of whites. In Bambamarca, in contrast, the percentage is smaller and almost equal to the percentage that believes that no particular ethnic group dominates. The results for media are similar to those for big private firms.

The analysis across ethnic groups is especially revealing when we examine the percentage of people who believe that people from the ethnic groups to which they have assigned themselves, have power or not. With the exception of local government, indigenous people see themselves as powerless. Whites are the group with the highest self-perception of power in the police, the army, the private sector and the media. In all institutions, *mestizos* see themselves as more powerful than *cholos* do. In local government, *mestizos* see themselves as even more powerful than whites see themselves (50 per cent vs. 30 per cent, respectively). In the case of central government, self-perceptions of power are relatively similar among whites (33 per cent), *mestizos* (33 per cent) and *cholos* (26 per cent); but the contrast with indigenous self-perception is remarkable (3 per cent).

The interviews enable us to deepen our understanding of how power is perceived. In contrast with the survey, the question in the interviews was open ('who do you think has power in the country and in your community?'). The responses show that power is certainly perceived both as political and economic. Only one mentioned race or ethnic characteristics. The absence of responses addressing the question from an ethnic approach is notable when the question is put in an open form. Political power was directly associated with the President (for the country) and the mayor (for the locality). The emphasis on the President is very strong in the testimonies, especially in Bambamarca. For instance, for Liliam power is first 'in God' and then 'in the President'[20] and for Fatima 'the President has the power in the country as parents do in their home'.[21]

In Huanta, the President and political power were seen as very important as well, but were generally seen as subordinate to economic power. Beatriz from Huanta said that the United States had power over Peru in the economy, while within Peru, power belonged to 'private firms'.[22] Lucio said that the rich and the government hold power, but added that the government works for 'the rich' not for the 'people'[23] and finally Pablo affirmed that big private firms hold power and buy the politicians and the media. He told us that some years ago, the people from Bambamarca organized a strike to protest against Yanacocha (a private gold mining company working in the area). According to him the strike lasted for a whole week and was accompanied by demonstrations and protests, but the media, bought off by the firm, did not give it publicity.[24]

Karla from SJL was the only one who mentioned ethnic and racial characteristics. For her, power belongs to the big businessmen and she describes them as 'white, fair-haired and dressed in a suit'. These groups are more powerful than others; in her opinion, 'white people are more involved in politics because they have more relations, relatives that help, access to education, and more opportunities'.[25]

Whether in ethnic or in other ways, the survey registered that 57 per cent of our interviewees believe the government discriminates against certain groups and 61 per cent think it favours some groups. Discrimination was mostly expressed in terms of class (52 per cent referred to 'the poor') rather than in ethnic terms; and favouritism in political (64 per cent referred to 'political affiliates') rather than in class or ethnic terms.

There were some significant differences between the three cases. The question was open and tended to be answered in class terms, but the emphasis on class discrimination ('the poor') was stronger in

Bambamarca than in Huanta and Lima, where the emphasis on ethnic discrimination was notable and significantly larger (Table 3.12). In the same way, a stronger perception of ethnic discrimination was perceived by *cholos* than by the *mestizos* (Table 3.12). There are no significant differences across cases with respect to government favouritism; the emphasis in all cases is on political contacts and affiliations.

Thus we see overall a picture of perceived discrimination and unequal power, but the picture is much sharper for our marginal communities in Lima than for either of our two Sierra groups. The Lima informants were more aware of ethnicity and of its negative side, of discrimination in jobs and of power residing in the hands of whites. Huanta and Bambamarca were closer to each other, with Bambamarca somewhat less likely to see ethnic discrimination or the dominance of a particular ethnic group, even in the private sector.

Conclusion

In these two chapters, we have attempted to gain a bird's eye view of group inequalities and ethnicity in Peru, using the 'window' of our regional surveys. We have attempted to bring together two aspects impossible to reconcile – on the one hand, ethnic identity in Peru is never clear-cut – people are always *'en proceso'*, in a process of 'modernizing', which they see as leaving behind their rural/peasant/Andean roots, yet at the same time there is pride in those roots. These two dimensions can coexist in the same person.

On the other hand, inequalities based in ethnic origins *are* a reality, but to prove that, we have to measure the unmeasurable – using statistics means defining groups precisely that simply cannot be so defined.

Using our proxies for ethnic origin – place of birth and surname – we find clear evidence of group inequality based on race and culture. The evidence is consistent between our quantitative measures and people's own perceptions, as we have documented through our survey and our interviews. Ethnicity matters, in both measures. There is exclusion from the labour market: both measures indicate it. People perceive exclusion: the quantitative work suggests that exclusion is principally a product of unequal access to education, though wage discrimination also plays a part.

The group inequality based in culture and ethnicity puts people of indigenous origin disproportionately in the bottom third of the income distribution. Indigenous people are heavily under-represented in formal sector jobs. Indigenous women still do poorly in accessing even primary

Table 3.12 Government and perception of forms of group discrimination (percentages)

	Class ('the poor')	Ethnic (indigenous and Cholo)	Political (the Opposition)	Others	Total (100 per cent)
Location					
Huanta	47.9	20.2	18.1	13.8	94
Bambamarca	64.4	5.1	9.3	21.2	118
San Juan de Lurigancho	43.8	18.8	18.8	18.8	112
Gender[a]					
Female	55.6	10.5	15.0	19.0	153
Male	49.7	17.5	15.2	17.5	171
Ethnic[a]					
White	44.1	17.6	8.8	29.4	34
Mestizo	60.4	10.7	14.1	14.7	177
Cholo	36.1	23.0	18.0	23.0	61
Indigenous	50.0	13.5	13.5	17.3	52

[a] Differences are significant at 95 per cent level.
Source: CRISE Perception Survey (Peru).

education. Indigenous men have unequal access to secondary level and beyond. Health indicators show less inequality of access, reflecting significant progress in provision of health care in rural areas – but we lack outcome data.

The political indicators are perhaps the most surprising. Despite significant equalization of opportunity in the past thirty years, in terms of the vote and local level democracy, indigenous names are very poorly represented at all levels of government and judiciary. The problem has been that inclusion has occurred at the level of the individual; as a group, indigenous people still lack representation, an issue we will dig into more deeply in the following chapters.

As seen from these marginal communities, the world is run by rich, white people. A self-concept that does not aspire is central to disempowerment and easily understood in terms of the prevalent attitudes of prejudice and discrimination. And such attitudes get reproduced within groups: this has been one of our most powerful findings so far. If people climb by pushing down those behind them, this is a strong force destructive of group interest and collective action. The individualizing pressures of the market aid and abet this. But there are other elements at work here, in the way institutions have been created over time in forms that exclude indigenous people, in economic and political terms. To advance our analysis, we need in the remainder of the book to see how that evolution has occurred and why. But first we need to explore more deeply the pivotal role of education in group inequalities.

Notes

1. The methodology developed here was first presented in Figueroa and Barrón (2005), which is the basis for the analysis undertaken here.
2. The poverty line is defined according to a base line of 1997, for which a minimum food consumption basket was calculated, and from that a minimum general consumption. The 2001 and 2003 surveys work from this base, correcting for price changes. The extremely poor have insufficient income for the food basket, the poor, for the total minimum consumption basket.
3. As commented in the previous note, the methodology is the same, though there are detailed problems to do with seasonality which would not affect the comparison made here.
4. An independent research and data-gathering agency based in Lima.
5. We have not reproduced the data for 1992, as the survey for that year seriously under-represented the Sierra areas affected by violence – see Hall and Patrinos 2006.
6. Note that this measure of underemployment refers only to one of the components of the excess labour supply and is different from the conventional measure of underemployment, which usually refers to incomes from work that are lower than the minimum wage.

7. The female EAP for rural areas is usually underestimated (Figueroa 2001), but this does not seem to be the case in the 2002 ENAHO. The estimated male/female ratio is very similar for urban and rural Peru (between 1.2 and 1.3), for different ranges of ages: from 14 on, from 25 on, from 14 to 65, and from 25 to 65.
8. However, the regulations for the constitution of Congress have changed over the years. Under the Constitution of 1979, the country had a bicameral Congress formed by a Senate of 60 members and a Chamber of Deputies of 180 members. Both were elected for five-year terms and the elections coincided with the Presidential election. Under this Constitution, party-list proportional representation was used for both chambers: national basis for the Senate and departmental representation for the lower house. After Fujimori's Auto-Coup of 1992, the Democratic Constitutional Congress of 1993 established a single chamber of 120 members, all members to be elected in a single national circumscription. In 2001 Congress returned to the proportional mechanism of departmental representation but with a single chamber. Twenty electoral districts were formed, each representing one department.
9. Peru's territory is divided into 25 regions (formerly, departments) and then subdivided into 180 provinces. The latter are divided in 1,747 districts. This is the situation today, but it has changed over time.
10. External Relations and Economy and Finances were created following Independence. Justice, Education and Transportation & Communication were created in the 19th century. In the first half of the 20th century, the ministries of Interior, Agriculture, Health, Labour and Social Affairs, Navy, Army and Airforce were formed. During the Military government of Velasco Alvarado (1968–1974), several ministries related to the area of production were initiated: Industry, Commerce & Tourism, Energy and Mining, Fishing, and Housing and Construction. The Ministry of the Presidency was created in 1985 by Alan Garcia and kept by Alberto Fujimori, but abolished in 2001. The three elements of the Armed Forces were united in the Ministry of Defence in 1987 and the Ministry of Women and Human Development created in 1996 was renamed to the Ministry of Social Promotion in 2001.
11. The judicial branch of government is headed by a 16-member Supreme Court in Lima. The National Council of the Judiciary appoints judges to this court. Higher courts in departmental capitals review appeals from decisions by lower courts. Courts of first instance are located in provincial capitals and are divided into civil, penal, and special chambers. In addition, the judiciary has created several temporary specialized courts in an attempt to reduce the large backlog of cases pending final court action. At the bottom level are the literate and illiterate peace judges. The prosecutors are also part of the system and they belong to each of the different levels of the judiciary system.
12. See web site http://www.cnm.gob.pe/cnm.
13. In their first year in Congress, Hilaria Supa and Maria Sumire have worked with some success to encourage indigenous members of Congress to come forward and acknowledge their identity and speak for indigenous rights. Their efforts have achieved victories such as a Quechua-speaking telephone service in the Congress switchboard, as well as wide committee work on issues affecting marginal people (environment, disability, extractives, etc.).

The discrimination faced has been notable (Interview, Hilaria Supa, Congress, Lima, 30 November 2007).

14. Interviews with Marco Balvín, Bambamarca (20 June 2006); Pablo Cavero, Bambamarca (21/06/06); Simon Barreto, Bambamarca (22 June 2006); Soledad Tello, Huanta (28 June 2006); Karen Valcazar, SJL (15 June 2006) and Karla Ramos, SJL (16 June 2006).
15. Interview with Jacinta Cáceres, Huanta, Ayacucho (27 June 2006).
16. Interview with Fátima Aguirre, SJL, Lima (17 June 2006).
17. Interview with Gertudris Valverde, Bambamarca, Cajamarca (22 June 2006).
18. Interview with Soledad Tello, Huanta, Ayacucho (28 June 2006).
19. This is certainly associated with the presidency of Alejandro Toledo, in office at the time of the survey, who has repeatedly pointed to his indigenous and/ or *cholo* origin.
20. Interview with Liliam Benicio, Bambamarca, Cajamarca (21 June 2006).
21. Interview with Fátima Talavera, Bambamarca, Cajamarca (21 June 2006).
22. Interview with Beatriz Calderón, Huanta, Ayacucho (27 June 2006).
23. Interview with Lucio León, Huanta, Ayacucho (28 June 2006).
24. Interview with Pablo Cavero, Bambamarca, Cajamarca (21 June 2006).
25. Interview with Karla Ramos, SJL, Lima (16 June 2006).

4
Persistent Inequalities in Education*

From the Peruvian peasant to the World Bank, education has been seen as the single most important element to end inequalities and poverty and provide not only true social mobility but also integration. We will show in Chapter 5 how the hope of national integration through education drove the Peruvian government's social expenditure during the whole twentieth century. This chapter first documents the desire of marginal groups for education and confronts this with the reality: the data show persistent group inequalities in education and its rewards. Then we analyse and document the reasons why, with the aid of a model developed by Adolfo Figueroa. The chapter then concludes and reviews the argument through Chapters 2–4.

In our fieldwork we encountered as a constant recurring theme the sacrifices indigenous people were intent on making to acquire education for their children. Judging by the interviews, the poorest indigenous Highlanders make the greatest effort to access education. Poor Highlander children either walk hours to reach school, especially to attend secondary school or to avoid 'multiyear' primary schools (which tend to be of a very low quality), or they live alone in rented rooms in the town. Sonia, a teacher from Huanta teaching 11-year-old children, told us that indigenous people from the Highlands rent rooms in Huanta so their children can attend the school there: "they are far away from their homes, are disorganized in their appearance and dirty. The other children insult them and they get depressed because their houses are far away and their parents are poor".[1] This testimony was repeated by other teachers in Huanta.

Juana from Bambamarca has sent three of her four children to Lima, although she has mixed feelings about her children liking their new

*As explained in the Preface, Adolfo Figueroa is co-author of this chapter.

life there. She has visited them four times (18 hours at least by bus) and is working hard to pay for her children's education. Neptalí Tipto, who has almost finished secondary school, walks and takes a bus to go to school in Huanta instead of just attending the school in Luricocha (which is closer to his town). He is proud of attending school in Huanta: 'I am the only one in Llanza', he said.[2]

To What End?

Having seen such an effort, and sensing the expectations that lie behind it, the figures and the qualitative evidence on outcomes are poignant. It is not that enrolment has not increased: it has. Table 4.1 uses the methodology and assumptions explained in Chapter 3, grouping people according to their place of birth, which we argue there to be the least inadequate proxy for ethnic origin in contemporary Peru. We remind the reader that 'indigenous' is shorthand for those born in the rural areas of Peru regardless of where they lived at the time of the survey, 'white' is shorthand for those born in Lima core, and '*mestizo*' is shorthand for the rest.

The data corroborate the progress in literacy for 'indigenous' men (92 per cent literate as compared to 98 per cent of non-indigenous men). But Table 4.1 shows that nevertheless, the secondary education gap is

Table 4.1 Literacy and level of schooling by ethnic group (percentage literate for each group)

	Literacy rate 15+	**Level of schooling for age 25+**		
		No level	**Primary only**	**Secondary or more**
'White'				
Male	99.1	0.0	4.1	95.9
Female	99.5	0.6	8.2	91.2
Total	99.3	0.3	6.4	93.3
'Mestizo'				
Male	98.2	1.0	16.4	82.6
Female	95.1	5.0	19.8	75.2
Total	96.6	3.1	18.3	78.6
'Indigenous'				
Male	91.7	6.2	43.0	50.8
Female	75.6	21.4	63.4	35.2
Total	83.5	14.1	63.1	42.8

Source: Barrón (2008), and data supplied by the author, working with the ENAHO 2002 survey.

Table 4.2 Years of schooling by age and by ethnic group

	Age bracket				**Total 25–65**
	25–34	**35–44**	**45–54**	**55–65**	
'White'					
Male	13.9	14.4	12.1	13.9	13.8
Female	13.9	14.4	10.8	10.4	13.4
Total	13.9	14.4	11.4	11.6	13.6
'Mestizo'					
Male	12.0	11.9	11.4	9.7	11.6
Female	12.1	11.5	9.8	8.1	11.0
Total	12.1	11.7	10.5	8.9	11.2
'Indigenous'					
Male	10.9	8.9	8.0	5.5	8.6
Female	9.9	7.1	5.0	3.1	6.6
Total	10.4	8.0	6.5	4.3	7.6

Source: Barrón (2008), and data supplied by the author, working with the 2002 ENAHO household survey data.

still marked, even for men, where 'indigenous' men's achievement of secondary level is half the 'white' level for the 25+ population. The gender difference shows where the severe problem still lies. A quarter of 'indigenous' women are illiterate and only one third are reaching secondary level. Our own survey of four sites found a similar picture with regard to gender: of those with primary education or less, 73 per cent of the indigenous group were women, and 79 per cent of the group self-defined as *cholo*. Knowing what we do about the externalities attached to women's education, this is a serious aspect of the embeddedness of inequality. Issues of human rights apart, it is well known that educating women – even to primary level – has beneficial effects on family health and on the education of the next generation.[3]

Table 4.2 shows the degree of progress over time. Among young people, the group inequality gap in terms of years of schooling has become almost non-existent. The indigenous/white ratio is 0.4 for the over 55s, and is only 0.8 for the 25–34 age group. The gap also falls over the generations for women, though it is enormous for older women.

Thus in the first basic but important steps of enrolment and literacy, we see significant progress though with some gap remaining. But we can also see how recent the improvement is. In relation to our preoccupation with the embedding of inequality over time, young indigenous women growing up and having families in the 1950s and 1960s were still receiving very limited education, including in quantity of school years.

Table 4.3 Enrolled students failing or dropping out in the school year 2004[a] (as per cent of those matriculated)

	Rate of failures	Rate of drop outs
Residential Lima	4.6	2.7
Rest of Lima	6.8	4.2
Local core (provincial capitals)	7.0	4.2
Rest of coast	7.0	5.0
Rest of Amazon	11.0	8.0
Rest of North and Central Andes	10.4	8.5
Rest of Southern Andes	8.6	7.6
Total	8.2	6.0

[a] The data for 1998 and 2001 show a similar pattern.
Source: Data from ESCALE, MINEDU.

When we explore more data on attainment, the story is less impressive. Table 4.3 shows regional failure and drop out rates, using the same geographical divisions to proxy for ethnic origin.[4] It will be seen that the drop-out rate in indigenous regions is some three times the rate in the better off areas of Lima, and the failure rate is over twice as high.

The Education Ministry has begun to do regular evaluations of educational outcomes in maths and communication. The data, contrasting students at the primary level with an indigenous mother tongue with those whose first language is Spanish, come with a health warning but are striking:[5] the 2004 National Evaluation finds a negative association between indigenous mother tongue and performance that is statistically significant, controlling for socioeconomic level, how rural the school is, and the other variables of the study (MINEDU 2007: 18).

Further, while enrolments, at least for men, are reaching parity, the income consequences of years in school are not. Tables 4.4 and 4.5 are very important. Table 4.4 presents data on incomes by level of education and by social group, and supports the existence of a positive relationship between the mean income and the level of education for the whole population. In addition, this positive relationship can also be observed in each of the three ethnic groups. But the curves relating income and education are distinct. Figueroa (2008) demonstrates that the observed relation between incomes and education is statistically separable for each ethnic group and shows that for each level of education the mean income is greater in the group of 'whites', which is greater than in the group of '*mestizos*', which in turn is greater than in the group of 'indigenous'. Table 4.5 shows that in contrast to Table 4.1, where we showed that the youngest age group experienced almost no gap in years of education,

Table 4.4 Mean income by education level and social group, 2003 (1000 people, soles/month, and percentages)

	'Indigenous'		'Mestizos'		'Whites'		Total		
	N (%)	Mean income	N (%)	Mean income	N (%)	Mean income	N	%	Mean income
Education Level									
None	9.6	171	1.9	297	0.0		604	7.1	180
Primary	41.0	330	13.1	479	1.0	137	2,704	32.0	346
Secondary	32.7	592	44.0	710	22.7	798	2,998	35.4	637
Technical	9.6	844	17.2	912	15.8	965	1,001	11.9	876
University	7.1	1,529	23.8	2,005	60.5	2,721	1,148	13.6	1,943
Total	100.0	535	100.0	1,015	100.0	1,981	8,464	100.0	717
Total N	5,841		2,330		293		8,464		
%	69.0		27.5		3.5		100.0		
Years of education									
Mean	7.6		11.4		14.2			9.0	
Median	8.0		11.0		15.0			11.0	

N = population, 25 or more years of age (sample expansion); mean income is monthly, soles, October 2003.
Source: Figueroa (2008, Table 2), with data from ENAHO (2003).

Table 4.5 Mean income by age bracket and social group, 2003 (soles)

	Age bracket								Total	
	25–34		35–44		45–54		55–65			
Group	N	Mean Income	N	Mean Income	N	Mean Income	N	Mean Income	N	Mean Income
'Indigenous'	1,551	530	1,636	596	1,260	623	850	473	5,297	563
'Mestizo'	912	771	670	987	449	1,195	218	1,626	2,249	1003
'White'	146	1,456	111	2,455	29	2,982	6	1,648	291	1991
Total	2,609	666	2,417	790	1,738	810	1,074	713	7,837	743
Ratio income I/W	0.4		0.2		0.2		0.3		0.3	
Ratio income M/W	0.5		0.4		0.4		1.0		0.5	

N = Economically active population (million people). Mean income is soles/month.
Source: Figueroa (2008, Table 6b), with data from ENAHO (2003).

Table 4.6 Wages of blue-collar workers by education level and ethnic group, 2003 (mean levels)

	'Indigenous'		'Mestizos'	
Level of education	**N (%)**	**Mean Wages Soles**	**N (%)**	**Mean Wages Soles**
None	6	306[a]	1.8	349[a]
Primary	37.5	489	21.6	518
Secondary	46.7	616	59.4	651
Technical	8.1	695[a]	13.8	712
University	1.7	763[a]	3.4	796[a]
Total	100.0		100.0	
Total N (1000s)	**1,163**		**482**	
per cent of EAP	19.9		20.7	
Years of education				
Mean		8		9.7
Median		9		11

[a] Small number of observations, 10 per cent or less.
Source: Figueroa (2008, Table 3a).

here there is no real sign of the gap in returns to that education improving over time. (All relationships are statistically significant and the significance testing is presented in the appendix to Figueroa (2008).)

In addition to household income, analysed in Table 4.5, we can look at wages. The data on wages of blue collar workers are given in Table 4.6, for the relevant groups, '*mestizo*' and 'indigenous', and again, the relation is statistically significant.[6] At a given level of education, 'm' earn more than 'i'.

Another way to look at returns to education is to look at quantitative exclusion from the labour market – in other words, unemployment and underemployment. In Chapter 3 we presented data on this exclusion controlling for education. Now we show (Table 4.6) that indigenous workers receive lower wages than non-indigenous for a given level of education. Figueroa (2008) uses a chi-square test and demonstrates the statistical significance of the findings.

What is Going On? A Framework and the Evidence

To help analyse these results, we make a fundamental distinction, already signalled above. Inequalities between groups may arise on the one hand from differing chances to acquire education in the first place. This can be decomposed into the chance of achieving years of schooling, and the

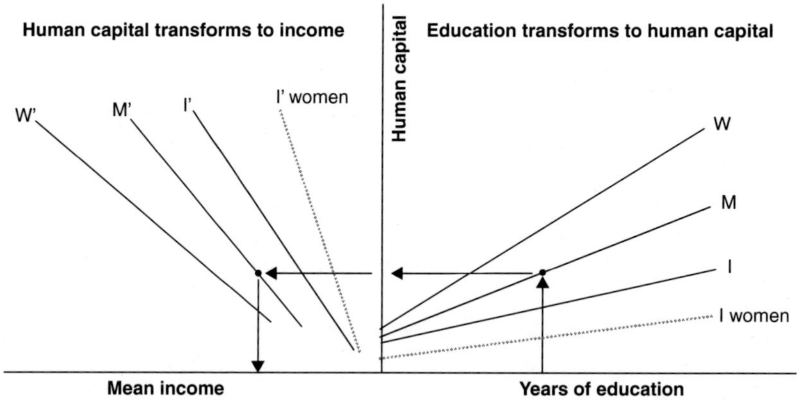

Figure 4.1 Theoretical relations between education, human capital and mean income

ability/freedom to make something of it – i.e. convert years of schooling into human capital, broadly defined. (We include here in human capital a wide range of functionings, ranging from confidence and self-esteem to contacts and networks, as well as the more usual skills.) On the other hand, the ability to use a given level of human capital to acquire income or other social and political assets may also vary between groups. We can represent this graphically using the framework developed by Figueroa (2008). Figure 4.1 uses the same abstraction as in earlier tables, converting the world into 'whites', '*mestizo*', and 'indigenous'. In the right-hand segment Figueroa represents the very different amounts of human and/or social capital that years of education represent for each group. In the left-hand segment he represents the differing transformation of that capital into income, taking income as a proxy for a wider range of benefits (citizenship, for example).

As we have suggested with Table 4.1 above, if the functions are further decomposed by gender, an additional gap may open up, which we suspect is particularly pronounced in the right-hand segment, but appears in both segments. We develop this aspect as we proceed. We shall explore how far and why indigenous women are at a different place on their curve from their male counterparts, having less access to years of schooling, but also operating on a curve which is lower than the male curve.

Differing chances of acquiring schooling

In the right-hand segment, the position on each group's curve is first of all driven by the availability of school facilities (we take up below the dimension of quality). Inadequate supply means problems of quality, which we return to below, but also the challenge of distance. We have seen in our stories of motivation how people struggle to overcome problems of distance, and at what cost. Another typical case is Eva Salazar, living in the community of Occana in Lauricocha (15 minutes from Huanta by car). She told us that she couldn't finish secondary school: 'I couldn't do it any more', she said. She used to wake up at 3.00 in the morning to cook the family meal and at 6.00 a.m. begin her walk to school. The walk was about an hour under the sun and her face was frequently burnt.[7]

Again, Carmela told us[8] that for her, her formative experience was being sent to Juliaca at age 8 to live with her older brother aged 12 and her younger sister aged 6, to go to school. They lived completely on their own – their parents gave them money but sometimes the money ran out. She remembers vividly (suddenly she is almost crying) a terrible time of floods – with high food prices and cut off from the family, they were desperate, sharing a little bit of mashed potato.

As these cases demonstrate, it is often the *cost* of access that is the key source of inequality – a cost that has a monetary component, but more importantly, a huge cost in terms of family life, values, isolation, and experiences of discrimination without a supportive environment. Here we are concerned with how that whole experience might affect years of schooling acquired, but there are also much deeper and traumatic effects, which we come to below, as part of the transformation issue.

A further important point is that access is far from gender-neutral. Kathy in San Juan de Lurigancho told us how she stopped her secretarial course, to go out and work to help contribute to her brother's education.[9] A further powerful intergenerational story from García (2003) speaks for itself. The author is talking to Gloria, now a parent herself, who was raped at school by her male teacher. 'Ashamed, she had never told her parents about his abuse, but she had also refused to return to school, and because of this she had been severely punished by her father. She continues: "My brothers also took advantage of the fact that my father hit me, so they would beat me up too and call me stupid because I did not go to school. But I knew it would be worse if they knew why I did not want to go. I was afraid they would hit me harder for that"' (p. 81).

Because of this she was now only sending her sons to school. So abuse deprived two generations of girls of access to education.

Differing chances: transformation of schooling years into human capital

Various studies have documented the poverty of resources in rural areas, and in public schools as opposed to private schools, distinctions which overlap with the gap we are concerned with here (Cueto *et al.* 1997, MINEDU Peru 2007, Rivera 1979). But the more important gap is in quality of supply. Here there is abundant evidence on the difficulty of getting committed and well qualified teachers to go to the more remote areas, the extent of learning by rote in small rural schools, and the lack of appropriate textbooks – or even of textbooks per se.[10] School visitors in the Highlands comment on the fact that whenever they arrive, 'recreo', or recreation, is likely to be going on. This reflects the lack of resources, including a lack of teachers.[11]

One thing is the variable quality of supply, but another just as important is the ability to make something of what is supplied. As we saw in our earlier examples illustrating the gender dimension of group inequality, the family can make a difference to access, through attitudes. But the family and its socioeconomic condition and its attitudes are central intervening variables in transformation. As shown in Table 3.2 in the previous chapter, ethnicity does correlate with poverty: indigenous groups therefore have fewer opportunities to improve the learning ability of their children through nutrition, health, early intellectual stimulation and language, than their white/*mestizo* counterparts.

Nutrition has a direct effect on the development of the brain and the cognitive skills of individuals; it also has an indirect effect through illness episodes. Recent research has found a significant negative correlation between school performance and the degree of malnutrition based on a sample of students in Lima, Puno-city and Puno-countryside. Further, on average, illness episodes will be less frequent in children living in Lima-core than in the Andes. The evidence for Peruvian health provision makes it abundantly clear that access to resources is extremely unequal between regions and between urban and rural areas, in ways which penalize above all the rural indigenous population.[12] A report by a group of physicians on maternal mortality, for example, concludes from case studies in Puno and Huancavelica, that 'Lack of available, accessible, acceptable and quality healthcare, including EmOC [emergency obstetric care], is a primary contributor to the ways in which women in Peru – and especially rural indigenous women – experience poverty and exclusion' (PHR 2007).

Differences in health condition are also associated with environmental health, which is not neutral in relation to socioeconomic condition. Lima-core families can avoid problems that involve environmental health damage (quality of water and drainage, and air pollution) through 'exit' behaviour (in the well-known *exit-voice* terminology of Albert Hirschman), because they are able to construct exclusive residential neighbourhoods. Indigenous families in peripheral areas can only try to solve the problem using their 'voice', that is, demands, protests, etc. – and we have documented political group inequalities above.

Another condition influencing children's ability to gain from education is language. First, coming from an environment where the first language is not the dominant language is a major source of inequality. This is made worse by the way the issue of bilingual education has played out in Peru. Unfortunately, the issue of bilingual education has been seriously compromised by communication difficulties. García (2003) reports on research in the Sierra of Cusco, showing how the honourable efforts of bilingual education activists were completely misinterpreted by indigenous parents, who could only see that their children needed Spanish to progress. One meeting she reported on is so instructive it is worth quoting at length. A teacher from the bilingual programme had come to discuss the programme with the community. The men spoke first, acknowledging the potential benefits of learning Spanish. Then the teacher expounded on the value of parental involvement. Then, 'one of the mothers present gathered her skirts, picked herself up from the ground, and began to speak in Quechua:

> "Our husbands have not made themselves clear. We do not think this change is good for our children. They speak Quechua with us, and they should speak Spanish in school. That is what school is for. If it is for teaching Quechua, why should we waste our time sending our children to school, when they can speak at home? And being a citizen means speaking Spanish."

Finished, she sat down abruptly and her husband stood up to speak next:

> "As my wife has said, we are not in favour of this change. We think that now teachers are not expected to do any work and that you want our children to stay poor and be like us. What I want most for my son is that he is not a campesino like me. And being an indian is worse! So you shouldn't tell [our children] to be indian!"' (p.78).

The failure to accept or even hear the argument that children would learn Spanish better if they first acquired literacy skills in their own language is a failure totally intelligible in terms of the history we have related, which reasonably gives rise to the fears lying behind the above quote. But the failure of communication has meant poor parental reinforcement of the strategy, in for example making appointments and reinforcing teachers' messages. The lack of support has combined with shortages of resources to make bilingual education an ineffective strategy to combat the serious educational limitations involved when your language is not the dominant language. This is reinforced if your first language is one that has only recently begun to acquire a written culture.[13]

This affects the ability to make something of the opportunity provided by enrolment. The impact of initial conditions may be even more profound, however, when it interacts with the discrimination frequently manifested in our interviews. We learnt how children often experience the first hostile impact of a discriminating urban context when they are sent away to school, and the consequences for internalization of low self-esteem, loss of confidence, etc., are that much greater when the child is on his or her own in a foreign world.[14]

Soledad, a 38-year-old *cholo* teacher in Huanta, experienced this discrimination herself. The first year she attended school, she could not speak Spanish very well, and, on one occasion, could not do the homework because she had not understood the teacher's instructions. She did not have the strength to explain the reason for her failure and the teacher beat her against the blackboard. The rest of the class laughed and she did not come back to school until the following year. She remembers that her first years at school were not pleasant. The students insulted her because of her language and her parents' occupation (peasants). Only at the end of the second year does she remember feeling more comfortable with Spanish, and better overall.[15]

There is probably a gender dimension here. While our field interviews were not intended to cover a representative sample, it is surely informative that the poignant stories of discrimination making school painful and unrewarding came from young women. Although internalized discrimination and resulting lack of self-esteem can clearly affect both genders, girls in the indigenous culture seemed particularly vulnerable.[16]

We have been considering the transformation of education into effective human capital from the perspective of school-age children. Another dimension of that transformation is *adult* illiteracy, of enormous importance in terms of basic rights but also for the way it holds back family health, intergenerational effects on attitudes and stimulus to children's learning. The costs, in terms of loss of potential benefits, are particularly high in the case of women's illiteracy and form an important part of the embedding we are documenting throughout this book. The obstacles to progress in adult literacy are very similar to those we have been highlighting – fear, prejudice, lack of confidence – but extra elements are worth noting, in particular poor public policy. Adult literacy programmes over time in Peru have been a disaster,[17] culminating in Fujimori's efforts that rejected NGOs and mobilized the army, and used gifts of food to get people to classes, then faked the data, claiming a fall in illiteracy from 12 per cent in 1993 to 8.7 per cent in 1998. This was the basis on which Peru was awarded the Korean 'King Sejong' prize by UNESCO, handed over on World Literacy Day in 1999 (Portugal 2004: 7).

This shocking outcome stimulated a radically different approach, important for what it shows can be done. The transition government of Paniagua exposed the fraud and initiated a simple programme developed by NGOs and based on self-help, empowerment and use of local people. Communities chose their own class leader from among themselves; the classes used people's own life experience, 'displacing teaching with dead words' (Portugal 2004: 22). No food or other benefits in kind were provided – yet people flocked to the classes. An NGO evaluation after a few months rated the programme a success in terms of enthusiasm, empowerment and the testimonies of the participants. Portugal recounts a poignant story of a 60-year-old indigenous shepherdess. With some difficulty, she was persuaded to take part in a very simple game where the leader calls out 'the people command that...' and all do it. She took her turn to be leader, and after a time burst into tears. Why are you crying, they asked. '"I've never been in charge of anything before and no one has ever paid attention to me. Only my sheep obey me"'(Portugal 2004: 99).[18]

However, with the transference of literacy programmes from the Ministry of Women's Affairs to the Ministry of Education in 2002, the programme was under threat after only six months, amid protests from participants (Portugal 2004: 27).[19]

The transformation of educational assets into income and other benefits

We now see why for many reasons the functions in the right-hand segment of Figure 4.1 are distinct, showing a clear gap in levels that is in significant part ethnically determined. The capacity of different groups to take advantage of education and transform it into human capital, or capabilities, is distinct. We should turn now to the left-hand segment of Figure 4.1. The transformation of human capital into incomes operates through the market system. The general relation is positive: the higher the human capital, the higher the income level will be. This reflects the positive economic return of investing in human capital. This economic return is the result of the positive effect that human capital has on labour productivity. This effect operates through three channels: the first is the complementarity that exists between human capital and physical capital because human capital makes the machine more productive; the second is the signalling function, and the third refers to the complementarity between human capital and the adoption of new technologies because new technologies are incorporated in new machines, the operation of which requires workers with a higher level of human capital.

In the hierarchical society illustrated here, if the children of the most and least privileged groups in ethnic terms are compared, then the privileged group receives on average a higher income on entering the labour market, for a given level of human capital. This relation is shown in the left-hand segment of Figure 4.1. Curves W′, M′, I′ represent these transformations. These curves are all sloping upward, showing positive relations between human capital and mean incomes, but they also show that the relations are hierarchical by social groups.

The hierarchy of relations is firstly the outcome of unequal initial asset endowments. Greater endowments of physical capital and social capital (social networks) will imply greater access to factor markets (labour, credit and insurance markets) and greater economic opportunities for doing business.[20]

But the unequal outcome may also be the result of employers' choice. This does not necessarily imply discrimination by employers at the point of purchase in the labour market (though as citizens they will have participated in a system which discriminates in many ways, to produce part of that inequality in human capital). But it may do: Ñopo *et al.* (2004) for example find evidence of ethnic discrimination in the labour market. But Figueroa argues that different levels of income/wages for the same level of human capital could have its origins in a problem of incomplete information that rules in the labour market. For example, a consumer preference for non-indigenous waiters might determine the choices made by the restaurant owner. Or consumer preference might limit the income opportunities of indigenous producers of quinua or kiwicha, traditional Sierra products. As a consequence, segmentation would appear in the labour market: given equal levels of human capital, indigenous people would secure an inferior wage rate compared to *mestizos* (Figueroa 2008).

The data we have do not allow us to separate the effect of education on human capital from the relation between human capital and earnings. But the relation between income/wages and years of education is clear. We have already demonstrated it in Tables 4.4–4.6 above, for family incomes and for wages, and in perhaps the strongest evidence, the numbers excluded from the formal labour market. This allows us to make the important if limited claim that the data do not contradict the model of relationships depicted in Figure 4.1.

Conclusion

This chapter has discouraging conclusions. What the world perceives as the key instrument to reverse inequality, by its effect on capabilities and employability as well as on attitudes, motivation and norms, is itself trapped in considerable measure by the structure in which it is rooted. Poverty may be reduced, but *inequality of opportunity* is not. We found this evidenced in our quantitative work and in the perceptions data, which confirm inequality of *access*.

We found also a marked gender difference. Indigenous men still suffer a serious educational handicap compared to their non-indigenous peer group – and indigenous/*chola* women were heavily over-represented among illiterates and those with only primary education. This latter is particularly serious for its intergenerational effects via its influence on family health, education and attitudes.

We have also concluded that there is a separable and further source of inequality: the returns to any given quantity of education are lower for indigenous than non-indigenous. So a first conclusion concerns the overwhelming importance of the structural conditions that determine your place on 'your' curve.

An important analytical conclusion from this chapter is the value of decomposing the sources of inequality into differing chances to acquire education in the first place, and the chance to use education to acquire income and/or other social or political assets. Although policy has not been the main focus of our analysis, this distinction is very helpful in that context. For example, a popular education policy in Latin America today is a form of affirmative action. It consists in applying measures of discrimination (positive) in favour of the poor so that their children can have access to school, giving subsidies to poor families on condition that their children should remain in school, compensating for many years of discrimination in the opposite direction. Our analysis shows that if this only leads to a move along the I curve, it will probably be ineffective in Peru. If bringing children (and parents) into the school were the means for attacking the underlying aspects we have highlighted here, then affirmative action would imply a displacement of curve I towards curve M and both towards curve W.

To make the same point in other words: we can increase the quantity of education for indigenous children (and adults) – a move along the I curve. But the policy will be much more powerful if it can improve the quality of education of indigenous people – a *shift* of the I curve – and increase employment opportunities, moving the I and M curves toward curve W.

Health services constitute another essential factor in the accumulation of human capital. One of the factors underlying the relations shown in Figure 4.1 is the supply of health services. The analytical distinctions mentioned above concerning policies associated with both equal opportunity and affirmative action also apply to the case of health service supply. One way to displace the curves of human capital accumulation is by increasing the quantity and quality of health services offered to the poor.

While our findings have generally been negative, they have not been entirely so. We found instances of small innovations that do bring real change. Where we have found positive experiences in education itself, these have mostly signalled measures that cost rather little but require considerable sensitivity to encourage. The literacy programme of 2002, for example, was proving enormously popular and having considerable effect – yet it was very simple. Again, García's study on bilingual education in the Sierra found instances of women getting together and forming their own groups, determined to learn to read and write in order to support their children (García 2003: 81ff). When the desire is so strong, surely it can be accompanied and fostered? This could allow the curve of the I group to inch upward in a particularly sustainable way.

Finally, a reflection on the three chapters we have just presented: we are well aware that in these three chapters we have attempted two tasks in direct opposition to each other. On the one hand we have found it of central importance to try to depict the subtle, complex, often suppressed and contradictory nature of ethnicity in Peru – which signals the difficulty of the precise definitions needed for quantitative measurement. On the other, we have pushed ahead with quantitative measures, making in some degree arbitrary assumptions. But we found it was worthwhile. The complexity will turn out to be an integral part of our analysis of the embedding of inequality, while the efforts at measurement, both of horizontal inequalities themselves and of the strength of perceptions of inequality of opportunity, have produced sufficiently striking results to suggest that quantification is valuable, and will be more so if a data base can now be built up over time.

As to complexity, we know that identities are always multiple, but it was possible to tease out through complex and overlapping terminology that ethnicity is an important *component* of identity in the communities we studied, and that it interacts and overlaps with geography: "we came from the Sierra" was a common phrase. Key elements *shaping* identity, self-esteem and the desire to suppress identity are prejudice and discrimination, and we have reported the strong results we found, above all from our interviews. What we had not fully expected was the extent of prejudice *within* groups, in particular the prejudice of the urban indigenous/*cholo*s against the rural countryfolk they have left behind. We came to understand how far this is a central accompaniment of the migratory processes which have transformed the ethnic panorama of Peru.

As to measurement, we explained and justified our geographical proxy, and showed how, using it, national data yield a striking ethnic perspective on income distribution and poverty. While 39 per cent of the 'white' population belong to the top decile of income, the 'indigenous' population has 6 per cent, and 49 per cent in the bottom group. As to poverty, 24 per cent of 'indigenous' are extremely poor compared with 2 per cent of 'whites'. The absolute gap of twenty points matches the gap found in the outstanding earlier work of Trivelli (2005), using a different definition of ethnic groups.

We went on to present our findings on health, education, access to employment and to politics, the latter producing perhaps the most surprising degree of inequality, after years of formal democracy and the universal vote. We deepened our exploration of educational HIs: one of the findings that has most impressed us has been how far education remains part of the problem as well as the solution. Here is where the extra burden born by indigenous women is most clear: access to education and ability to profit from it is still far from equal among indigenous women and men. We analysed the issue of inequality both between indigenous and non-indigenous and between men and women, in terms of three gaps: there may be differences in access to education; years of education may not translate equally into capabilities, or human capital; and capabilities may not translate equally into opportunities of income, citizenship or other components of well-being.

Finally, we presented our results on perceptions of unequal opportunities. Half of our informants thought that ethnic background affected the chance of getting a job – in the Lima group over 70 per cent thought ethnicity was significant. Among the relatively marginal populations we were studying, overwhelmingly the perception is that whites have power in the private sector and the media and in government except for local government. Apart from local government, indigenous people in our cases felt powerless.

Out of this material, reflecting a very complex reality, we draw several points to highlight for the analysis we are now about to undertake, of the deep embedding of horizontal inequality. First, horizontal inequalities are today deep and pervasive, and are surprisingly so in the political realm. Second, there are multiple disadvantages for indigenous women, in education but also in employment, possibly in health, and in the political realm. Third, discrimination and prejudice with ethnic roots are deep and pervasive. Decades of a discourse of class rather than ethnic divide might well deceive, but the ethnic component of the divide is demonstrated in our survey results and other work. Fourth, discrimination and prejudice are within as well as between groups – which leads to the fifth and final point: there are contradictory aspects at work, above all as a result of migration. As an urban migrant, the same person may well prize his or her Andean/indigenous heritage – and wish to differentiate him- or herself sharply from the rural countryfolk left behind.

Armed with this understanding of horizontal inequalities, ethnicity, identity and prejudice, how come inequality is quite so deep and impervious to change? For this we need a historical analysis of the intertwining of economic, political, geographical and cultural factors over time. It is our contention that 'embedding' can only be understood in terms of the dynamic interactions over a long period of these different and all equally crucial aspects of the Peruvian story. We need to explore how institutions evolve and interact with socioeconomic and geographical structures, to shape policy and the options and lives of indigenous people.

Notes

1. Interview with Soledad Tello, Huanta, Ayacucho (28 June 2006).
2. Interview with Neptalí Tipto, Huanta, Ayacucho (28 June 2006).
3. See for example Frost et al. (2005) for an authoritative survey.
4. Unfortunately in the MINEDU data set, we cannot classify by place of birth. So the data are not completely comparable with our other tables.
5. The study is done for the fourth grade of primary school. The Minedu explain that the group of 'indigenous mother tongue' was not a representative sample of that population (personal communication, Patricia Arregui, 28 March 2009).
6. Figueroa (2008), where the data and the significance testing are presented. We have not included white collar earnings here. The number of

'indigenous' employees in the category is so small as to make it not very significant for our purposes.

7. Interview with Eva Salazar, Huanta, Ayacucho (27 June 2007).
8. Interview with Carmela Taype, Huancane Puno (10 April 2007).
9. Interview with Karen Valcazar, SJL, Lima (15 June 2006).
10. Ansión (2006) reviews the evidence.
11. Conversation with Barbara Hunt, consultant with the Ministry of Education 2000 and former Inspector of Schools in Boston, September 2007.
12. Rivera (1979). For evidence on how health expenditure is concentrated by region and by income strata, see Ewig (2004), Tamayo and Francke (1997).
13. Indigenous languages in Peru have traditionally been oral. Searle (1995) argues that complex abstract thoughts require words and symbols, which develop with more fluency in a culture that is both written and oral. This issue is discussed more fully in Figueroa (2008).
14. This was well expressed to us in interview in Huancané (various, 2007).
15. Interview with Soledad Tello, Huanta, Ayacucho (28 June 2006).
16. We only encountered one episode where gender roles were reversed. Beatriz, a *mestizo* teacher in Huanta, described the situation of a 6-year-old girl insulting an indian boy, calling him *chuto* and foolish (*bruto*), and making him cry. She said such situations were always happening (but we did not ask her about the gender dimension).
17. See Portugal (2004) for a damning and compelling indictment.
18. It was too early to measure outcomes in terms of literacy itself.
19. Presumably because the degree of decentralization and the use of unqualified teachers were both seen as threats.
20. A theory which explains the differences in endowments and in the accumulation of social capital, defined as social networks, between social groups is presented in Figueroa (2008).

5

The Historical Embedding of Group Inequalities: From the Colony to the War with Chile*

One hundred years ago, many important characteristics of the ethnic structure and attitudes towards ethnicity were already well-embedded. Where stories need to start is always a difficult matter – inequalities predate the colony, of course – but we consider that the particular shape the ethnic divide and the associated institutions have taken in Peru owes a great deal to the way the Spanish administered their colony and the institutions that were created. And the focus on the Coast and Lima that developed with Independence also laid down fundamental aspects for the polity as well as the economy. First we explore the ambiguities of the Spanish system of indirect rule – through local leaders, whose position became quite two-sided: the precursor of the institution of the '*gamonal*', or local power broker and boss. We explore how the need for labour drove the creation of a system of control and exploitation that was unrelenting and maintained with vigour. We note the role of religion as part of the 'cement'. We explore the differences with what was to become Bolivia, differences which centre in the diverging nature of the 'intermediary' system. Then we consider how following Independence, new elements developed – in particular the increasing concentration of the polity and economy on Lima and the Coast, compounded by guano. But the new structures in the economy and the polity went alongside the survival and increasingly rooted institution of the intermediary – now the '*gamonal*'. The combination of the geographic and ethnic marginalization of the Sierra in the new economic and political pattern of growth, with the continuing institutions of domination and control within the Sierra, led to a deepening of forces of exclusion, which would be in no way tackled by the new philosophy

*As explained in the Preface, Carlos Contreras is co-author of this chapter.

of 'assimilation' which emerged once the war with Chile led to new fears about the consequences of exclusion.

The Colony: The Embedding of Inequality and a Hostile Terrain for Indigenous Political Mobilization

From a rich and complex colonial history, we wish to draw out two important dimensions for our present topic. The first is the depth of the embedding of ethnic inequality and attitudes, a strong conditioning of subsequent events. The second is the creation of unfavourable conditions for the evolution of a vigorous indigenous political movement in Peru, a story we find is rewardingly told by contrast. What was to become Bolivia on Independence – 'Upper Peru' – and the future Peru as we know it – called at this time 'Lower Peru' – had perhaps a surprisingly divergent set of characteristics and resulting political evolution.

The creation and embedding of group inequalities

While the 'original peoples' encountered by the Spanish conquerors in the sixteenth century were hardly egalitarian in their political economy,[1] the coming of the Spanish conquerors imposed an indirect colonial rule that introduced strong new elements of between-group inequality in the course of three centuries, deeply rooted in new ethnic differences.[2] The Spanish Crown attempted to build a colonial apartheid, on the one hand the Republic of Spaniards, on the other indians,[3] only related by the control of the State represented by Spanish authorities known as *corregidores*, who controlled commercial relations and the collection of tribute.[4]

In stark outline, the process of colonization came close to wiping out the indigenous population. A conservative but authoritative estimate puts the pre-conquest population at 2,738,673 and 601,645 by 1630 (Cook 1981), a fall due to epidemics, to the violence of the Conquest, and to the disruption of established ways of living in a difficult environment. Village indians were uprooted by forced labour of various forms, and by the migration undertaken to escape it.[5] The decline continued, only reversing in the course of the eighteenth century (O'Phelan 1985, Sanchez-Albornoz 1974). This scarcity of labour was a major preoccupation for the Spaniards, for whom the exploitation of Peru's silver wealth was the reason for the colony, and a great user of labour. Thus land abundance and labour scarcity provided the context for the evolving treatment of the indigenous population and for the terms on which it related to the dominant white population. To achieve cheap labour in these circumstances, institutional development was necessary. This took the form of the 'reducción': the resettling of scattered populations in villages with associated collective land holdings, with a presiding indian authority responsible for enforcing labour and tribute payments. Through the Catholic priest, there was also enforcement of 'ethical standards' – how the Spaniards thought indigenous people should behave.[6] The resettlement involved large numbers: for example, 21,000 indigenous inhabitants of Cusco were brought from 309 villages into 40 resettlements.[7] Platt (1982) describes this as a 'pact of reciprocity' whereby indigenous peoples received rights to their land and recognition of their community authorities, in return for an increasingly harsh system of taxation, in cash and kind. The exactions exclusively imposed on the indigenous population were the *mita*, the tribute and the *reparto*. The *mita* was the requirement on each community to provide labour principally for the mines, though other forms also existed to supply labour to the haciendas and the early industries of the colony. The 'tribute' was the payment in cash or kind at the heart of the revenue-raising. The *reparto* was a system whereby indigenous people bought goods on credit, then repaid the loan in labour or in kind at an inflated implicit price. This extended markets and allowed indians access to new goods, but led to serious abuse (Larson 2004). The *reparto* was in wide use by the eighteenth century though only legalized in 1756 and abolished in 1783.[8]

Despite the fall in the number of indigenous, the dominant group of whites was always a minority, never more than an eighth of the population: they took care to maintain this position, seeing their privileges and exclusivity as rooted in their small numbers (Morner 1980). The system was consolidated by the religious factor. Aggressive evangelization amounted to a form of cultural violence.[9] The Spaniards worked hard to promote a culture of superiority: they knew themselves to be superior not only because they held the reins of government and controlled resources, but also because they were closer to God. A telling parable from the sixteenth century compares Europe and America as two sisters. The first is beautiful and gracious and rapidly receives a visit from Christ who weds her soul. The second has to compensate for her ugliness and country manners by offerings of mountains of gold and silver to tempt possession.[10]

Whereas in some other societies, religion overlaps with and overtly deepens ethnically-based group inequalities, here it played a subtle role, nominally unifying, but in fact reinforcing inequalities, and making rebellion the more difficult by the power of its ideology.[11]

The system of exploitation was in part imposed *through* the indigenous local elite (Glave 1992, Lavallé 2004). The *caciques* were 'noble indians', whose inherited position was used by the Spanish, who gave them responsibilities for collecting taxes and delivering the *mita*, as well as rights to land and to the use of the communal labour force (O'Phelan 1985: 139). These people were key in facilitating the indirect system of Colonial rule and exploitation, and held an ambiguous position between the two worlds, a position which by the later years of the Colony was playing out significantly differently in the two parts of the country, as we shall see.

But the ambiguities went further. The apartheid attempted by the Spaniards was imperfect and during these three centuries the dual caste system gradually eroded and Peruvian society took on the characteristics of a tripartite society, a caste segmentation of indians, *mestizo*s and Spaniards with numerous ties between the groups, both commercial and cultural. As the expanding colonial economy led to urbanization and migration, so the *mestizo* population grew and found spaces as the Bourbon reforms centralized government and taxation. They became small town mayors, tax collectors and postmasters (Sala I Vila 1996). The progressive destruction and collapse of indigenous elites in Lower Peru left a space, to be filled by this new group – bilingual *mestizo*s, landowners at the top of the hierarchical structure, judges, lawyers, police, merchants, teachers, among others, often located in the urban centre of a province.

The mixing of blood was driven by the shortage of Spanish women, and was a preoccupation for the Spanish authorities, who could see that it upset their bi-polar world. The mixing had two forms: upper class marriages with rich or politically important indian families and unofficial relations that could be 'a form of sport' for the dominant population, in Samañiego's graphic phrase (1974: 410). Products of such illicit unions were usually not recognized by their father and grew up in the community of their mother. *Mestizo*s thus held an ambiguous position from an early date – on the one hand representing progress and closeness to the desired status of white for the indigenous population, on the other, looked on with suspicion by the white population, and described as 'people with destroyed lives' – '*hombres de vidas destruidas*'.[12]

Rebellion and repression

From the strong group inequalities implicit in three centuries of such exploitation came both acceptance and restlessness. The indigenous population combined accommodation to the new colonial system with diverse manifestations of discontent, and on occasion, open rebellion. The portfolio of 'everyday resistance' included absenteeism, small thefts and unwilling compliance with orders.[13] Stern's study of Huamanga in the first century of the colony shows the skill with which indians used the formalistic legal system to reduce the burden of tax, including forced labour, by manipulation of the population counted.[14] The eighteenth century story of rebellions and revolts has been brilliantly captured in the literature, notably in the writing of Stern, O'Phelan and Flores Galindo, while Thomson and Serulnikov document Upper Peru's rebellion. O'Phelan shows how there were distinct periods of loosening of restrictions allowing a flourishing of indigenous culture, each followed by renewed efforts by the authorities to regain control. These efforts at renewed control produced rebellion: she identifies three waves or 'conjunctures' of rebellion – 1726–37, 1751–56, and then the important events from 1777 on, culminating in the Great Rebellion of 1780–81, centred in Cusco and then in La Paz. She convincingly shows the relationship of the waves of rebellion to the tightening of exploitation – the reimposition of horizontal inequalities causing violent conflict. The horizontal inequalities included the cultural: lack of respect for traditions and the indignities imposed.[15]

However, the revolts in Lower Peru were fragmented and local (Flores Galindo 1986: 120) – until increasing pressure *also* on the *mestizo* and creole populations[16] led to an alliance between indigenous and *mestizo* groups and a strength of leadership that allowed the *cacique* Jose Gabriel Condorcanqui Túpac Amaru to be crowned Inca King as direct descendant of the last native sovereign, who had been executed by Virrey Toledo in 1572 in the main plaza in Cusco. Strong elements of an Incan utopia were present.[17] Thus the 1781 rebellion in Peru itself – i.e. Lower Peru – was led by the indigenous elite in alliance with *mestizo*s and creoles and was ambiguously based on 'the King's orders' – so Túpac Amaru claimed – to end bad government, and yet also on the notion of the Spaniards as usurpers of the true kingship.[18] It led to terrible repression: the elite family networks behind Túpac Amaru and his associates had to be exterminated.[19] Killed they were, in brutal ritual fashion, and thereafter elite families also were denied access to the education that had always been denied the masses.

The contrast with Upper Peru makes clear how poor a scenario this was for the development of an indigenous political movement. In Lower Peru the rebellion was led by a *cacique*, and the *cacique* system in the north of Peru and in Cusco still had sway and mobilizing power, with all its ambiguities, the more so as its economic status improved in the eighteenth century.[20] As Mallon (1992: 44) explains, the legitimacy of this indigenous ruling class contrasted with the position of the *caciques* in Upper Peru – the future Bolivia. In the latter, internal contradictions had by this date significantly weakened the institution of *cacicazgo*, as the more robust Aymaran communities demanded accountability and a representative role from their *caciques* which the latter were not prepared for.[21] The impact of demographic collapse was far less disastrous here than in Lower Peru (Cook 1981).The robustness is signalled by the fact that many *ayllus* were reconstituted into the new villages or *reducciones* of the Colonial structure, a sign of their coherence, whereas in the region of Cusco huge numbers of indigenous people were physically moved. Thomson documents that the rebellion in La Paz, which culminated in a 184-day siege of La Paz,[22] was led by an illiterate peasant-cum-trader, Túpac Katari,[23] with almost no support from the local *caciques*. In Chayanta the leader Tomas Katari was illiterate and not of noble indian lineage (Serulnikov 2006: 232–3). These movements had a downwards accountability to the people which was different in kind from the Cusco story. From the early days, *caciques* and their families and property were subject to attack as friends of the Spaniards (Thomson 2002: 217). The goal of self-rule was clear and unambiguous, anticipating the moment when "[they] alone will rule".[24] *Mestizo*s and creoles were frequently under threat, made to wear indian clothing, chew coca and in the case of Caquiaviri swear obedience to the indians (pp.158, 172). Thomson's analysis is that this clear aspiration for self-rule would be kept alive and "manifested repeatedly in Republican history" (pp.10, 12).

This was promising terrain for later political life. In 'Lower' Peru by contrast, indigenous people faced the weakening of their leadership and networks. Already, the best option often appeared to be to bribe an official and get redefined as a *mestizo*, or leave one's community since as a '*forastero*' or stranger, you were no longer subject to the *mita* and only to half the indian head tax. (Already, *mestizaje* was identified with losing one's original identity.) It is notable that in the future Bolivia those who chose the *forastero* route (and there were many) also chose to stay close to their *ayllu* and maintain their links (Thomson 2002).

Independence, Guano and a Growing Divide: From Independence to 'the Aristocratic Republic', 1821 to the 1890s

Peru was freed from Spanish rule by the victory of the Liberators, with the decisive Battle of Ayacucho in 1824. 'Independence' for Peru was a somewhat odd animal – brought from outside and not requested.[25] The liberation did not happen in one go: San Martin arrived from

Argentina in 1820 and Bolivar met him in Guayaquil, coming from the North, but the Spanish Viceroy Jose de la Serra remained in power in the Sierra with his base in Cusco until 1824, while in the meantime the first Congress of the independent country was installed in Lima in 1822 and the first constitution was proclaimed in 1823. Lima changed hands five times. The Liberators left without completing the defeat of royalist forces, and Bolivar was called on and eventually arrived late in 1823, to launch the final battle of the war.[26] The population was very divided, but not on clear lines of ethnic identity, or indeed any other. Before the Battle of Ayacucho, provision was made for people to salute and say (provisional) goodbyes to relatives on the opposing side (Contreras 2000: 65, 67). Indigenous groups formed the troops of both armies: many *serranos*, indigenous and non-indigenous, were royalist. The first years of Independence were extremely unstable and lacking in a 'project' – after all, no internal group had launched the country on this route.[27] In the first years, between 1826 and 1854, there were fifteen presidents, all military men and often *mestizo*s who had risen through the ranks in the course of the war. There were six constitutions.

In addition, a complex regulatory system had disappeared, with resulting intense disorder in the state; the result of this combined with the cost of the war was economic recession. The economic cost of the war was great, in destruction and dislocation as well as the cost to the community of supporting men under arms for an extended period.[28] Many Spaniards left, depriving the local economy of skills. As for the role of the state, silver in particular had relied on a quite complex state role for the supply of inputs: this had all disappeared. So did a state system for fixed price purchasing of silver (Contreras and Cueto 1999: 83). Silver was the key revenue earner and exports hardly grew.

We now turn to consider what kind of change was really at play here. What we shall find is that there was far less real change than might be expected. With Independence, there was effectively no change in the rules governing the ownership of resources – lands, mines, trade concessions. We shall see that the reality came close to a simple change of hands in the control of booty, with no change in the social relations of production. What did occur was a certain relaxation of taxation, giving a degree of relief, above all to the rural population – but leaving the state without resources for intervention.

Point counterpoint

As a degree of stability eventually arrived and the 'new' country began to find a shape, both change and continuity were evident. First, change.

A formative event was the emergence by 1839 of Lima as the new capital – not Cusco. With the designation of Lima as capital and full acceptance of the role of Lima, an important implication for our story becomes clear: up to that point, the strength and focus of the country had been the Sierra. While Lima had had an indisputable political primacy during the Colony, the Sierran elites had controlled the key economic resource, indigenous labour, and the Sierra had supplied foodstuffs and textiles. The economic dominance of the Sierra already began to shift with the decline of mining relative to commerce (Kendall Brown 2008; Fisher 1977), and the more so once Potosi was placed under the administration of the Virrey of Buenos Aires in 1776. With Independence, and the eventual political dominance of the Coastal elite, and specifically Lima, the configuration of the country radically changed. From that point on, the politics and economics of the new geographical formation would have huge implications for horizontal inequalities. From now on, the inequalities experienced by indigenous peoples in their local context of domination and deprivation, would be *compounded* by the impact of the working out of another inequality: between Coast and Sierra – a burden of 'double inequality' indeed.

When recovery did come about, with guano, given the sensitivity of the political economy to the new focus on Lima, it is an extraordinary irony of history that the first export boom of the newly-independent colony was one that could hardly have had less need of the Sierra. Guano, an excellent fertilizer much in demand at the time in Europe, is simply bird dung, which by the mid-nineteenth century had accumulated to form islands off the Peruvian coast. The guano was 'mined' in intolerable conditions by Chinese coolies transported in the same ships that carried the guano. It produced huge revenues for the Peruvian public purse (Table 5.1 below). Because the capital and labour came from abroad, no local processing was required, and because the labour was semi-slave labour so wages were non-existent, the only (but very significant) linkage to the Peruvian economy operated through the fiscal revenues which accrued to the central government in Lima.[29] Such revenues gradually permitted the consolidation of Lima's power, financing police and administrative outposts throughout the country, and putting 'the rest of the nation under the influence of its centralising military and bureaucracy' (Larson 2004: 151).

From now on, the opening to trade would mean consumer goods from elsewhere displacing those produced in the Sierra, and with the arrival of coolie labour from 1849 on and demographic growth, the power given by control over indigenous labour would slowly decline.

Table 5.1 Government revenues during the Guano Age (per cent of total)

	Customs	Guano	Loans	Others	Total (1000 pesos)
1846	26.3	8.4	0.0	65.3	6,113
1847	40.1	0.0	0.0	59.9	5,005
1851	29.1	28.7	0.0	42.1	7,636
1852	35.8	37.9	0.0	26.3	8,699
1861	15.3	80.0	0.0	5.0	21,246
1862	16.3	70.1	6.0	7.6	19,949
1863	13.4	42.6	37.5	6.6	26,235
1866	19.4	67.4	0.0	13.2	20,128
1868	10.9	65.7	17.2	6.2	32,370
1871	12.1	83.5[a]	0.0	4.4	51,181
1872	10.9	50.8[a]	31.1	7.1	67,987
1873	12.2	73.9[a]	10.2	3.7	67,710
1876	12.5	57.3[a]	18.8	11.4	44,246
1877	30.6	29.1	5.2	35.1	22,500

[a] Includes advances made on guano as well as current earnings.
Source: Adapted from Hunt (1973: 70, Table 8). See Hunt for original sources.

This shift in the economic and political dynamics embedded the importance of the Coast, allowing Peru to grow while ignoring the Sierra – and *a fortiori* the Selva. The embedding of this approach to economic management was for the long run one of the deepest elements of 'institutional evolution'.

With the new structure, and supporting it, and of course contradictory to the supposed liberal ideology of the time, went a culture of despising the people of the Sierra, a prejudice that to an extent also applied to the regional elites, never trusted by the Lima elite. The latter was increasingly characterized by a mix of *mestizo* and white, as the new elite took shape, with a strong presence of military men, often *mestizo*. The domination of this *criollo* elite of Lima would mark the ethnic relations of the new Republic. Further, the old regional elites had at least been subject to certain redistributive pressures arising from their obligations to dependents as 'Lord of the Manor'. The new elite was less subject to such obligations, a change helped over time by the greater weakness of the Church under the new order.

The change therefore was radical, in policy attitudes as well as political and economic realities. But there was also powerful continuity. One element of continuity underlay what would appear to be change: with Independence – in principle – there was to be a move from a mercantilist regime where non-market mechanisms dominated internally, to a so-called 'liberal' regime. The colonial system had been embedded in power relations and maintained by violence. With Independence, the Coastal elite that now unsurely held the reins of power had inherited, but hardly bought into, the liberal reforms of the Liberator Bolivar. Early actions included the abolition of all differentiation by race in public policy ('We are all Peruvians'), the declaration that all children born in Peru to slaves would be free, and changes in property rights. Indigenous communities no longer had legal status and '*caciques*' lost both status and lands.

The ambiguities of the attempted shift in culture are eloquently analysed by Larson (2004: 142–4). It will be no surprise that the shift in culture was not enforced, and in practice labour relations continued to be shaped by feudal power structures, in different forms and responding to different pressures in distinct regions of the Sierra. Debt bondage evolved a little from its colonial forms but remained very much alive as a means of securing labour, to re-emerge as a key mechanism to feed the export boom of the 1890s, consisting of sugar and cotton. '*Enganche*' – meaning 'hooking' – was the vivid name given to the process of obtaining indigenous labour both for the mines and for the Coast, with the use of *mestizo* labour contractors and a mechanism of debt to keep the hook in place.[30]

But even more deeply, while the power of the Sierran elite was indeed being eroded at one level by the shift of the political and economic focus to Lima, at another the very shift of focus of the 'modernizing' trading economy saw the traditional institutions of the Sierra – above all, the dominating role of a small group of intermediaries, principally landowners – left unchallenged. New power brokers emerged to fill the space left as the indigenous elite was further undermined. They continued the colonial tradition of monopoly in the mobilization of favours from the central power. These new actors gradually came to be known as '*gamonales*'.[31] Privilege was secured by keeping the size of the intermediary group small. Indigenous opportunities to access land, education, decision making, or to mobilize collectively were intermediated by these power brokers in many diverse forms of political patronage and clientelism, exploitation and protection, based on their economic, political, cultural and military power both in the hacienda and often also at the level of the provincial administration. Individual indigenous might be co-opted into the system, finding themselves subtly led to reject their antecedents and collaborate in their own progress at the expense of their fellow indigenous.[32] In this pervasive and embracing system, gradually known as '*gamonalismo*', land ownership was important but not the defining characteristic. However, 'Firstly, by becoming the owner of the pasture-lands, Don Santos also becomes the master of the Indians who dwell there. Secondly, respect is due to him on this double account. And thirdly, this order of things which the law of man bids us respect is respected also by God in his heaven' (Bourricaud 1970: 32–3). So the *gamonal* had power not just by virtue of delegated authority, but in himself. He was more appropriately viewed as an ally of the central state, than as a functionary (Ibarra 2002).

The depth of this element of continuity, and its significance for the domination and marginalization of indigenous people, cannot be overemphasized. The next section explains how with the lifting of the head tax and reduced demand for land and labour in the Sierra, certain opportunities were opened up for indigenous people, though very briefly: the limited response is hardly a surprise given the continuing oppressive social structure and the lack of infrastructure to unite the country and to make the Sierra competitive.

Short-lived opportunity, conflict and renewed repression

The new focus of the economy and polity on Lima and the Coast, it is argued in the literature, did at least lift a little pressure from the Sierra. But the 'easing' only really helped that part of the Central Highlands already well connected to Lima and the Coast – the Mantaro Valley, Jauja, Huancayo, Tarma – and the relief was very short – twelve years, for example, in the case of the head tax on indigenous people.

Revenue from guano only began to be significant by the early 1850s (Table 5.1). In the first years after Independence, revenue needs were desperate and the decision was taken to retain the head tax of the colony but to rename it the '*contribución indigena*', a euphemism for the indigenous tax. There was also a '*contribución de castas*'.[33] But collecting the tax was difficult: in the colony the collection mechanisms had relied on a social fabric that had been disrupted by Independence. In 1854 the rising revenues from guano allowed the ending of the tax. As a result, communities were able to reduce their integration into the market, once the need for cash payment was reduced, and this is what some did.[34]

Another 'pressure' taken off was mining. Exports of silver stagnated through the mid-century. To grave supply-side problems was added the real exchange rate overvaluation as guano boomed.[35] The stagnation of mining presumably reduced demand for foodstuffs from the surrounding area, but at the same time indigenous small-scale miners were able to increase their footing in the sector. Cerro de Pasco remained in European hands, but in other cases local miners maintained their place.

The nineteenth-century social history of the Sierra is shaped by the varying regional impact of different booms in the international demand for commodities. Land concentration and pressure for labour were in different ways the result of rising demand from sugar estates in the North and by the 1860s the wool boom in the South. It was the central Sierra where the indigenous population benefited most as the pressure was reduced on land, labour and mineral resources. At least in parts of the Central Sierra this was a time for consolidation and even possibly improvement in the quality of life.[36] In the South and North, the hacienda system seems to have remained entrenched, but in the Central region, some individuals moved out from their communities and secured title to land (Contreras 1988: 540). Income estimates at the time of the 1827 matricula gave a ratio of non-indigenous to indigenous monetary income of 2:1 (Gootenberg 1991: 45). Given some demonetization in some areas but also some increased monetization in others, it is impossible to say how the ratio moved in the following decades, but more importantly and more securely, we can say that in the Central Sierra access to resources improved for the indigenous population. There was some recovery in population: the national rate of population increase was 1.2 per cent a year 1827–76. The percentage of indigenous in the growing population was 62 per cent in 1827 and 58 per cent in 1876 – but in the meantime a wave of epidemics had hit the Sierra again in the 1850s, reputedly accounting for 300,000 indigenous dead.[37] Although no improvements occurred in education or health provision, this release of pressure over access to resources coincides with relative peace, as HI theory would predict: no serious conflict between indigenous people and the authorities broke out after 1815 until 1867.[38]

However, conflict did eventually break out. The occasion for that conflict was the reimposition of the head tax in 1866,[39] ahead of the collapse of guano, as Table 5.1 shows. The earlier abolition of the head tax had deprived regional elites of their principal source of public income and was the source of much conflict with the centre, which led to its reimposition. The specific focus of revolt was Huancané, in the department of Puno in the South. Here severe drought was aggravating pressures on peasants, but conflict was also surfacing as the wool market boomed in the 1860s, with a growing number of merchants hungrily searching out sources of cheap wool.[40] The conflict was hardly simply a reaction to increasing market pressures, as some have suggested, since the 'market era' still continued to be something of a myth. Landlords and merchants both still used unpaid indian services and indigenous people had many scores to settle, including servitude.[41]

The reaction to the revolt was punitive. An emergency 'Law of Terror' was passed and mass killing and imprisonment followed. Whole villages were uprooted and exiled to labour camps in the Selva (Larson 2004: 158). The uprising was brutally repressed, and its leader, Juan Bustamante, was stoned to death.[42]

What we are seeing, then, is that it can well be economic *recovery* that generates conflict in this historical context of deeply exploitative social and economic relationships, as the whole regional economy is visibly growing in response to the world economy, and yet again harsh means and practices are used to keep indigenous incomes from growing too.

However, for the economy as a whole, prosperity was now at an end. Guano collapsed because of substitutes; the railways had been built with debt backed by guano, so government debt now became a heavy problem. Yet with the exception of a few routes, the expensive railway adventure failed to reach the Sierra. Although the Sierra cities were in the original plans, lack of state capacity and minimum accountability contributed to the failure (Contreras and Cueto 1999: 123). While no significant loss of community lands was registered until the 1850s, in the South, wool was expanding but in highly conflictual circumstances, with indigenous communities often being displaced (Jacobsen 1997).

War with Chile

On top of economic problems and internal conflict now came a major international conflict, the War of the Pacific. This was a resource war with Chile 1879–83, over possession of the nitrate fields, resulting in occupation by Chilean troops of the Coast and Central Sierra and an expensive defeat.[43]

The War is an important moment in our story. The effect of Chilean troops arriving in the Central Sierra was to spark an indigenous mobilization to defend the country (Mallon 1987), building on the elements of autonomy we have seen developing in the Central Highlands. The nature of the 'consciousness' behind this movement has been much disputed,[44] but it seems improbable it was anything other than nationalist and patriotic. But even during the war, relations with the *mestizo*/white elite went sour, and the issue transformed into class/ethnic conflict. This was prolonged for three years after the signing of a peace accord with Chile (Manrique 1988). Elites rapidly realized that indigenous mobilization and autonomy represented a greater danger than Chile, and began to press for peace with Chile at any price (Mallon 1987).

The impact at national level was profound: among the elites, the indigenous were blamed for the defeat, with all the emotional impact that such a view was bound to have, given the need for a scapegoat in the face of a very strong defeat and a punitive settlement. Ricardo Palma writing to Pierola in 1881 was explicit: 'The principal cause of the great defeat is that the majority of Peru is composed of a wretched and degraded race that we once attempted to dignify and ennoble. The Indian lacks a patriotic sense; he is a born enemy of the white and of the man of the coast.'[45]

The political result was a new bonding of Lima with regional elites, whose need for reinforcement to deal with 'the indian threat' was suddenly vividly perceived. This helped to consolidate the emerging institution of *gamonalismo*. For the first time throughout the Sierra, this was now clearly the most important mechanism of domination. The consolidation was furthered by the decline in the practice of appointing military officers to the local post of 'prefect', following the lowered prestige of the military after the defeat by Chile and the low level of trust by the Lima elite in this group.[46] The state was increasingly conscious of the value of delegation at the local level to the group holding the monopoly of power, thus legitimizing its power and reproducing boundaries that mixed class and ethnic elements (Bourricaud 1970, Larson 2004, Réñique 2004). The local *gamonales* competed among themselves for power, based on their capacity to mobilize favour from the central power. The formation of these 'circuits of privatised public power', as O'Donnell (1999) has called this type of delegated power, permitted or at least tolerated by the state, was to have profound implications in the next century as the state tried at various times and in various ways to penetrate the Sierra with its own institutions, as we shall see in the next two chapters.

Meanwhile, indigenous people learnt more thoroughly than ever to distrust their regional elites. Perversely, given Lima's new-found alliance with these groups, this strengthened a culture of going straight to Lima and specifically to the President himself. This responded to the monarchical tradition of the Inca regime, which led naturally to a 'filial' relationship with the 'king', and to the patrimonial Spanish colonial state and the symbolic power of benevolent patriarchy in the Spanish King. Thus the inherited vertical system of patronage was strengthened and continued to channel indigenous resentment and appeal – a deep source of continuity in patron/client relations that had structured hierarchy and inequality from the pinnacle to the base of colonial power relations. Various presidents knew well how to build on this. At another level, however, a possibly more productive consequence of the War was a growing realization that the 'indian problem' needed dealing with in terms other than crude repression. An emblematic event was the response to the rebellion of Atusparia by the two successive governments which confronted him.[47] The revolt was over the efforts of the local authorities to collect the *contribución personal,* once again imposed to fund the War. President Iglesias (1882–5) applied force, sending troops from Lima; the incoming President Caceres in 1886 removed Atusparia from gaol and invited him to his house, where they embraced – an embrace that was to become a symbol of the reconciliation of the two Perus. On leaving, Atusparia entrusted his son to the President as godfather and educator (Stein 1988; Thurner 1997).

In this shift of attitude among elites following the war was the birth of the '*civilista*' movement, to dominate Peruvian politics until the 1920s.[48] From this point, the Coastal *civilista* elite succeeded in imposing its discourse and its programme. In the 1880s the conclusion was that immigration should be the answer, to 'dilute' and improve this 'barbarous' people. Already then, however, it was becoming obvious that Peru was never going to compete successfully for the huge waves of immigrants coming into Brazil, the Southern cone and some countries of the Caribbean. So the new philosophy became civilization and assimilation through education, meaning schools but also wider elements, such as education in hygiene as a way of dealing with issues of health and nutrition. The decentralization wave that accompanied the end of the guano boom thus included the beginnings of paternalistic central pushing of responsibilities on to the regions, with very limited resources. A 'school tax' was decreed, and all local taxes went to the departmental authorities, which now had responsibility for education and health (Contreras 1996: 215–9). How far this succeeded in modernizing HIs is part of the twentieth century story, the subject of the next chapter.

Conclusion

This chapter has explored how both the Colony and the first decades after Independence shaped both horizontal inequalities and the institutions that were now to embed and condition such inequalities. We have shown how the Colony had a profound effect in subjugating and fragmenting the indigenous population, in creating institutions of prejudice, forced labour and taxation that reinforced the political, economic and social inequalities, and in virtually destroying the leadership of indigenous peoples, by death and by repression. We have shown how with Independence, large themes of continuity and change came into play. The powerful change was the establishment of Lima as the key centre of power and the capital of the new Republic, with all that lay behind that, and the resulting domination of the Coast, consolidated by the guano boom. Peru was reshaped in these years both in its polity and economy, with major consequences for all the people of the Sierra, elites and indigenous communities alike. But the paradox was that the very shift of focus to the Coast allowed a fundamental continuity in social structures in the Sierra. No forces of modernization challenged the essential reproduction of the colonial system of power brokers: intermediaries who monopolized access to power, privilege and opportunity. The weakening of the indigenous elite and their internal forms of governance – further weakened after Independence – gave new opportunities for this intermediary institution to become established. Thus the institution of '*gamonalismo*' came gradually to dominate Sierra life, and specifically indigenous people. Land was important in that domination – but the institution of *gamonalismo* was far more than land ownership or elite power: it was about reinforcing mechanisms of monopolization of access to power and opportunity, supported in a web of obligations and possibilities that sucked people into its culture and attitudes. Thus indigenous individuals might find themselves 'co-opted' – sucked in – and bettering themselves by collaborating in the disempowering of their fellows.

We thus see two crucial lines of institutional evolution by the beginning of the twentieth century, already embedded in decades of attitudes and enforced norms: first, that 'Peru' can do without the Sierra, and second, that 'the *gamonal* is the master of the indians'. Both characteristics will be fundamental in shaping the burden of 'double inequality' as we turn to horizontal inequalities in the twentieth century.

Notes

1. There were inequalities between Coastal people and *Serranos*, or people of the Sierra, between 'valley' people and those of the '*puna*' or high pastures: divisions which are manifest today. The within-group inequalities were also great. See Rostworowski (1993).
2. 'Indirect' in terms of the hierarchy of control via native officials. But the Spanish in Latin America also implemented very direct control in some areas, more so than in other colonial experiences, especially in the aspect of religion. And the local leaders implementing the indirect control came low in the hierarchy and their area and manner of operation was strictly local.
3. In Peru the indigenous people in fact came from different ethnicities and cultures, but were placed by the Spanish in the single 'indian' category. Only a few years previously the Inca empire had tried to integrate all these different kingdoms and groups, but at the moment the Spaniards arrived,

the exercise was only unevenly successful and the development of a unified Quechua language and process was interrupted.

4. The establishment of this system was consolidated by the policies of the Viceroy Toledo who significantly reduced the power of the *encomienda* system that was predominant until his arrival.
5. See Assadourian (1994), Flores Galindo (1986: 39), Glave (1992), Larson (2004) among others. For once, 'decimation', the taking out of one in ten, is a weak word for a situation where almost eight of every ten people died.
6. The priest was the only non-indigenous who could spend the night in the community, and so oversee important aspects of community life.
7. Cotlear (1989) citing Morse (1984).
8. As one of the consequences of the rebellion of Túpac Amaru.
9. For the cultural and religious politics of Spanish colonialism in the Andes, see Silverblatt (1987), Spalding (1984).
10. 'El anonime de Yucay', written in 1571 and cited by Assadourian (1994).
11. This draws on ideas developed by Martinez (2004).
12. The phrase is recorded by Flores Galindo as that of a colonial functionary. Ares and Gruzinski (1997) is an important reference on the subtleties of 'life between two worlds'.
13. For the case of mining see Glave (1992), Tandeter (1992).
14. Stern (1993) argues that these successes weakened the possibility of a more radical challenge to the system.
15. See Larson 2004 on 'economia moral'; Kendall Brown (2008) on the region of Arequipa.
16. '*Mestizo*' meant one parent of indigenous origin and one of Spanish or creole origin. 'Creole' meant a person of Spanish descent born in Peru. For the reforms, see Flores Galindo (1986, Chapter 2); O'Phelan (1985: 234).
17. Flores Galindo (1986: 93). He describes the elements of utopian vision which ran through the movement: Cusco in the 18th century became the centre of a new flourishing identity. Inca symbols, colours and techniques were incorporated in craft-making, clothes design, painting and other artistic expressions. The *'Comentarios Reales'* of Garcilosa de la Vega had enormous influence in elite reinterpretation and reconstruction of a neo-Inca identity that was disseminated through popular expressions such as theatrical and folklore representations, in which 'the Inca' and 'the Tahuantinsuyo' were idealistically elevated as symbols of generous justice opposing European abuse.
18. Túpac Amaru's coronation edict proclaimed that 'the kings of Castile have usurped the Crown and dominions of my people for close to three centuries.' Quoted in Thomson (2002: 164). See also Stavig (1999), Szeminski (1987), Walker 1999.
19. O'Phelan (1985: 234–6) documents the networks.
20. Flores Galindo (1986: 115–6); O'Phelan (1985).
21. Serulnikov (2006) shows how the Chayanta rebellion in 1780 (to the North of Potosi) was against the *caciques,* for example against their upsetting of norms over control of access to resources.
22. In two stages – see Thomson (2002).
23. He traded in coca and baize cloth. Túpac Amaru was also a trader but at another level: he owned a string of mules.

24. 'Indians themselves spoke expectantly of the time when "they alone would rule"' (Thomson 2002: 231, citing AGI Buenos Aires 319, Cuaderno no.4 fols 60v, 77).
25. This section draws on Contreras and Cueto (1999, Chapter 1).
26. The last royalist stronghold was in fact the fort of Callao, which held out till January 1826.
27. Contreras and Cueto (1999: 42). Not that there were no continuing revolutionary intents from within: there were, notably in Cusco in 1814–15. See Contreras and Cueto (1999: 44–6).
28. A population of one and a half million was supporting some 25,000 men at arms over nearly 15 years (Contreras and Cueto 1999: 70).
29. Hunt (1973) provides careful documentation of this.
30. Contractors would loan the cash to make the journey, the beginning of indebtedness. The contract signed would typically be for seven years. This was rapidly followed by a build up of debt in the company store, so that a worker was soon truly snared, and pursued with violence if he or she fled. See Klaren (1976); Gonzalez (1980).
31. The term '*gamonal*' is first located in use in 1863, in the *Revista Americana* in Lima. The *gamonal* is there described as 'the satrap of the parish'. The word is borrowed from the natural sciences, where it means a parasitic plant. Pablo Macera is responsible for the elucidation. See Ibarra (2002); also Burga and Flores Galindo (1979).
32. Thus an indigenous person might conceivably, though improbably, emerge as a *gamonal*, after several generations of 'whitening', marriage and schooling, but only by enforcing 'indianness' on others.
33. '*Casta*' signified all who paid neither the indigenous tribute, nor the property and industrial taxes.
34. Contreras (1988: 521–2). His analysis is based on Jauja in the Central Highlands. See also Contreras (1996a).
35. Given the bi-metallic exchange standard of the period the Dutch disease effect of the guano boom came through internal inflation. See Hunt (1973) for documentation.
36. This is well argued by Mallon (1987), and by Gootenberg (1991).
37. This is based on a fascinating and detailed analysis by Gootenberg based on the heretofore unexploited matricula, or fiscal census, of 1827. He is able to correct the famous estimates of Kubler for 1795–1876, which left out 14 provinces including Puno. See Gootenberg (1991).
38. An exception is the *iquichano* revolt in Huanta in 1825 against the new republican regime (Klaren 2000), but it was very localized.
39. This time as an individual head tax without ethnic characteristics (Contreras and Cueto 1999: 118).
40. As Larson vividly puts it: 'scouring the arid plateau for cheap wool' (Larson 2004: 157).
41. The interpretation of this event is disputed in the literature, with some authors claiming that it was principally a dispute between rival local *caciques*, making use of the indian grievances. See McEvoy (1999).
42. See Jacobsen in Jackson (ed.) (1997), Larson (2004: 158), Réñique (2004, Chapter 1). Bustamante was the son of an indigenous mother and a Spaniard, of whom, he said, he knew little or nothing (Réñique 2004: 28).

He identified with his indigenous roots. Today he would have been termed a *cholo*. He had, however, an exceptional education and had travelled widely. See McEvoy (1999).

43. Lima was occupied for about three-and-a-half years, Peru had to concede the nitrate territories to Chile and pay a large indemnization in guano.
44. Indigenous did fight on both sides. But Manrique (1988) has a convincing analysis arguing against the theses of Bonilla and Favre. The latter interpret the entire episode of indigenous mobilization as a class/ethnic phenomenon. Manrique points out that if this were the case, more would have joined the Chilean side.
45. Quoted by Larson (2004: 196).
46. There was also a move to professionalize the army around the turn of the century, taking them out of public posts.
47. The revolt was based in the Callejon de Huaylas in the Northern Sierra. The indian mayors who went to petition the authorities, led by Atusparia, were humiliated by the cutting of their braided hair, a practice deliberately reminiscent of the Colony. Tens of thousands of indigenous peasants then took the city of Huaraz and other cities of the department (Stein 1988, Thurner 1997).
48. Formally 'born' in 1871, under the name of the '*Sociedad Independencia Electoral*', the following year it took the name *civilista*. It was in disarray during the War, and formally reappeared in 1894.

6

The Embedding of Regional Inequality and the Consequences for Group Inequalities: The 1890s to the 1960s*

We have signalled how central to the fate of indigenous people was the emergence of Lima as the capital in independent Peru. As the growth path which was to dominate the twentieth century took shape decade by decade, so the domination of the Coast and of Lima was reinforced. A pattern of growth emerged which had no need of modernizing the Sierra, and still less the Selva. At the same time and of equal significance, '*gamonalismo*' came gradually to dominate the power of state intermediation in the Sierra. Both crucial lines of institutional evolution shaped and reshaped state institutions in various ways. They became part of the infrastructure upon which other less 'foundational' institutions, such as major public policies, were constructed.[1] One consequence of the pattern of growth was the failure to develop state capacities to understand what was needed to develop the Sierra. A further important consequence was that the state used the traditional intermediaries for the channelling of resources. Indigenous peoples had access to such resources on terms shaped by the clientelistic and discriminating culture which prevailed. The pattern of growth and its institutional consequences led unavoidably to change, and also left a legacy of lack of capacity, weak leadership and norms of discrimination and paternalism that prevented the developments that might have modified the pattern in favour of the indigenous population. This chapter documents these processes.

The previous chapter began to delineate how regional and ethnic inequality intersect. In this chapter, we need to explore carefully how regional inequality evolved and why, to show how the elite of the Sierra now became severely affected as the Sierra as a whole suffered increasingly in the inter-regional dynamics, political and economic.

---

*As explained in the Preface, Carlos Contreras is co-author of this chapter.

As the elites suffered, the embedded repressive structures meant the indigenous suffered even more, which left only two options – to migrate, or retreat back into the hacienda.

The key to the process was the evolution of commodity exports. The growth of exports is given in Table 6.1. It will be seen that the end of the nineteenth century and the early years of the twentieth century did provide elements of growth for non-Coastal Peru, in the form of rubber and wool. But these were severely excluding in their nature. As we saw in the last chapter, in the case of wool, the expansion generated fierce competition for both land and labour, leading to increased marginalization of the indigenous population throughout southern Peru (Larson 2004). However, by the end of the 1920s there was no element of direct stimulus to growth left. Wool was in terminal decline by the 1920s, the market eroded by synthetic substitutes. The one commodity in demand from the Selva, rubber, crashed earlier and for the same reason, together with competition from Asian plantations – though rubber had provided a threat rather than an opportunity for the indigenous people of the Selva (Santos-Granero and Barclay 2002). Cocaine was also a significant export up to the first decade of the twentieth century: its suppression after 1910, under pressure from the United States, added to growing competition from Java, affected agriculture in the Sierra (Gootenberg 1999).[2]

Ironically, as wool collapsed, the unfavourable equity consequences of the earlier boom were not reversed, the typical asymmetry of boom and bust. While competition for land and labour lessened – which in itself favoured the indigenous population – the oligarchic politics and

Table 6.1 Main export products, 1890–1960 (per cent of total exports)

Year	Silver	Copper	Lead and zinc	Hydrocarbons	Sugar and cotton	Wool	Rubber
1890	33	1	0	0	37	15	13
1900	22	18	0	0	39	7	13
1910	10	18	0	2	34	7	18
1920	5	7	0	5	72	2	1
1930	4	10	7	30	29	3	0
1940	10	19	3	25	28	5	0
1950	4	5	11	13	51	4	0
1960	5	21	9	4	28	2	0

Note: 1940 figures for metals correspond to 1939.
Sources: Thorp and Bertram (1978), *Extracto Estadístico* and BCR *Memoria.*

clientelistic structures and practices shaped to profit from the earlier expansion kept the indigenous population in a subservient role. Once the violent protests of the 1920s were repressed, it was not until the 1950s and 1960s that indigenous peasant unrest would start to be a challenge to the institution of *gamonalismo* as it began to collapse, and even then the emerging signs of unrest were fragmentary and uncoordinated.

The whole of Peru suffered, of course, as the model faltered briefly in the 1930s, as in all Latin America, but the impact of the Great Depression of 1929 was less than in any other country of some size (Thorp 2000), and Peru fairly rapidly resumed its pattern of primary export-led growth.[3] From the mid-twentieth century, the major products leading growth were centred on – or off – the Coast, with the one important exception of metal mining. Thus oil, cotton, sugar and fishmeal in their turn brought expansion and prosperity to the Coast. And as throughout the world, mining now became larger scale, more capital-intensive and, as a result, more dominated by foreigners. Opportunities for local populations were increasingly limited: the need for labour declined, equipment was brought from abroad, and the infrastructure was already largely in place early in the century. More access roads were built – roads designed to take mining products to the Coast, not develop the Highlands.[4]

Economic exclusion was compounded by political exclusion, as in the Electoral law of 1895, which restricted the vote to the literate population. As we see in Table 6.2, the literate population was largely concentrated in the Coast. The majority of the Sierra people and the bulk of indigenous were disenfranchised and political voice was concentrated in a small elite. By such means and such an evolution, a hostile geography was compounded by the politics and economics associated with the pattern of development. This began to seem insuperable for the indigenous population.

In all this process reducing the importance of the Sierra, migration from the Sierra was both consequence and cause. The earliest version of the export-led model at least needed labour from the Sierra, but even that positive impact was already weakened by the arrival of 'coolie' labour in the nineteenth century. Such labour demand was significantly reduced by the 1930s and came to an end by the 1960s, with population growth on the Coast and with migration.[5] Table 6.3 shows the growth of population accelerating during the course of the century, with pronounced migratory flows occurring after 1940, reducing the growth of the Sierra population to 1.2 per cent a year from 1940. This was a consequence of the economic model concentrating activities in the Coast,

Table 6.2 Regional distribution of registered voters, 1940, 1963 (total numbers and percentages)

Regions [a]	1940 (%)	1963 (%)	Population share 1961 census
Coast			
Lima	26	39	
Total Coast	**51**	**63**	**38**
Total Sierra	**42**	**30**	**51**
Total Selva	**7**	**7**	**11**
Total registered	100	100	100
Absolute number	392381	2070727	

[a] According to the location of capital city of the department.
Note that the classification is at the departmental level, which is less than accurate.
Coast: Callao, Ica, La Libertad, Lambayeque, Lima, Moquegua, Piura, Tacna, Tumbes.
Sierra: Ancash, Apurímac, Arequipa, Ayacucho, Cajamarca, Cusco, Huancavelica, Junín, Pasco, Puno.
Selva: Amazonas, Huánuco, Loreto, Madre de Dios, San Martín.
Source: Own elaboration, using Basadre (1980: 161) and data from the *Anuario Estadístico* (1966: 973, and Table 6.3).

Table 6.3 Regional distribution of population

	Percentage distribution		Average annual growth rates	
	1876	**1961**	**1876 to 1940**	**1940 to 1961**
Sierra	69.0	50.6	1.2	1.2
Selva	8.2	11.1	1.6	2.8
Coast	22.7	38.2	1.6	3.9
Major coastal valleys			1.6	2.0
Lima-Callao			2.2	5.1

Note: The regional distribution is done as in the previous table.
Source: Adapted from Hunt (1977, Table 4-1).

but reinforced the domination of the Coast, as the more educated and more entrepreneurial tended to migrate. We come below to the consequences for leadership.

Similarly, the increased concentration of growth on the Coast weakened elites in the Sierra: this also led to migration and undermined a process of modernization in the Sierra that eventually could have developed and strengthened new regional political voices to contest the model, as we argue below.

We now develop these themes in turn. First we analyse the macro level: the way the state evolved and the way the economy evolved. Then we look in detail at the policy response to the 'indian problem', as it was being defined by the end of the previous century. Next we trace the political and social consequences of these events at the local level, in particular the consequences of the pattern of integration to the international economy, and the impact of migration on identities and political mobilization. Finally we explore the intersection of local political developments with those at national level and the fate of the reformist efforts which resulted. By the end of the 1960s, the situation is one of national incoherence and ineffectiveness, into which steps the military government of General Velasco: the story of the following chapter.

The Emerging Growth Path and its Consequences for Growth in the Sierra and for Inequality

We have demonstrated elsewhere the pronounced negative characteristics of this form of export-led expansion, despite the reasonable growth provided (Thorp and Bertram 1978). Here we highlight two: the kind of state which was to emerge and the kind of economic policy, above all that shaping the relation with the international market.

The first, the nature of the state, was indirectly of huge importance for our analysis of group inequalities. Its evolution was profoundly shaped by the lack of a felt need among business elites for a developmental state and by a political system increasingly responsive to an electorate concentrated in the Coast. The influence of the needs of the Sierra was zero – the vast bulk of the population of the Sierra was without a vote, and the business elite that had major influence was based in the Coast. Their interests were clear: the rapid expansion of sugar, cotton, oil and copper in the first thirty years of the new century needed a state that could maintain order, including securing property rights, in the modern sectors of the Coast and above all in Lima.[6] But the needs for infrastructure – transport, power and marketing – were largely covered by foreign firms, and what is more, foreign firms prepared to give space to local elites.[7] The mining elite of Peru – a collection of serious and qualified entrepreneurs – for the most part rationally opted for profitable partnerships with foreign capital, or sold out and used the cash to develop enterprises on the Coast, as did Rizo Patron.[8] The developing culture of close partnership with and reliance on foreigners is captured (unintentionally) in a quote from Augusto Weisse, distinguished member of the business elite, as he decided in 1964 to move into fishmeal in partnership with Mecom, a Texan oilman: 'This business has always smelled highly to me. But if Mr. Mecom is interested, why then, it smells like a rose.'[9]

Such a pattern of development, where a perceived need to develop the state's role was not shared by the 'doers' – the business elite – is an underlying explanation of why by the 1960s the underlying institutions needed to frame and support a flourishing modern economy were weak, if not absent. As in all medium and large countries in Latin America, the 1930s were a time of institution building, partly in response to crisis but also to international influences such as the Kemmerer Missions.[10] A Central Bank had already been created in 1922 under the Kemmerer aegis: in 1931 a Banking Superintendency was put in place. But the governments of General Benavides (1933–39) and Manuel Prado (1939–45) also contributed much to the creation of modern Ministries.[11] Health and Education Ministries were created in 1935, an Agrarian Bank was created in 1931, an Industrial Bank in 1936, a Mining Bank in 1940, and a Ministry of Agriculture in 1944, to name but a few of the innovations introduced.

However, the incipient development state was severely damaged by a chaotic period of policy-making in the years immediately following the Second World War, when Bustamante y Rivero attempted to govern with Aprista allies, resulting in a period of exceptional internal contradictions, which sent the business and political elites resolutely back to laissez faire.[12] The coup of 1948 led to the government of General Odría, a solidly right-wing and pro-market administration dedicated to smoothing the path of foreign capital.

Both Odría, and the earlier government of Leguía, 1919–29, reinforced the centralism of the model, concentrating activity in the Coast but above all on Lima. The governments that followed in the 1930s and 40s in no way undermined this centralism: the protection of industry was increased but the protection was greatest for Lima.[13] This responded to growing populist politics in the Coast where most of the electorate was concentrated (Aljovín and López 2005, Basadre 1980). The result was that over the whole period there was an increased concentration on Lima. For example, data on the number of industrial establishments show that whereas in 1943, 43 per cent were in Lima, in 1954 the figure was 75 per cent.[14]

The outcome of the whole period from the 1920s to the 1960s was continuing institutional neglect of the Sierra, apart from schools and institutions of order. Police posts in particular were put in place throughout the Sierra during these years. And schools were gradually being built: we return below to this important part of the story. But looked at in a comparative Latin American perspective, the Peruvian public sector experienced limited development promotion and correspondingly little learning by doing. Institutions in the fields of technological support or credit for industry, or efficient taxing and spending, were underdeveloped, and/or limited to Lima and the Coast.[15]

The second characteristic of the period we need to highlight here, policies shaping the relation with the international market, was of more direct and obvious relevance to our inequality story. The opportunities for primary exports were sufficiently plentiful that a model based on cheap imports and lack of protection seemed entirely rational, particularly given the perception of Peru as a small market – a perception aggravated of course by the marginalizing of the Sierra.[16] Again in comparative Latin American terms, Peru had low levels of protection up to the end of the 1960s and a plentiful supply of dollars providing a high exchange rate. As urban populations grew (again an important topic we explore below) it made good political sense and (seemingly) economic sense to allow cheap food imports, often to the point of subsidy.[17]

It was not that no one was thinking strategically about the Sierra: they were. Following the War with Chile, a new group of intellectuals had emerged, positivist in their thinking, in line with the current fashion of the time in Latin America. These were not the romantic historians and writers of the guano era, but engineers, geographers, economists and doctors, who brought new diagnoses of backwardness and saw a clear role for the Highlands.[18,19] In their thinking, the Coast, given its comparative advantage in sugar and cotton, should specialize in export agriculture, while the Sierra should produce the food for both regions. They were well aware of what this implied in terms of good physical communication between the two regions and measures to increase the productivity of agriculture and livestock industries.

However, these views never translated into a significant programme to overcome the barriers, not helped by falling international transport costs or the nature of the model itself, which as we show below further weakened the ability of regional elites to build a consensus around the need for and nature of a modernization project.

The same positivist mentality was also present in some cities of the interior, such as Ayacucho and Cusco, where the North American Albert Giesecke brought about a revolution in the University of San Antonio Abad in the early years of the twentieth century. However, once again the increasing centralism, reinforced by the new wave of exporting, left these intellectuals without political weight and consequent capacity to influence. As the twentieth century progressed, attempts at change based on regional forces did occur, notably both in the 1930s and early

1940s, but never achieved coherence as a regional project (Portocarrero 1983, Réñique 2004).

The impact of economic policies on Sierran growth and on inequality

The impact of trade policies on the Sierra was particularly severe. It was most felt in food, with major consequences for the indigenous population. The native wheat and milk industries were the most devastated. Ayacucho's agriculture was brought to a standstill by inflows of imported wheat, as well as goods from other regions (Degregori 1990). The whole South of Peru initially benefited from the Nestlé Corporation's processing plant installed in 1943, but as the company increasingly mixed imports of powdered milk with national milk, so the local dairy industry began to suffer. In the North, the traditional exports of food to the Coast also suffered from increased imports. This led to a switch to a livestock and dairy industry. Nestlé's subsidiary PERULAC set up a treatment plant in Cajamarca at the end of the 1940s (Deere 1990: 151). But the same problems hit with a delay: to anticipate our story, by the 1980s free trade policies generated an acceleration of the switch to powdered milk imports, and Cajamarcan dairy producers were also suffering.[20] The Mantaro Valley in the Central Sierra experienced benefits as well as costs from its increased access to Lima but the net balance was a situation of 'growth without capacity to accumulate' as described by Samañiego (1974). He documents how the small independent indigenous producers of the valley found they needed to do seasonal cash work, in the mines and on the Coast, to be able to buy the consumer goods increasingly available from Lima via the Central Highway – but could never earn enough from this to save and invest and so increase productivity.

The Huancayo textile industry is an interesting indicator of regional processes.[21] By far the most significant of regional industrial experiences, it began in the 1930s based on supplying the modest local market generated by mining. By the 1960s it was in severe decline as a result of competition.

What did begin to flourish was commerce. The railways of the late nineteenth century and early twentieth century, and the roads built in the 1920s, were allowing penetration of the Sierra, but the 'balance of trade' was usually unequal and in favour of the Coast. Degregori quotes Miro Quesada: they served 'not as entry points but as exit routes.'[22] From the 1930s busy new towns grew up at key junctions, of which a notable case is Juliaca in Puno, described as an 'Andean Chimbote', the latter being in that period the booming fishmeal town on the Coast north of

Lima (Réñique 2004: 160). The population of Juliaca grew from 7,000 in 1940 to over 20,000 in 1961 (Dew 1969: 33). But this urban commercial growth went hand in hand with economic crisis for many haciendas, above all in the South where wool could not be replaced with another commodity. The growth of commerce also caused continued decline in the artisan textile industry of the Sierra. The number of women engaged in rural handicraft – reasonably to be assumed indigenous – declined between 1876 and 1940 by 40,000, from 15 per cent to 6 per cent of the labour force (Hunt 1974: 4). These families lost an important secondary income source and the women returned to subsistence activities.

Documenting what happened to incomes in the Sierra and the indigenous population of the Coast before 1940 is beyond the skill even of such a brave reconstructor as Hunt – he does have one Sierra wage series, for wheat, which certainly shows the gap between the Sierra and the Coast but unfortunately is only available for the 1930s.[23] But what we know about the decline of Sierra agriculture and artisan activity suggests that even before strong demographic growth began, conditions were not good for indigenous compared to non-indigenous, though an immense regional diversity makes generalizations difficult.[24] Deere (1990) has analysed the accounts of a hacienda for 1917 (Hacienda Combayo) in the relatively prosperous North, Cajamarca. She is able to show that (subject to all the difficulties of such a comparison) incomes of smallholders in 1973 were if anything lower than the earnings of *peones* in 1917, while 'rich' indigenous peasants gained (p.289). Women's earning opportunities declined and they were giving more time to subsistence activities for the family.[25] She concludes that the prosperity brought by dairy expansion in the mid decades of the century generated few jobs and very unequalizing growth (p.291).

After 1950, we have the income distribution work of Webb. The data in Table 6.4 come from his *magnum opus* in which he re-estimated the national income accounts from 1950. Here we see that the most deprived group, Sierra small farmers, experienced zero real income growth, while the numerically expanding urban informal sector experienced slow income growth compared to the modern sector.[26] This, however, is also largely hypothesis, working to a benchmark of 1961, for which year we do have data.

So, while there were areas of growth, and also instances of strong community resilience, overall the Sierra lost out to the Coast, and growth, where and when it occurred, was unequal within the Sierra as well as between Coast and Sierra, giving little sign of improvement for the majority of the indigenous population.

Table 6.4 Trends in per capita real income, 1950–66 (percentage)

Labour force groups	**Annual per capita rate of growth of real income, 1950–66**
Modern sector[a]	
Wage earners	4.9
Government employees	3.6
White collar	3.3
Urban traditional	
Wage-earners	2.5
Self-employed	1.9
White collar	1.8
Domestic servants	1.6
Rural traditional	
Coastal wage-earners	4.1
Sierra and Selva wage earners	1.5
Small farmers	0.8
coast and hinterland	2.0
other regions	
-- 0–5 hectares	0.0
-- 5–50 hectares	2.7

[a] Webb takes registered, or reporting, firms, plus government minus all agriculture except sugar.
Source: Adapted from Webb (1974: 35).

Of course, Coastal growth itself was unequal in its impact, as Webb's data show. The urban traditional sector grew far more slowly than the formal. And this was compounded in welfare terms by the fact that the wage-related benefits (sick pay, vacation pay) introduced in the 1910s and 1920s (as generally in Latin America) applied only to the formal sector. What was intended in its genesis as a progressive measure, became with time part of the inequality problem, as the informal sector grew in the post-war period. Such legislation had never benefited the rural indigenous peasants, and now as indigenous people migrated and joined the ranks of the informals, they continued to be excluded.

The Approach of the State to Group Inequalities: Assimilation through Hygiene and Education

The Civilista government which oversaw the first three decades of export-led growth had a clear policy of assimilation of indigenous people and saw the Sierra as the heart of that challenge. Its leaders believed deeply that citizenship was open to all, and the state needed to provide channels of access to all (Contreras 1996). In the necessary 'civilizing' process education was key. It was also important to improve the quantity and quality of the labour force, and in this hygiene was important, to reduce infant mortality and improve nutrition standards. At the same time we have described the fear of national disintegration produced by the War of the Pacific; hence railways and roads were to complement the civilizing policies in health and education.

Under Leguía 1919–29 in particular, there were also more specific measures, but not well implemented. Leguía, looking for popular support in Lima, tried to project the image of an inflexible reformer and the indigenous protector that was to end abuses and guarantee peace in the country. Indeed, during the first years of his regime, a large amount of indigenous legislation was promulgated. He created the office of indigenous affairs in the Ministerio de Fomento and the office *Patronato de la Raza* to deal with indigenous claims and problems and gave legal status to indigenous communities for the first time since Independence.[27] Most of these policies were not implemented (Kapsoli 1987, Stern 1998). Indigenous people commissioned by their communities came to complain about the abuses of local authorities and the Committee *'pro-indigena'* would help them with the contact with the President, their accommodation and food during their days in Lima (Davies 1974). Commissions were created to investigate abuses of indigenous populations in the regions. On several occasions significant reports were produced, such as that of José Antonio Encinas (see Réñique 2004: 69), but they had no impact on the situation of abuse and exploitation. On the contrary, pressured by Sierra local elites concentrated in the National Congress, Leguía ended up outlawing the Committee *'pro-indigena'* and imprisoned many of its leaders (García 2005: 70)

The two most significant legislative efforts targeting the indigenous population in an apparently positive sense, were the Communities Law of 1920 and the *Ley de Yanaconaje* – Sharecroppers' Law – of 1947. The first established that indigenous communities should be recognized as owners of the land they occupied. The second strengthened the rights of sharecroppers, prohibiting their eviction, giving them permanent contracts and requiring landlords to pay a monetary wage. In both cases, the legislation represented a bid for social peace, in the face of protest. However, both cases, by going against the immediate interests of the Sierran elite (in one case by the threat to immobilize land, in the other labour), set back the agenda, by further alienating the regional elites who were central to any potential modernizing project within a mixed system.[28, 29]

The other arm of the assimilation strategy was the use of social programmes. The increase in spending on education is shown in Table 6.5. Up to 1935, education is combined with justice and health in the national budget, but it will be seen that once the data are disaggregated, education is almost two thirds of the total, and rises from some ten per cent of total public spending at the turn of the century to thirty per cent by the 1960s.

As the table shows, the rate of increase in the share of social spending slowed with the 1920s, in line with the distinct interests of the Leguía government (urban construction, public buildings, large projects). Spending picked up again after 1940 and its nature changed. The 1940 census demonstrated the failure of this spending in the important field of literacy, which led to a different approach. The census results are shown in Table 6.6.

It will be seen that by 1940 the results were disappointing. The heavily indigenous departments of the South – Apurímac, Ayacucho, Cusco, Huancavelica, Puno – showed far less improvement than the average, and at an average of over 80 per cent illiterate,[30] the indigenous population was severely disadvantaged. More shocking still, the percentage of 6–14year-olds receiving instruction *fell* in Ayacucho, Huancavelica and Puno and remained constant in Cusco (Contreras 1996: 41, Table 7).

After 1945, the shock of these figures pushed the subsequent government to rethink, and Valcarcel at the Ministry of Education led a shift in policy, focusing far more on bilingual education and drawing teachers from the local community. The increase in the number of schools and teachers was commendably parallel in the Coast and Sierra between the 1940s and the 1960s. But by 1961 the Sierra was still showing far higher figures of illiteracy than the Coast. Two thirds of the illiterate were girls (Contreras 1996: 26).

The problem was that spending was occurring without the wider changes in the institution of *gamonalismo* needed to give such expenditure a chance. The traditional approach in rural Highland communities was that schooling 'would make your child disrespectful'. Added to *gamonalismo* was the gender discrimination to be expected at such a date: girls in particular were felt to be at risk, and indeed sexual abuse by teachers is well documented.[31] As a result of all these aspects affecting the quality of education, the most gifted teachers might with reason prefer urban jobs and the private sector, so compounding the problem of quality. Teaching was typically by rote and the use of fear. Outside school, in a Highland rural community, there would typically be no books or newspapers to encourage literacy skills.

Table 6.5 Central government spending by principal sectors, 1900–60 (percentage shares)

Years	Education	Health	Promotion and Public Works	Agriculture	Armed Forces	Government and Police	Finance and Trade	Others	TOTAL
1900	1.2	n.d.	3.0	n.d.	25.4	24.1	27.8	18.4	100.0
1910	8.0	0.0	6.1	n.d.	20.5	19.4	15.6	30.4	100.0
1920[a]	8.1	1.2	8.3	0.5	15.8	12.4	34.3	19.5	100.0
1930	7.6	1.7	6.5	0.4	17.3	15.7	38.9	11.9	100.0
1940	10.8	3.7	4.5	0.8	22.7	20.3	26.7	10.6	100.0
1950	14.1	4.1	4.6	1.8	22.6	16.3	24.1	12.4	100.0
1960	26.0	4.1	3.2	3.2	21.6	18.6	16.1	7.3	100.0

[a] Data for 1919.

Source: Balanza y Cuenta General de la República (Archivo General de la Nación), various years.

Table 6.6 Illiteracy rates[a] by region[b] (per cent of adult population of region)

Year	Lima	Other Coast	North and Central Sierra	Southern Sierra	Selva
1876	45.4	74.0	85.8	91.8	85.8
1940	10.6	40.6	66.2	79.8	51.0
1961	10.5	28.3	50.8	61.8	39.3
1972	10.3	23.0	43.8	49.6	34.4

[a] Illiteracy rates: I_{1876} = (do not read or write) / total population; I_{1940} and I_{1961} = (do not read or write and older than 6)/ population older than 6; I_{1972} = (do not read or write and older than 5)/ population older than 5.
[b] The regional split has been made at the provincial level. Lima = Lima and Callao provinces; North and Central Sierra = Sierra provinces of the departments of Lima, Junín and departments north of them; Southern Sierra = Sierra – North and Central Sierra. The Coast is taken to be those Coastal provinces with mean altitude below 1,001 meters above sea level. As 'Selva' we classified all Amazonas, Loreto, Ucayali, San Martín, and Madre de Dios provinces, and the provinces of Jaen, Leoncio Prado and Satipo. The results do not change significantly if Andean provinces with both Highlands and rainforest are reclassified from Sierra to Selva.
Source: Own elaboration with data from the National Censuses.

Thus we see that despite serious efforts, group inequalities in education did not significantly improve by the 1960s. There was more improvement in health conditions. The work of the Rockefeller Foundation throughout Latin America in the 1920s to the 1940s had an impact through increasing availability of vaccines and campaigns such as those to exterminate mosquitos.[32] However, the disparities in life expectancy and child mortality are still great, where data are available. The anti-malaria campaign is interesting for horizontal inequalities: malaria fell from the first cause of death in 1945 to the tenth in 1955, but deaths from malaria *rose* in the Sierra as a result of migration, as temporary migrants returning to the Sierra carried infection with them (Cueto 1997: 165).

The earliest data on health care we have found, for 1943, are presented in Table 6.7. They do not show outcomes, unfortunately, but inputs: availability of services. They show a huge inequality in how far the formal health care system reached into the different regions.

Political inequalities were reduced with the introduction of elections in the municipal level, but the main problem remained: while voting was conditional on literacy, and inequalities in literacy were not improving, this important step remained a potential gain rather than actual.

So policies, either through the protection of indigenous populations or through their assimilation and civilization via education and health

Table 6.7 Regional variations in availability of health care, 1943[a]

	Number of people per doctor	per cent without medical attention
Coast	2,110	37 per cent
Sierra	18,978	84 per cent
Selva	11,690	62 per cent

[a] Coast = Callao, Ica, La Libertad, Lambayeque, Lima, Moquegua, Piura, Tacna, Tumbes. It therefore includes some Sierra populations, so reducing the observed inequality. Note that in this case we were not able to refine the classification as we did in Table 6.6 above, by doing it at the level of province.
Source: Own elaboration with data from the *Extracto Estadistico* 1943.

policies, were well-intentioned but ineffective: they were also misguided. Those promoting them did not grasp how far something more radical than policies of education and hygiene by themselves was required. Institutional structures that distorted incentives and made people fearful and incapable of availing themselves of opportunities needed to be challenged: the state was not ready for this.[33] By the 1960s the indigenous people of the Sierra had low levels of literacy and minimal access to health care, while direct interventions in the regulation of land and labour were either not implemented or typically had perverse effects. We turn now to the repercussions of this, first at the local level.

The Social and Political Repercussions of the Pattern of Export-Led Growth

The process we have here described had major social and political repercussions. The two we need to consider here are the migration of elites and also of the more educated and talented of the indigenous population, and the increasing divide within indigenous people themselves, between those who remained in agriculture, indigenous peasants, and those who now became the backbone of an aspirational '*cholo*' culture. As we demonstrate below, both processes, in different and complex ways, eroded the terrain for generating indigenous or Andean 'imagined communities'. With that, the chance of moderating the Coast's neglect of the Sierra became almost non-existent.

Different Sierra regions had different histories. In the South the impact of the decline of wool was to make many landlords lose interest in their lands, become more effectively absentee, and sometimes migrate to Lima, Arequipa or even Europe. Here from time to time they would receive news that '*cuadrillos de bandoleros indigenas*' had robbed them of their livestock, as vividly described in 1928 by a speaker at the annual conference of the *Sociedad de Ingenieros del Perú*.[34] As property rights came under attack, so investment was further discouraged. Some landowners sold all or part of their land, others effectively abandoned it. In the Central Highlands, for instance, in Ayacucho with the decline of agriculture there was also emigration, though less pronounced, and many indigenous people remained in conditions of servitude in the absence of the landlords. Sometimes better off but still modest *mestizo*s or indigenous would acquire land and reproduce conditions of servitude, in a way that could be more provocative of conflict, since the workers were likely to be less accepting of the new bosses than they were of the traditional owners.[35] In areas of the Central Sierra more connected to the Coast, some moved, others stayed, in a situation of increasing economic pressure, which meant that oppression of their workers tended to increase.[36] In Piura, the *hacienda* workers focused more on their terms of employment than on issues of ownership, supported in this by the Partido Socialista. But the outcome was the same.[37] Insight into regional elite fortunes and the relative weight of the Highlands and the Coast can be drawn from an innovative piece of work analysing the data collected on death in relation to the imposition of the inheritance tax.[38] This supports our picture of regional elites that suffer relatively and migrate, undermining the political and economic base for an autonomous growth process in the Highlands – while the Selva appears totally excluded. The study analyses the 800 largest fortunes in Peru left by those dying between 1916 and 1969. Of these, only 12 per cent are people born in the Highlands – and none in the Selva, not surprisingly. But more tellingly, the detailed analysis of the 100 largest fortunes yields only seven Peruvians born in the Highlands, three of whom had invested their wealth in Coastal urban property or land. The three who left Sierra land to their descendants were all women, dying in Lima or abroad. The remaining one was the key mining entrepreneur, Proaño, whose battles were fought exclusively around protection of his mining interests.[39]

We see that the weakening of the Sierran elites had diverse consequences for our analysis. In the North and parts of the Central Highlands, it could provide opportunities for small independent farmers to access land. In others the old power structure was maintained or even tightened. But on balance it certainly meant that those who could have lobbied Lima for more resources were instead opting out.

The elite may have been moving or opting out – but the numbers of the less well off who also chose to move were swelling even more vigorously. By the end of the 1960s Apurímac and Ayacucho were losing population the most rapidly, with annual net out-migration at 16.5 per thousand and 14 per thousand respectively. Then came Huancavelica, Ancash and Cajamarca with 13.4, 11.9 and 11.6 per thousand in their turn (Degregori 1990: 32). It is clear in numerous studies that it was the better educated and the better off who migrated (Degregori 1990: 40). Samañiego provides careful survey data for the Central Sierra demonstrating this for the 1960s (1974: 267).

The process of migration, and the accompanying process of economic differentiation, had profound consequences for indigenous identity and for relations within the indigenous community. There were in fact several processes at work in the area of identity. At one level there was an evolution in perceptions. At another, there was the impact of migration, either to the Coastal cities or to large cities within the Sierra – and the evolution of identity within the remaining rural community.

The Census of 1940 declared that there were 53 per cent whites and *mestizos* and 46 per cent indians.[40] Most indians lived in their communities far from urban areas and only exceptionally visited the largest cities (even less Lima). The *mestizos* lived in the largest cities including Lima, but many lived also in the small towns in the 'periphery' surrounded by indian communities. The white population lived mostly in the main cities, highly concentrated in Lima. Migration broke up this landscape and the whole structure of ethnic boundaries was transformed into the very complicated setting we have today.

Taking first the level of perceptions, a project of *mestizo* national hegemony was already taking shape (García 2005, Mallon 1992). By the end of the 1960s, the word *mestizo* no longer referred to a racial category – a person with European-white and aboriginal ancestors – but instead referred to a cultural and class-based process of acculturation. Basadre, the most influential historian of the republican period, expressed this idea very clearly: 'Even today, if you see someone of pure Indian blood in the fields, using a plough, pasturing his sheep and dressed in short trousers, you are seeing a process of cultural *mestizaje*' (Basadre and Yepes 2003). *Mestizaje* became thereby a process of scaling up from the 'indian' situation of exclusion and exploitation to a life of citizenship and progress through the learning of Spanish, education and migration to urban centres. This class-based construction of cultural differences has made it very problematic for Peruvians to disentangle class from ethnicity.

Thus the 'racial' content that the *mestizo* category once had was transformed into a 'cultural' content that expressed a hierarchical combination of both western and aboriginal cultures. *Mestizos* were supposed to embrace the customs, technologies and ways of life of the white-*mestizo* dominant society, but at the same time pay tribute to their origins by the glorification of the indigenous past. Indigenous culture was transformed into cultural products to be found in museums, commemorations, folklore, products for tourism and the history of the Incas.[41] It was not a matter of living languages and forms of organizations, nor the recreation of traditions and knowledge as they entered into contact with other cultures. Vargas Llosa (1990: 52) illustrates very well the power of this conception and its continued significant influence on intellectuals and politicians: 'Indian peasants live in such a primitive way that communication is practically impossible. It is only when they move to the cities that they have the opportunity to mingle with the other Peru. The price they must pay for integration is high – renunciation of their culture, their language, their belief, their traditions and customs and the adoption of the culture of their ancient masters. After one generation they become *mestizos*, and they are no longer indians'.

However, this conceptualization in no way did justice to the reality. It was not only that state efforts for integration "remained mostly on the table" (Mallon 1992), but that the physical process of migration was producing something much more complex. Quijano (1980) has argued that urban areas in Peru saw a massive process of 'cholification' in the last third of the 20th century as a significant number of indigenous abandoned the countryside and rejected their association with 'indianness', as a vision of the rural peasant, illiterate and monolingual. His description is based on migrants to Lima, but the same processes were at work in migration to the larger cities of the Sierra. Migrants adapted to the predominant western culture as a means of improving their socioeconomic situation, but at the same time they contested total identification with the 'acculturated' *mestizos* who had forgotten their origins and their communities and were ashamed of their traditions. *Cholos* clung to their customs, which defined them as Andeans, and took pride in their Andean identity. The new *cholo* identity thus contested the class-based construction within which ethnicity was framed.

The leading work on how indigenous identity has been redefined and contested in urban areas is De la Cadena (2000). Drawing on extensive historical documentation and ethnographic research in contemporary Cusco, she explores the meaning of being indigenous-*mestizo,* and argues that contemporary *cuzqueño* workers have recreated and redefined its meaning.[42] The terrain of *'choledad'*, however, is highly disputed. *Cholos* were not the product of the process of *mestizaje*, but of its failure. Indigenous migrants erupted into 'modern' Peru and constructed a new and contesting *'cholo'* identity in a society that had not yet overcome its 'oligarchic' prejudices. In Chapter 2 we showed that *cholos* in Lima and in other urban provincial centres, such as Huanta and Bambamarca, in an effort to avoid discrimination, reproduce racism and discriminatory practices against those 'less literate', and 'less urban' than themselves. And as these are very fluid and subjective 'boundaries' and *cholo*s themselves were living on the 'borders' of urbanity/rurality, educated/non-educated, modern/non-modern, they rapidly found themselves victims of the discrimination they practised against others. This happened particularly as they moved from smaller to larger and more urbanized centres.[43]

Thus by the 1960s distinct processes were coming together to produce a terrain of greater fragmentation among indigenous peoples that resulted in the complexity and fluidity we tried to capture in Chapter 2. The division of interests between urban populations valuing cheap food imports and rural populations living from food production, the migration and weakening of the *mestizo* elites, the drain of the more educated of the indigenous population, and the growth of a *cholo* culture that was internally contradictory and built itself on superiority to 'the indian' – all these meant a complex breaking up of the social and ethnic landscape.

To take our analysis further, we need to understand the role of national level actors, and it is to this that we now turn in the final section.

The Beginnings of Class-Based Mobilization in the Countryside, and the Intersection with National Politics

We have been documenting the high degree of economic and social differentiation between the Coast and the Sierra. This differentiation shaped different types of political mobilization.[44] In the Central and Northern Coast as well as in the Central Highlands, the plantation economy – mainly cotton and sugar – and mining eroded the basis of the traditional system and in large part displaced archaic forms of production and the related social relations. These sectors favoured the concentration of employees in a labour regime, thereby opening spaces for processes of unionization and political participation. The APRA played an important role among these organized rural workers, but the situation was not one of total co-option. For instance, the sugar workers organized in the *Federación de Trabajadores Azucareros del Perú* (FTAP) were highly concentrated, so were able to negotiate with management with relative autonomy from the APRA. However, the rest of rural-sector workers, members of the *Federación Campesina del Perú* (FENCAP), faced greater geographic dispersion and lack of homogeneity. These characteristics undermined the capacity of the FENCAP to mobilize their own resources and they were therefore more dependent on their collaborator, the APRA.[45] The FENCAP expanded in the 1950s, incorporating diverse more traditional peasant organizations.[46]

The situation in by far the greater part of the Northern and Southern Sierra was completely different, where the traditional system was maintained. However, as we have argued above, with the absence of anything to replace wool and the decreasing need of politicians in Lima for their political support, the power of these landlords had decreased by the second half of the 1950s and a wave of mobilization occurred among indigenous peasants in these areas: a nice example of this loss of power is given by Craig (1969). Indigenous peasants in the valley of La Convención, organized in unions, mobilized to push the local elites to complain to the national government. President Prado, rather than sending a contingent of the army to maintain order, as was expected by the local elites and as had typically occurred in the past, sent an investigating commission. Politicians were increasingly tolerating the formation of class-based representation in direct opposition to the local elites in Sierra. Their goal was to build a popular base of support independent of the one controlled by the APRA in the Coast. Thus social mobilization in these areas is not directly related to modernization, but to the collapse of the traditional economy, and the strong and transformative influences arriving from outside (Hobsbawm 1969).

The expansion of education, the increasing urban–rural relationships and the diffusion of anti-oligarchic ideologies and Marxist parties led to the formation of critical views of the old regime (Cotler and Portocarrero 1976). As a result of these changes and the return to electoral democracy in 1965, associational activities became more active by the end of the decade and new groups in the political arena demanded deeper reforms (Cotler 1995).[47] *Acción Popular* emerged as an organized structure alternative to APRA in the electoral terrain, but leftwing groups were also to become rapidly an alternative to APRA in grassroots mobilization during these years. These leftwing groups were not a united force; they were a plethora of new factions that emerged in the 1960s to compete with the traditional Communist Party of Peru (PCP). A variety of Maoist,[48] Troskyist[49] and Guevarist[50] organizations outflanked the PCP on the left, challenging the party's strategic moderation and its doctrinal loyalty to the Soviet Union (Roberts 1992).

For most of the 1960s, land reform efforts were repeatedly blocked by the conservative coalition UNO–Odriísta–APRA, supporting landed elites, but the issue of land reform was present in all presidential campaigns from 1956 to 1963. The rapid erosion of landed elites' power was clear (Mar and Mejía 1980: 294).[51] From 1956, simultaneous land invasions by indigenous peasants across the country stunned Lima. Close to one hundred land invasions were reported in the period 1959–1966, and 77 happened in the last six months of 1963 (Cotler and Portocarrero 1976: 292). Indigenous peasants grew in organizational capacities through their contacts with urban organizations, unions and the political parties of the Left, assimilating their forms of organization and tactics. For the first time, they built organizations at the regional level. The first were created in Cusco in 1961 and in Cajamarca in the same year, as 'peasant' (not indigenous) organizations.[52] Two years later a Federation was created in Ayacucho and in 1967 it brought together indigenous peasant communities at the regional level. Other federations were created in Pasco, Junín and Ancash (Mar and Mejía 1980: 71). This cycle of rural Sierra mobilization was controlled by the government, by carrying out a partial land reform, with a military intervention in the key regions of turmoil.[53] Though the land reform was very narrow, the state achieved its goal of containing indigenous peasants' mobilization and neutralizing their newly created organizations.[54]

Land struggle in much of the Central Sierra has been well documented (Guzmán and Vargas 1981, Tullis 1970). Reviewing the data gathered by Guzmán and Vargas, we can see that these mobilization events from 1956 to 1964 were still very spontaneous and dispersed, but gradually began to reveal an evolution in their form of organization (peasant unions) and their repertoires (strikes). With the years, petitions became strikes and strikes became invasions of land. Mobilization was temporarily controlled in 1964 with military action, and also with the initiation of a partial agrarian reform in the most mobilized areas. These protests succeeded in their main goal – the further weakening of the hacienda system. They met with police responses and deaths, but the decision of the elites to seek profit opportunities elsewhere – which was already manifest – and the fragmented nature of the rebellions presumably explains the lack of escalation. Guzmán and Vargas document seven different types of indigenous peasant movements from 1956 to 1965, all very disarticulated. Their view is that the movements were stronger in the South, where the lack of connection to the national level and the small voting power of the population led to repressive responses. By the end of 1963, each and every land invasion in the South was being violently dislodged (pp.16ff).

The political mobilization described above was never violent on the scale of earlier collective action. In the 1920s the crisis of wool, and the tightening web of oppression which often resulted, produced severe episodes of violent protest, repressed with a severity to be echoed in the 1980s and the reaction to Sendero. But between the 1920s and the 1960s the elements of violence were small-scale and isolated, though conflictual relations were part of the incentive to landlords to absent themselves and generally lose interest: the combination of memories of repression and the decision of owners to pull out probably reduced the level of violence. But collective action was a constant: a good example of a typical process is given by the case of Pomacocha in Cangallo, Ayacucho, as related by Degregori (1990: 104). The 1,162 families were 'subject to the most abject forms of servitude'. Collective action started among the *colonos* in 1942 with memoranda written to the Ministry of Labour. The level of activity was persistent over the years, with numerous unsuccessful written protests, though activity had to cease during the Odría period. By 1959 links were being made to the new Peasants' Confederation, through their children's connections in Lima – an interesting dimension of migration. At this point the workers' own analysis was that they had been living a continuous process of 'movements without direction'.[55] In the 1960s action escalated to a land invasion, a strike and the expulsion of police from the estate.

Conclusion: The End of an Era

A key theme of this chapter has been the way the economy and polity intersected in the shaping of particular institutions. As this institutional evolution developed in the first seven decades of the twentieth century, political and economic inequality between Coast and Sierra was embedded in a manner that made it almost impossible even to imagine any prospect of an alternative growth path of more benefit to the indigenous population of the Sierra. Throughout the analysis, whatever we have said for the Sierra has been *a fortiori* true for the Selva too. In this process, the weakening of opportunities for new elites in the Sierra, migration patterns, economic policies favouring imported food and the failure of education policies all played their part. So too did the evolution of complex indigenous/*cholo* identities, and the continued subtle but pervasive attitudes of discrimination that sustained hierarchies. We have shown how the evolving identities and the shape of the evolving economy led to a process of increasing complexity and fluidity of indigenous identities. We have also shown how a significant mobilization gained strength among indigenous peasant populations, though repressed by military action and in some measure appeased by partial agrarian reform.

This historical analysis can now enrich the understanding we achieved in Chapters 2–4, where we were able to show from qualitative and quantitative data how deep are group or horizontal inequalities today. Over time, they have worsened but most significantly, have become more entrenched and thereby intractable, as geography, politics and economics have interacted. The analytics of the process provide convincing evidence. The dynamics of group inequalities are about the way in which the Sierra has been increasingly marginal to the centres of power, accumulation and actors' decision-taking, and the way the failure to modify patterns of domination and exploitation, in particular the mechanisms of *gamonalismo* and *clientelismo*, have left the indigenous population within the Sierra in a position of powerlessness and poverty. This has happened despite a rise in social expenditure, much of the explanation being captured in Table 6.6, which shows the poor return to literacy from the expansion of education in the Sierra. In summary, over time the analysis encapsulated in Figure 4.1 above takes on additional dimensions, each one part of a vicious circle. Over time, more is spent per capita on social services in the Coast than the Sierra, so a gap persists although it lessens with time, and this gap has an ethnic dimension. However, over time, the less favourable outcomes from given expenditure on health and education in the Sierra result in a bigger continuing gap in literacy and other social indicators (literacy is observable in Table 6.6). This gap reflects several inter-related aspects: the impact of discrimination, distance and isolation on quality of delivery, the failure to change the social structure, and the fact that the most educated tend to migrate, eventually to the Coast. Literacy levels also translate unequally over time into political voice as the most politically articulate migrate. Given assets in the labour market translate unequally into income over time, because of differences in infrastructure and market access. Differences in political weight translate into continuing disparities in resource allocation.

A turning point

Peru by the end of the 1960s was at a turning point. In political and economic terms, the pattern of development of the previous century-and-a-half was no longer working. The export-led growth model that had produced reasonable growth during nearly a century, in a symbiotic relation with foreign capital, was ceasing to deliver in either political or economic terms. Relations with foreign capital were accumulating to a sharp point of tension, focused on the controversy over the contract with the International Petroleum Company to exploit the Brea-Parinas oilfields (Thorp and Bertram 1978: 226). And social pressures in the countryside were growing, aggravated by the half-hearted agrarian reform measures of the Belaúnde government. Violent dislodging of land invaders was not proving a satisfactory answer.

The crisis of the export economy model was a crisis of supply, reflecting in part underlying tensions generated by incoherent nationalist sentiments that frightened foreign investors without producing a way forward. We have tried to show how it was that the very success and solidity of export-led growth, based on national elites allied with foreign capital, was an obstacle to the greater articulation of diverse views and the integration of alternative interests into the political system. As nationalist sentiment now surged, this negative dimension led to incoherence: the worst of all worlds since foreign investors had no confidence in political coherence or stability, and the answer was not to invest. The resulting lack of investment in mining meant that a supply crisis built up, while lack of available land on the Coast and overfishing of the sea were producing similar problems on other fronts.[56] The clumsy efforts at stimulating industry and years of overvaluation in times of export plenty had left an industrial sector that was not competitive and hardly about to rescue the ship with new non-traditional products. There was a pervading sense, grounded in these realities, that the country's traditional oligarchy had failed and a radical new focus and vision of structural reform was what was needed. There was a widespread view that the old model was 'bankrupt' in political and economic terms. Popular mobilization to speak up for the dispossessed in such a model was lively but still fragmented, lacking a coherent political voice. From that point until the present century, Peru has been in a frustrating search for a route through, beginning with the military coup of General Juan Velasco in October 1968. The way the search for solutions and the failures along the way have interacted with the issue of group inequality is what we probe in the next chapter.

Notes

1. Pierson (2004) argues that major public policies represent very substantial extensions of political authority that further alter the incentives of and resources of political authors.

2. Peru's exports of crude cocaine fell from 34 tons in 1940–8 to less than 22 tons over the following four years (Gootenberg 1999: 51).
3. Prices of Peru's principal commodities recovered relatively fast even in the 1930s (Thorp 2000: 83).
4. The northernmost parts of the Coast – Tumbes and Piura – suffered something of the same isolation as the Sierra, though they did have petroleum. The first airport outside Lima was in Talara in 1928.
5. The literature shows *enganche* still in use in the 1930s, but declining. See Deere (1990: 45–50) for a detailed description of the institution as it was being used up to the 1950s. Also Gonzáles (1980); Klaren (1976).
6. Order in the Sierra was maintained by the institution of *gamonalismo*, as we have explained – the Peruvian version of indirect rule.
7. The insightful contrast here is with Chile, where it did not suit the interests of the US multinationals involved in copper to allow locals to participate, and as a consequence, a feature of Chile's development was a local bourgeoisie interested in encouraging the national government into a developmental role to provide opportunities (Thorp 1998: Chapter 3).
8. See Low (1976) for an unusual and enterprising piece of work tracing what happened to the men who sold their mines to Cerro de Pasco Copper Corporation in the early years of the century – and the few who did not.
9. *Peruvian Times* 5 March 1964, back cover.
10. Peru was no exception to the general trend in Latin America in the 1920s–30s, when the setting up of Central Banks, Banking Superintendencies and *Contralorías* was widespread under the aegis of the Kemmerer Missions, advisory missions led by Edwin Kemmerer with a reach far beyond Latin America (Drake 1989).
11. See Schmidt (1984) for a full account of these institutional developments.
12. See Caravedo (1978: 63); Thorp and Bertram (1978: Chapter 10). This was the outstanding instance of a regional elite – from Arequipa – exercising political influence, but ultimately without success.
13. This was largely because the customs administration was more efficient in Lima than in the other coastal ports (Caravedo 1976: 90).
14. Caravedo (1978: 105). Bank loan data show the same evidence of concentration: in 1945 77 per cent of commercial bank loans were in Lima. The Arequipeño share fell from 24 per cent in 1945 to 18 per cent in 1955 (p.93).
15. See Thorp (1998) for the regional comparison.
16. In population terms Chile was smaller but significantly more industrialized.
17. Thorp and Bertram (1978: Chapters 10–13). Imports of wheat and flour, for instance, rose from 9 per cent of imports in 1936 to 14 per cent in 1948 (Thorp and Bertram 1978: 200). On the problems of agriculture in the Sierra, see for instance Caballero (1981), Manrique (1987), Martínez-Alier (1977).
18. Among the well-known members of this new generation, we can mention Joaquín Capelo, Carlos Wiese, José Rodríguez, José Payán, Javier Prado, Alejandro Garland, Luis Carranza, Alberto Ulloa. The Faculty of Political Science and Administration of the University of San Marcos and the School of Engineering (both founded in the years immediately before the War with Chile) produced various promotions who shortly thereafter filled the ranks of the state bureaucracy, especially the Ministries of Finance and Development.

19. On the economic thought of this period, see Nils Jacobsen, 'Pensamiento económico y políticas económicas en el Perú, 1885-1899: los límites a la ortodoxia liberal', in Contreras and Glave (eds) (2002). The yearbooks which began to be published after 1903 by the new ministry of development (headed by Alejandro Garland, up to 1908), are excellent illustrations of the development programme proposed by the new group.
20. Deere (1990) documents this process, in a regional history of unusual richness in its micro detail and interweaving of social and economic processes. On the issue of food imports in general, see Lajo (1983).
21. Documented with much micro detail by Roberts, Chapter 5 of Long and Roberts (1978).
22. 'No de puerta de entrada sino de puerta de salida' – quoted by Degregori (1990: 30).
23. For 1940, it gives 0.67 soles as compared to 1.62 in cotton picking or 1.87 as a sugar field worker.
24. See the numerous case studies carried out by Matos Mar and his team at the Instituto de Estudios Peruanos. An excellent set of case studies of the vitality of some local communities in the Central Sierra is Long and Roberts (1978).
25. The modern dairy industry needed 'male' skills.
26. There are no direct time series data for informal or subsistence workers for this period. The 1961 census gives a benchmark and everything has to be extrapolated backwards. We have argued elsewhere, based on food consumption data, that Webb's calculations may be too optimistic in regard to the income growth of the poorest groups, but the point is, we do not have good evidence.
27. This recognition was incorporated in the Constitution of 1921.
28. This interpretation is provisional and requires further research, but appears an important strand in exploring how short-term measures favouring the indigenous population were inadequate for their long-term progress, because the measures lacked a coherent politics supporting them. In fact in this case the Law was not enforced and was not therefore the key mechanism immobilizing the land market. The main immobilizing mechanism was low productivity, which meant that landowners could only make a profit by controlling large amounts of land and labour.
29. By the 1960s, a completely different motivation brought an interest in land tenure back to the agenda, as the rural protest we describe below gained force, if not coherence. The land reform passed in 1964 was in its original form very modest, and political opposition reduced its bite still more, such that by the end of the 60s only 4 per cent of the land in principle subject to reform had been transferred (Matos Mar and Mejía 1980). Repression had rapidly proved a more adequate response.
30. In the Southern Sierra, if the average over all the population was 79.8 per cent illiterate, it can reasonably be assumed that the figure for the indigenous population was higher.
31. See the monographs written in the 1960s by the Instituto Indigenista Peruano.
32. Cueto (1997: 61) comments that although their work had impact, their sensitivity to community factors was poor.

33. Ainsworth, an American academic and good friend of the Cusqueño and Limeño intellectuals espousing these policies, supported the policies as far as they went but predicted their failure, arguing that for example the proposed Bureau of Indigenous Affairs would have neither the appetite nor the means to take away *gamonales*' powers (Ainsworth 1920).
34. Carlos Barreda, cited by Réñique (2004: 135).
35. Degregori (1990: 105) quotes the example of Orcasitas in Ayacucho, where seven families were in a '*colonato-servil*' relationship with a *mestizo* peasant as their boss.
36. Alberti and Sánchez (1974: 207). Tullis (1970) describes for the case of Yanamarca how the *return* of an absentee landlord, attempting to enforce the traditional system, might be the occasion for resistance to flare up.
37. Apel (1957) gives a detailed account based on complaints filed with the Ministry of Justice and Labour in Piura.
38. Portocarrero (2006). The archive comprises wills but also documents such as valuations.
39. Fernandini also turns up in the list and might be thought to count as Sierra given his mining wealth. He was in fact born in Ica, and had substantial coastal interests. Both men were satellite suppliers of the Oroya smelter, owned by Cerro de Pasco Copper Corporation (Thorp and Bertram 1978: 81).
40. White and *mestizo*s were reported together but the categories were mentioned as different. Other groups were seen as minorities.
41. Mallon (1992) correctly summarizes the 20th-century construction of the nation state in Peru as a process in which the 'indian' past was glorified, but contemporary 'indians' found they had to 'incorporate' themselves into society through education, agrarian reform, and state-sponsored development programmes.
42. Other authors have looked at these transformations in different contexts. Réñique (2004) explains in detail the history of Puno and how through the history of the struggle a new type of indigenous identity, the *cholo* of Juliaca, was constructed. Quijano (1980) and Nugent (1992) discuss the emergence of a new *cholo* or *chicha* identity in Peru in order to explain the same process of redefining the dominant *mestizo* identity.
43. For a more detailed account of this process of discrimination and reproduction of discrimination, see Paredes (2007: 10–19).
44. Based on Cotler and Portocarrero (1976).
45. From 1956, unions associated with APRA acquired official recognition from diverse governmental agencies and international organizations, including the International Labour Organization.
46. The '*sindicatos*' of the haciendas, the associations of small cultivators, associations of share croppers and indigenous communities.
47. This period is seen in the Peruvian literature as the origin of the party system that would dominate democratic politics from 1980 to 1992 (Cotler 1995, Tanaka 1998). During the 1960s, only *Acción Popular* represented an organized structure alternative to APRA in the electoral terrain, but leftwing groups were to become rapidly an alternative to APRA in grassroots mobilization during these years.
48. The Maoist movement emerged from a split of the PCP in 1964 founding the pro-Chinese *Red Flag* party (Bandera Roja-PCP). Sendero came from a further

split of this group in 1969 that led to the creation of the Red Fatherland PCP (Patria Roja-PCP) and the Shining PCP (Sendero Luminoso PCP).

49. Trotskyist organizations developed a base in the labour movement as well as in the peasant movement led by Hugo Blanco in the valley of La Convención in Cusco in the early 1960s. Like the Maoists, the Trotskyists suffered from repeated divisions and factionalism.
50. Influenced by the Cuban revolution, two guerrilla groups existed in Peru for an extremely short period. The *Movimiento de Izquierda Revolucionaria* (MIR) and the *Ejército de Liberación Nacional* (ELN) were both created in 1962. They initiated guerrilla operations in 1965 in areas of peasant protest, but, with little preparation and almost no linkages to popular organizations, they were rapidly defeated. MIR was founded by José de la Puente Uceda who left the APRA with a few other young members because of APRA's pact with Manuel Prado's 'oligarchic' government. Uceda was killed in action in 1965 and the group was dismantled. In the 1970s, members tried to reconstruct the party but with organizational links to popular movements.
51. Agricultural land continued to be highly concentrated in Peru at the beginning of the 1960s. According to the Census of 1961, private individual holdings made up 94.9 per cent of the holdings, and they contained 88.3 per cent of the land in farms. The remainder was land in various types of community landholdings. Of the individual landholdings, 70 per cent of the land was concentrated in 3,400 individual holdings with more than 500 hectares, representing less than 0.5 per cent of all individual holdings in the country (INEI, *Censo Nacional* 1961). For more detail see Alvarado (1989) and Brodsky and Oser (1968).
52. See the following chapter (p. 138) for the growing class discourse and its role in mobilization.
53. The violence spread as guerrilla groups (MIR and ELN) attempted to mount operations in the most convulsive areas such as Cusco and Ayacucho. It is not clear that they received support from the peasants. Traditional powers in the congress started to call for stronger repressive measures; hence from 1959 to 1963, the state carried out military operations to demobilize these areas, resulting in 32 peasants dead and thousands of people in prison. The guerrillas in 1965 added a dozen causalities to this fatal list, both among guerrilla's fighters and army forces (Degregori 1992: 414).
54. In the Central Highlands of Junín and Pasco, two properties of around 600,000 hectares were expropriated and in the valley of La Convención in Cusco a process of distribution was initiated (Cotler and Portocarrero 1976).
55. Document cited by Degregori (1990: 104).
56. We have shown elsewhere how each of these elements of supply-side problems was in reality a problem of a discontinuity in the complexity of investment and/or of state management, for which the previous decades had prepared neither the state nor the private sector. See Thorp and Bertram (1978: Chapter 14, also Chapters 11 and 12); Thorp (1991).

7
The Evolving Crisis and Consequences for Group Inequality, 1968–90

We have seen how forces for change in Peru emerged only in incoherent and fragmented form by the 1960s, though there were some constructive signs developing. Not only was political protest around land and labour issues increasingly vigorous, but also with municipal elections introduced in 1963, movement in political HIs seemed possible.

In this chapter we explore the years of missed opportunity and increasing chaos from 1968 to 1990. We show how indigenous movements emerged in the rural areas through class-based organizations and with significant development of leftwing parties. We explain how in the short term, this organization made possible indigenous peasants' mobilization, but in the long term eroded the possibilities for an indigenous movement to emerge in the Sierra. We show how political violence erupted and how violence and group inequalities interacted. We show how economic recession and hyperinflation combined with political violence to worsen group inequalities and further disempower grassroots political actors. These were the tragic pre-conditions for the Fujimori years and the accentuation of horizontal and vertical inequalities which they were to bring.

The story is thus one of opening and closing, and the closing comes largely through the power of institutional legacies, in the form of the inherited lack of capacity in the state, the vertical and paternalistic political culture and the norms of discrimination and prejudice. As we said in Chapter 1, we find institutions, formal and informal, and the politics behind them, to be what embeds inequality over time. Institutional legacies were now powerful in constraining and even reversing important openings toward change.

Unlikely actors – the military – played a major role in the first element of opening, implementing a radical agrarian reform. In the first section we show how the reform was based on a mistaken analysis plus a lack of political conviction that popular movements could be trusted, so leading to a stalled opening and in due course closure, as more conflict resulted. The traditional institutions of the rural area were not so easily defeated. In the second section we see how indigenous peasants organized, reaching for the first time a high level of centralization. We try to address how certain political collective identities were reinforced and others prevented. Other actors – the emerging Left – moved in to support mobilizing indigenous groups, but the leaders' formation in a vertical and paternalistic society made it not totally surprising that their use of top-down structures failed to strengthen either the capacity or the political identity of grassroots organizations. From then on the chapter moves to show how the different additional elements of closing more than accounted for the lack of progress through the two decades to 1990. A Maoist guerrilla movement was able to use the vulnerability generated by HIs, and by the history we have recounted, to provoke terrible violence, which in turn produced repression. In both action and reaction, inherited institutions of ethnic discrimination and prejudice played a role in the outcome: this is the story of the third section. In the fourth and fifth sections we show how economic recession and the increased fragility of political parties led to further elements of closure of opportunities. Economic recession, building on the existing pattern of growth and limited public sector capacity, reinforced exclusion from the labour force and discrimination against the rural sector via producer prices, making mobilization more difficult in the face of survival needs. The fifth section shows how political violence and the evolution of political parties themselves led to a closing down of political space, even before the events of the Fujimori era.

What can be observed through these accounts is that opportunities were taken up with vigour: there was no lack of effort to achieve change, whether by peaceful or violent means, and there was indeed some success in achieving change, in access to land, to voice and to education. But not only was there an impeding of progress through the institutional legacy, in the form of the inherited lack of capacity in the state, the vertical political culture and the norms of discrimination and prejudice: the net result through each story of closing was an actual worsening of inequality, especially horizontal inequality. Even before the events of the 1990s, the last state was arguably worse than the first – a further embedding of inequalities.

The Contradictory Policies of the State in the Rural Sector: Awakened Expectations and Mobilization

The military government which took power in a coup in October 1968 was deeply imbued with a structuralist analysis which saw the core of the development problem as one of ownership and concentration of power. Inequality, both in the town and in the countryside, could and should be tackled by redistribution. The role of detailed micro development strategies to complement such an approach was tragically neglected.

In line with this analysis, the new government implemented a number of significant nationalizations, including the International Petroleum Company and what they saw as key sectors to dynamize industrialization, such as mining, oil, electricity and railways. Worker ownership was introduced in the form of 'industrial communities' throughout the formal sector of the economy, with workers intended to have a progressively increasing share in the ownership, management and profits of the enterprise (Thorp and Bertram 1978: 302).

But the far more fundamental aspect of policy for the rural sector was the land reform. The experience of the army as it dealt with the waves of mobilization and the guerrillas of the 1960s, particularly in Cusco, persuaded the military that a serious land reform was needed to guarantee national security (Lowenthal 1975). The agrarian reform law (No. 17716) of 1970 was without doubt radical and represented the end of the hacienda system. At the same time it was full of contradictions. It eloquently promised land for indigenous people, but most of the land was not distributed to them. Rather, for the Coast, the Cooperativas Agrarias del Perú (CAPs) were designed as units of self-managed production under the control of workers, while for the traditional haciendas of the Highlands – where indigenous communities were more numerous – the larger groupings called *Sociedades Agrarias de Interés Social* (SAIS) were created, wherever the terrain permitted such groupings. The SAIS included the workers of the ex-hacienda and only some of the surrounding population. It did provide recognition of communal landholdings for indigenous communities,[1] but did so by reorganizing 'indigenous' into 'peasant' communities. Velasco condemned the use of ethnic terms, and instead promoted class-based identification, such as farmers, agricultural workers or peasants. Whether these policies made ethnic identification less likely is debatable, but since then both the state and civil society have overwhelmingly used the terminology of 'peasant' to refer to indigenous people in the rural area. Our solution to this problem has been to use the term 'indigenous peasants' to refer to indigenous peoples in the agrarian sector or rural areas, or to refer to them collectively with the term 'community'.[2]

In 1974 land reform was already a frustrating process. Only 9 per cent of the lands were distributed among indigenous peasant communities, and 13 per cent among other groups in the countryside, while the newly created SAIS received 43 per cent of the lands (Table 7.1). In addition, SAIS and CAPs received most of the total values of land and livestock. In 1974, the total value redistributed to SAIS was estimated at over two million soles, while the total value distributed to communities and other rural groups together was only 47 thousand soles (Arce 1985: 84). This was perceived as unfair and frustrating and indigenous peasants from inside and outside the state associations began to recognize that the SAIS were the new *hacendados,* a new 'state-hacienda'. Table 7.1 shows the estimated distribution of land in hectares for 1974 and 1980.

Further, profits were never significant enough to address the needs of communities and agricultural workers. Figueroa (1973) and Webb and Figueroa (1975) show that the former estates relied heavily on pre-capitalist modes of labour. Once salaried payments and centralized production were imposed, it was more difficult for cooperatives to reach the required level of efficiency and produce profits. The lack of adequate support services and technical understanding meant that the new cooperatives and the SAIS had very little chance of being economically viable, even without the level of conflict which resulted.

In political terms, with the land reform the government sought to create a new link between indigenous peasants and the state but without

Table 7.1 Estimated distribution of land by type of agricultural organization

Type of agricultural organization	**1974**		**1980**	
	Hectares	**%**	**Hectares**	**%**
CAPs	1,588,498	32	2,173,447	25
Other rural groups	646,039	13	1,893,352	22
Communities	442,967	9	857,399	10
SAIS	2,124,317	43	2,815,029	32
Individuals	125,149	3	685,203	8
State entities			376,164	4
Total (has)	**4,926,970**	**100**	**8,800,594**	**100**

Source: Arce (1985), using information from the Ministry of Agriculture, Agrarian Reform Unit, 1992: Ministry of Agriculture, *Dirección de Agricultura (Dirección de Tenencia de Tierra y Estructrura).*

the participation of the political parties, which were considered an outdated structure of patronage and manipulation of the peasantry (García-Sayán 1982). In 1972, the *Confederación Nacional Agraria* (CNA) was created as the one legitimate organ of expression for the agricultural sectors. Workers from CAPs and SAIS, independent farmers and officially recognized communities were all integrated in this organization. Pre-existent and more 'autonomous' class-based unions registered with the Ministry of Labour were left without a role in the new order of things. Indigenous peasants' unions and their regional federations were free to exist but they were formally stripped of their ability to represent indigenous peasants in any official capacity (Bourque and Palmer 1975). This was the case of the federations created during the agitation that preceded the military government. They had strong links to the Left, but failed to scale up effectively into larger or national organizations.[3]

At the local level, the government thought that the new cooperatives required a modern communal organization. The statute passed by the administration forced indigenous peasant communities to organize along cooperative lines, replacing the traditional *Junta communal* roles with new 'Administration and Vigilance Councils'. It also restricted elected positions in the new cooperatives to those who could read and write Spanish (Bourque and Palmer 1975: 190). The technicians held much power within the cooperatives because of their influence on the initial creation of the structures, their access to information, their over-representation on the vigilance committees, and state discretion in appointing the general manager. They often used their power to exercise clientelistic influence over the leaders of the indigenous peasants' communities or workers, garnering votes to reduce the benefits of other groups (Knight 1975). Further, the new 'modern' structure was not functional for resolving the internal problems of the community. Indigenous peasants were accustomed to organizing themselves around the need to distribute resources such as land, water and pastures. The traditional organizations solved problems of collective action and, to some extent, moderated unequal access to those resources. The new organizations and representatives responded to the directives of the cooperative but not necessarily to the members of the community.[4]

The contradictory discourses in regard to land redistribution and forms of representation created frustration: 'land for the tiller', 'the boss shouldn't live off your poverty', and 'social democratization with full participation' were the slogans of the revolutionary government. However lands were not redistributed and communal and local organization was disregarded.

In conclusion, during these seven years of experiment, the military government failed in its attempt to transform and modernize society in the countryside. Yashar (2005) has argued that corporatist forms of state–peasant relationship were also developed in Ecuador and Bolivia. By granting civil and social rights, these regimes unwittingly provided shelter for rural indigenous communities faced with the control of the state (p.57).[5] In Peru the 'corporatist' model of Velasco (1968–75) finally liberated indigenous peoples from the 'monopolized' control of power of local landlords by a radical land reform and by imposing class-based corporatist modes of interest intermediation with the state. Yet, at the same time, the agrarian reform and its corporatist organization were intended as means to incorporate and control the countryside, and in particular peasant communities. Cooperatives were developed precisely in those areas where the *hacienda* system was more prevalent and where indigenous peasants had the most vivid memories of traditional exploitation. These indigenous peasants moved from fighting the landlords to rejecting the intervention of the state. The consequences of the reforms were uneven across the Highlands: significant local autonomy was gained in the North, in clear contrast with the South, where most of the cooperatives were created (Paredes 2009). Probably the most anomalous consequence occurred in Ayacucho where traditional mechanisms of exploitation were reproduced by better-off indigenous peasants who benefited from the uneven redistribution of assets, providing a fruitful territory for Sendero to develop its project (Comisión de Verdad y Reconciliación 2003).

Unintentionally, in several parts of the country, but above all in the Southern Highlands, the reforms created motives for confrontation. The state recognized communities, and promoted rights to lands and organization. The discourse created expectations, not only among indigenous peasant communities, but in society in general. Such expectations were unevenly met. In this context, communities found a legitimate reason to mobilize. The invasions of lands started spontaneously in several parts of the territory, but these movements had their epicentre in the Southern Highlands, where indigenous peasants now also began to build class-based federations with extensive support from the parties of the Left, first in their provinces and then in their regions, and then across regions. These forces were invigorated by the radicalization of the 'official' agrarian organization, which now abandoned its 'official' role and adopted a contentious discourse (it was eventually outlawed in 1976). The Southern Highlands communities affiliated to the CCP or to the CAN began a process of unification. The potential for the building of an indigenous peasant movement in the Highlands was never greater than at this time.

The collapse of the military government, the return to elections in 1980 and the incorporation of popular parties into the system was an unexpected out-turn for the Left in Peru. Moreover, the high electoral turnout for various leftwing groups in the elections for the constitutional assembly in 1978 came as a great surprise for the Left. It was the next highest turnout that a leftwing party in Latin America had achieved after Chile in 1970, and its highest support was in the Southern Highlands. It indicated the degree of expansion of the Left in the previous decade among peasants in these regions. As a result, there was a growing consensus among the leadership that the Left must participate in elections as a united front, but the most radical of these groups had not yet renounced the idea of political revolution (Roberts 1992, Sanborn 1991). Before we consider the phenomenon of political violence, we need to reflect on the role of the Left and ask if the beginnings of political organization would amount to anything that might challenge group inequalities.

The Left, the Indigenous Class-Based Movement and the Growth of Networking

In the 1970s, there was a growing sense of a need for change, particularly among the young. We have seen that leftwing parties emerged as important pressure groups for the land reform in the 1960s. The sudden success of the Cuban revolution, the splintering of international communism, the evolution of progressive thinking in a section of the Catholic Church (the 'option for the poor'), and the increasing consciousness of the need for change in a long-lasting oligarchic society, all played their part in capturing the interest and imagination of a booming population of middle-class university students in the 1970s. Over and over, we heard in our interviews stories of young students embracing a deep and passionate zeal for transformation and for justice when they came close to the reality of an unjust system. Many recounted how progressive teachers, priests or nuns had inspired them to work in marginal areas, often initially as catechists, and that the experience had given them a passion for justice. Others emphasized the influence of peer groups and teachers at university. Yet others said that the party's insistence on their going into the field had been a formative experience for them.[6]

The work of these early leftwing groups in the countryside led to the first attempt to build a national class-based organization in the countryside.[7] Much of this new organization was the result of the work of the young militants of a party called Revolutionary Vanguard (VR), or 'Vanguardia'.[8] In the same year, 1974, an active member of VR and the leader of the peasant federation of Piura became the new president of the CCP, the Peasants' Confederation of Peru: Andres Luna Vargas. In that year's final resolution, the CCP established 'land occupations' as the principal strategy for peasant political action (CCP 1974). Silva from the Peasant Federation of Cusco described to us the process in Cusco: 'the Peasant Federation in Cusco founded in 1961 was practically undercover because of the political direction of this time. The PCP-Federation Red Flag saw the military government as a fascist option, with the result that leftwing social organizations had to become clandestine. But we succeeded in . . . reorganizing the Federation. It has meant hard work since 1971 to defeat a dogmatic and ultra leftist position. We also had to struggle with the state, which wanted to control peasants through corporatist organizations.' According to Del Mastro (1979), the CNA and its *ligas agrarias* expanded in the regions of the South between 1973 and 1975 (p.49). However, in the following years to 1974, the CCP experienced a process of change and expansion, reaching more than 200,000 members by 1977. The movement had a particular strength in the Southern Highlands but during the 1980s expanded over all the territory of the Sierra (see Paredes 2009).

The increasing conflict with the state around the cooperatives and land provided the opportunity for Vanguardia to supply indigenous peasants with organizational infrastructure and to help to create links among communities. These young militants from Vanguardia, generally young university students, created networks, built contacts with other organizations, disseminated information through bulletins and conferences, and developed an effective repertoire of political activism. However, the type of organization they helped to build was extremely vertical and ideological, something that would do untold damage to grassroots inclusion as time went on.

It would be wrong to assume that just because the Left was present in the Highlands, the result was the building of class-based organizations and political identities. History is, as so often, more complicated. We argue that in the initial years, the struggle for land drove the mobilization and provided the opportunity for Vanguardia to reinforce class-based political identity among indigenous peasant organizations. Vanguardia incorporated the fight for land successfully in their Marxist discourse, in which this struggle was the first step in the organization of a class-based movement aiming to base itself in a peasant–worker alliance. During these years the young leftwing activists and the indigenous peasants achieved and sustained this delicate balance by developing an ingenious and complex set of alignments (see Paredes 2009). As the lands were not devolved, in the eyes of the members of the communities the state became the new, even more powerful landlord. '*Wanuchun Asnu Cooperative*' (death for the cooperative, this old donkey) was the CCP slogan that resounded in the Highlands. This framing, however, made class identity more important. It resonated in the region, particularly in the South, because it was consistent with communities' uncomfortable experiences with the cooperatives and because there was nothing more vivid for indigenous peoples than land struggle. This stand, so effective among communities in the region, was also convenient for the VR and similar groups such as the MIR. While land reclamation and Marxist Leninist revolution are distinct traditions, VR was creative in incorporating land claims into their Marxist discourse against the new 'bourgeois' state, which had 'only' replaced the old 'oligarchic' state. Land for the communities was a way to empower the communities and their autonomous organizations would form the base of the people's state Vanguardia was looking to build.

Other leftwing parties, with a presence in the countryside, opposed these lines and considered the occupations a mistake. But beyond the land struggle, the leaders of Vanguardia allowed little space for debate. Today the actors confess that they were too taken up with their ideological struggles to realize the daily problems that indigenous peasants experience from their increasing interaction with a market economy (prices, credits, commercialization, etc.). Indigenous peasants' leaders gradually recognized this issue, but they could not get a hearing among their allies and even within their own organization.

In this context, the space for indigenous peasants to start experiencing and constructing a different political identity was ever narrower. Indigenous people do not 'naturally' construct indigenous political identities: as will all people, indigenous people share multiple spheres that organize routine life (social class, religion, region, profession, age). It is contention, and the way that people interpret, debate and build explanations during contention, that activates a particular sphere within which members and allies make and remake political identities. The reduced open spaces for debate and negotiation and the lack of an interpretation reflecting their own reality eroded the likelihood of indigenous people building an autonomous political identity with potential to connect their claims more widely and to provide a feeling of ownership over their organizations. Language and forms of local organization were always the base of any coordination and forms of action during mobilization for land struggle, but were somehow invisible. According to Oscar Mollohuanca, Mayor of Espinar 1998–2002 and founder member of the indigenous-based M'inka party, although in Espinar class-based ideology was dominant among the members of the party and in the official events of the peasant federation, communities did not lose their local indigenous character.[9] The base of the organization was built on kinship networks and a particular understanding of the value of land. The struggle for the land and for organizational autonomy was a strong source of political identity during these years. However, without open spaces to recreate meaning based on indigenous peasants' new claims, the opportunities to transform class-based political identity were few, even though with time the existing identity was increasingly less apt.[10] The testimony of Inocensio Mamami, a Cusqueño leader interviewed by García-Sayán (1982), illustrates the transcendence of the struggle for land for the identity of the group: 'Our fight is for land and liberation, a serious liberation for our children, so that they grow healthier. Our towns do not have water, or only yellow water. There is no school and there are no highways and we don't have the means to take care of our health. The hour has already arrived to fight to take care of all of these things. The work we do in our parcels of land is poorly rewarded, the produce from our land is sold for little, but what we buy from outside – the fertilizers, the seeds – costs more than we earn. For all these things we must continue fighting, all peasants organized and united as a single man. Now, the authorities are against us and for the *wiracochas* [*mistis*, that is *mestizos*] but we will hold these positions' (p.188).

According to Montoya (1989), questions about the culture, language and territory of indigenous peoples were also not totally absent from the discussions in the CCP, but they always ended up excluded from the official agenda. Following the Vth congress of the CCP in 1978, the CCP branch of Puno, named Tupak[11] Katari, held a meeting in which they claimed that the CCP did not recognize the Quechua and Aymara people as the basis for the Peruvian nation and the principal actors in the struggle in the countryside. Inside the CCP, but very marginalized, the Tupak Katari federation continued to stress the role of the Quechua and Aymara nations in later meetings.[12]

The official thesis of a party of 'cadres' inserted in the 'mass' and the real and dramatic differences that existed between the cadres and the indigenous peasant population unintentionally created an acutely differentiated organization, where the few were giving political direction and the peasants were 'the bases'. While the vertical organization was useful for the discipline it provided during the military government and the land invasions, indigenous leaders were overwhelmed and alienated by this type of organization at the moment of the return to democracy. The new democratic system inaugurated in 1980 brought universal suffrage and included all political forces, as well as the Left. Under the new rules, political and social leaders placed their hopes of representation in the political parties, particularly the United Left Front (IU). Given the organizational and symbolic resources that political parties of the Left had accumulated in the previous years of mobilization, the new system facilitated the absorption of indigenous peasants and other social organizations into the brokerage of these parties. The new system was formally democratic, but the parties were still vertical, ideological and prone to divisionism. Our informants in Cusco, Anta and Espinar registered repeatedly their sense of frustration at the top-down nature of the parties of the Left. For example, Wilber Rojas, Mayor of Anta in the department of Cusco, told us how the dogmatism of the national party alienated people like him. The agenda was imposed from Lima and he could not get his preoccupations into the debate. Crecencio-Merma in Espinar, former peasant leader and councillor in the municipality, gave a parallel description. He described how he constantly tried to push forward the agenda of '*los bases*', the grassroots – the need to improve productivity and provide employment. But he was repeatedly told that the important things are issues such as opposing the US and the forces of imperialism.[13]

Further, the fragility of this type of organization became obvious when disputes between parties of the Left became damaging for the organization as they tried to gain support for their own party's empowerment within the IU. In the early 1980s, disputes between parties became clear obstacles for the building of open spaces of debate among indigenous peasants and other social groups that were emerging outside and inside the rural sector. Without these open spaces of communication, solidarity and cultural cohesion of any type (ethnic- or class-based) is not likely to flourish. In addition, the Left made organizational resources easily available for indigenous peasants in the South to assist mobilization around land claims; indigenous peasants therefore had no need to develop their own formal structures. When electoral politics challenged the mutual goals of indigenous peasants and the Left, and the Left became more interested in party/electoral politics than in the building of the indigenous peasants' movements, indigenous peasant organizations did not have the organizational skills and the cohesion required to change the path.

The experience of the CCP movement contrasted with that of the indigenous peasant movement that developed in Cajamarca and spread towards the zones of the Highlands of the neighbouring departments of Amazonas, La Libertad, Lambayeque and Piura where contention around land issues was resolved relatively quickly by the mid-1970s (Paredes 2009). Indigenous peasant communities in Cajamarca, and to some extent also in the Highlands of Piura, were left alone for the first time now that landlords were gone. Community leaders became more interested in solving their immediate and communal problems, particularly the escalating cattle robbery that reached epidemic proportions in Cajamarca in the mid-1970s (Gitlitz and Rojas 1983, Gitlitz 1998). Thus new organizations such as the *rondas*, or community patrols,[14] developed at the micro level without significant influence from the Left. Without that support, the indigenous peasants in these regions had to build their own networks of organization to achieve their goals. This contrasts with the South, where a small number of committed cadres provided the brokerage.[15] The *rondas* in the Northern Highlands did not achieve the levels of organization of other regional movements in Ecuador and Bolivia; however, compared to the Southern Highlands where people struggled for decades to build a more prominent organization, the *rondas* were able to go from near invisibility to significant political prominence, and in the middle of violent internal conflict (see next section). They built, not an overt indigenous political identity, but a culturally-based identity using their local, communal and indigenous sense of solidarity. They became accepted as political actors by the state, which led to a broadening of the state's notion of citizenship. Elements such as customary law and communal governance structures have had to be taken seriously and given recognition.[16] However, the *rondas* were a regional movement and found it difficult to scale up into a national movement without response from the rest of the Sierra. That affected their strength as a regional movement.

In this section we have contrasted the evolution of politics 'on the ground' in different regions, always exploring how far indigenous peasants were acquiring voice and leadership. We found that the indigenous peasant movement in the Southern Highlands appeared exhausted and locked into its historical path. Awakened expectations with the Velasco reforms collapsed into frustration, as the 'old way of doing things' was reproduced, with state bureaucrats or better-off peasants assuming new roles. The struggle for land made the Left extremely attractive in the eyes of indigenous peasants. The vertical and ideological patterns of behaviour of the Left allowed peasants no space for 'learning by doing' and building their own networks and their own political identities.

In contrast, in the North, mobilization around land issues decreased and the influence of the Left at the micro and community level significantly declined by the mid-1970s.[17] The *ronderos* have created a powerful collective identity whose existence has challenged the exclusive recognition of individual citizen rights, and led to a degree of recognition of customary law and community governance practices. Such groups were able to expand and mobilize using new identities at the same time that the class-based indigenous peasant movement of the Highlands was collapsing. The resulting lack of reinforcement and the absence of common experiences supporting networks and alliances are key elements explaining the failure of indigenous collective action in Peru (see Paredes 2009).

The Phenomenon of Political Violence

Ironically, the return to democracy in 1980 coincided with the eruption of serious political violence. In Ayacucho a particular dynamic was going on.[18] Radical intellectuals interested in the reopening of the Universidad Nacional de San Cristobal de Huamanga (UNSCH) achieved their goal in 1959. The university was seen as a subversives' nest by the government, which attempted to cut funding. A huge protest succeeded and led to the formation of the Frente del Pueblo de Ayacucho in 1966, in recognition of the fact that issues of repression went far beyond the university. This was the first of such Popular Fronts. Here also the incipient CCP was particularly active (Degregori 1990, Guzmán and Vargas 1981) – not surprising since Ayacucho was Saturnino Paredes' headquarters and immediate area of influence. In an increasingly radical analysis and mobilization, and in contrast to the urban–rural divide emerging elsewhere, the university-based movement tended to draw together urban and rural interests.

It was here in Ayacucho, one of the poorest of the regions in the Central Highlands, that the first attack by Sendero occurred on the day of the election, in a tiny town. The two phenomena appear connected: the return to democracy propelled part of the Left into the legal system and drove the most radical group into armed conflict.[19] However, the culture of division continued throughout the 1980s, finally splitting the fragile unity of the Izquierda Unida – the so-called United Left. Unity was not helped by the immaturity of the movement at the point of return to democracy in 1980.[20]

The origins of Sendero are well documented, in the provincial university of Huamanga in Ayacucho. From there the movement gradually spread through Ayacucho, Apurímac, Huancavelica, Huánuco, Junín, and eventually to Lima in the mid-1980s.

The movement was created by the charismatic leadership and strong ideological conviction of Abimael Guzmán, as reflected in a 1980 speech:

> Never before have men had such a heroic destiny . . . To these men of today, these men that breathe, toil and combat, has fallen the task of sweeping the reactionaries from the face of the earth. It is the most luminous and glorious mission ever entrusted to any generation.[21]

The first stage to prepare for a people's war against the state consisted in recruiting cadres for the organization. Sendero did not look for them among indigenous peasants; instead it targeted the young indigenous who migrated to the city seeking education and something better than their parents' rural life.[22] Sendero's leadership began its recruitment in the early 1970s among young students and teachers in the University of Huamanga. The strategy consisted in implementing a 'pedagogical project' that presented a schematic vision of the world and of history that justified violence. Guzmán took advantage of his power as Director of General Studies to introduce courses inspired by the manuals of Marxism-Leninism elaborated by the Academy of Sciences of the USSR.[23] By such means, Sendero promoted a critical vision of Peruvian society that contributed to an acceptance of the role of violence, as revealed in the following testimony:

> when I entered the university, I found that dialectic materialism opens your eyes ... I understood better the process, the process of struggle, that the people have fought and will fight and that that fight is useful to achieve change. We studied the French revolution: yes, it was bloody, there were excesses, it was violent, but it served to transform the society and that is what counts.[24]

When Guzmán was expelled from the university in 1975, he and many of Sendero's leadership began intense political work in other parts of Ayacucho's society, in particular in the rural areas of the poor provinces of the Centre of Ayacucho (Vilcashuamán, Huancasancos, Cangallo and Victor Fajardo).[25] The initial approach in indigenous peasants' communities was also pedagogical. Portugal shows that in order to expand its project in rural areas, Sendero employed the large number of students of the Faculty of Education that had become militants during their university studies (Portugal 2008). Many of them were born in the rural towns where they settled as teachers, and were therefore considered 'children' of the community and easily accepted. In addition, students and teachers from other provinces settled in the same rural towns to reinforce the political work of local teachers, staying for long periods and participating in community chores in order to gain people's trust. In some cases, they even married people from the town, thus getting closer to the community. Once the population stopped seeing them as 'foreigners', they began their formal indoctrination through the people's schools, which taught techniques of war to people of the community and students and trained them to become members of the *Ejército Guerrillero Popular*, the military force of the party (Portugal 2008).

The discourse made rapid inroads given the rigid and conflictual nature of Ayacuchan rural society, where land reform had typically increased conflict.[26] Sendero was able to take advantage of these conflicts and disputed authority in the local communities to gain support from indigenous peasants in Ayacucho, Apurímac, Huancavelica and Junín, in the early days of the conflict. The movement had only to exacerbate ongoing conflicts for land between communities, quarrels over the control of resources in the surviving SAIS, and all types of resentments against better-off indigenous peasants who were seen to have benefited from the uneven redistribution of assets during previous governments. In the first three years of what was soon a war, Sendero had a fruitful territory to develop its plans in the conflictive countryside (CVR 2003).

The influence soon went beyond Ayacucho and the surrounding provinces. The universities provided fertile ground for political activism. The proliferation of political parties from the Left and student unions created an environment of permanent debate. However, the situation was not homogeneous within and among universities, and many students and teachers rejected Sendero's violent discourse. Public universities with large numbers of students from poor provinces of Peru were most open to Sendero's ideology. This was the case of the UNSCH in Ayacucho, the UNCP in Huancayo, the UNI and San Marcos (the UNMSM), both in Lima.

Sendero's political work also went beyond the classroom to other areas of the campus through strategic control of the canteens, university residences and transport services, which were gradually transformed into spaces for ideological debate and indoctrination. The discourse emphasized the improvement of food rations and transport services, winning the sympathy and support of students, especially the poorest who depended on these services to survive.

Sendero also earned respect among both indigenous peasants and student populations for its firm hand in imposing order, if by drastic methods. For the student, the emphasis was on the punishment of ineffective and corrupt teachers. Indigenous peasant communities initially supported Sendero in part because they were attracted by its discourse of re-establishing order through public punishments of members who broke the communities' norms (Portugal 2008). (Later, however, as Sendero made mistakes, such as killing leaders who still had legitimacy in their communities, and in general failing to respect community structures and customs, this support waned.)

The movement could also draw on another need: that for authority and order. Guzmán demanded total submission, in a quite personal sense: this appealed in particular to the young and poor migrants living in the university residences or in rented apartments away from their homes. It facilitated the process of conversion and identification with the 'new father and family'.

The appeal was of course also to a sense of injustice. 'Elizabeth' illustrates this in the testimonies collected by the Truth Commission: she migrated from Ayacucho with her parents because of the tensions there. Having first worked as a maid, she started in petty commerce, selling garments. Travelling to Huancayo she met *Senderistas* who persuaded her to join them. She did so 'because she was young and witnessed so many injustices that she sympathized with Sendero's discourse of fighting for social justice'.[27]

When the power of ideology and the use of clientelistic relationships proved insufficient to win adherents, Sendero resorted to the use of terror and coercion as means of co-option. The testimonies provide eloquent demonstrations of the vulnerability of an unorganized, ill-educated and fragile society, on the edge of subsistence, to the arrival of Sendero. The testimony of Armando, from Huanta, conveys the flavour of powerlessness (Box 7.1), as well as extreme techniques of violence and coercion.

Sendero did not differentiate by age or gender. Children were also abused and forced to join the party. The seizure and use of children in the hostilities was a generalized and systematic practice of Sendero from the beginning of the armed conflict, according to many testimonies, and intensified between 1983–5 and 1987–90. According to the database of the CVR, of the total kidnappings and conscriptions by Sendero where age was recorded, 20.5 per cent were children, and of all the acts undertaken against children by Sendero, conscription and kidnapping represented 42 per cent, 80 per cent of which occurred in the regions of Ayacucho, Huancavelica, Huánuco and Junín.

In summary, Sendero combined the power of ideology with the provision of material benefits that included appointments of teachers,

Box 7.1 Armando's testimony

The testimony of Armando narrates how he was ten years old when he and his family were living in Huanta and captured by around fifty *Senderistas* and taken to the jungle. They travelled for several days by foot and then by boat until they reached a small town.

> 'In that place, the *Senderistas* told us "here you are going to work" ... these are our lands because the government will not give us food. They grouped us in the squad N.1 in charge of comrade Tiburcio ... The squad was composed of twenty people who had working tools and two shotguns ... Every morning, all the families went out in groups to carry out assignments given by the chief of the group and during the night they did vigilance shifts. On Saturday and Sunday afternoons they met to study big red books about Marxism, Leninism, Maoism and *Pensamiento Gonzalo*. After one or two weeks the guerrillas came back and called an assembly where they gave us talks, that might last the whole day; they also taught us how we should escape towards the river or how to hide in case the army arrived.
>
> 'In Anapati we cultivated beans, yucca, maize and all kind of fruits. After the harvest, we distributed a proportion of the food to the guerrillas ... the *Senderistas* assessed the work of the conscripts; if they failed to carry out their jobs, they were punished with no food. The more educated people in the camp became part of the guerrilla force.'

His family continued praying and meditating according to their religion, until one of the chiefs of the squad found out and told them 'here, it is forbidden to profess any religion'. In these camps 'we met people from different places (Tambo, San Miguel, Huanta, etc.) who had been recruited like us ... There were families that had been there for years, and tired of that kind of life, many escaped.'

In 1992, Armando and his family decided to escape by boat through the Ene River. The *Senderistas* were waiting for them in the river mouth: '... they took us out and put a rope around my parents' necks, first they hanged my father, then my mother. My brother Vidal tried to escape and they shot him in the back while another seized me – "if you escape we are going to kill you like your brother" ... I started crying and could not speak ... They took me back and put me under the supervision of Mrs Tania, telling her "you are going to take care of this child that has no parents".'

Source: excerpts from Portugal (2008: 57–8) (with editing), using the CVR testimonies.

free transport and food in the universities' canteens, salaries and the possibility of social mobility, and other less tangible benefits such as the sense of belonging to a community and the opportunity to make history. In time, and under special circumstances, Sendero moved from intellectual and clientelist manipulation to the use of physical force and violence, spreading a culture of terror. The discourse was never ethnic, but in each element of the discourse and the strategy, people oppressed by socioeconomic, political and cultural inequalities were particularly vulnerable. This vulnerability was rooted in their ethnic and regional history.

Our stress on vulnerability is confirmed by our fieldwork in the Northern and Southern Highlands. We heard from our informants, both in Cajamarca and in Cusco, how the level of community organization led to group decisions to reject violence, and therefore the overtures of Sendero. This rejection grew out of the stronger community organization we have already commented on, and, in the case of Cajamarca, the work of progressive priests and nuns of the Catholic Church, cementing a culture of non-violence (Muñoz *et al.* 2007). By contrast, community organization was weak in Ayacucho and a particularly conflictual situation had emerged out of the perversities of the agrarian reform.

The response of the authorities and its feedback effects

The first attack by Sendero was on the day of Belaúnde's election in 1980. But no one in Lima, and especially in the corridors of power, had even a glimmering of how serious a challenge this was: it was all happening very far away. It took two years and seven months for Belaúnde to send in the armed forces. In the meantime the police were left to deal with the situation with completely inadequate resources and training. When the armed forces did enter the scene, there was still no recognition of the nature of the war. Sendero was drawing in the whole population in its principal zone of operation: this meant that what was needed was a plan for (re)gaining the support of the population, and adequate resources to avoid human rights abuses – basically, good resourcing of an intelligence effort. In fact there was no full backing from the legislative arm of government, and very limited resources. The person speaking out most lucidly against the armed forces going in was none other than the Minister of War, General Luis Cisneros Vizquerra. He saw clearly that with the lack of preparation and resources, the only possible result would be indiscriminate killing: 'They will kill sixty people – at most there will be three *senderistas* in the group – and surely the police will say that the sixty were *senderistas* ... I think this would be the worst alternative.'[28]

Lacking adequate intelligence, the armed forces could only try to regain territorial control. The CVR's analysis is that this led to 1983–4 being the most lethal years of the conflict, with high levels of abuse, as evidenced in many testimonies. Repressive strategies had multiple causes: however, the CVR is adamant that the ethnic prejudice developed over the years was in good part responsible for the severity of the abuse. They ascribe the military's use of torture principally to inadequate intelligence facilities, but in a culture which permitted violence, and where the treatment of 'indians' could be the more ferocious because they were considered inferior beings. This was true also for Sendero, described as using indigenous communities as 'cannon fodder'.[29]

Such abuses inevitably led to instances where, because of military abuse, people joined Sendero. A moving example comes from the detailed case histories compiled by Portocarrero (Portocarrero 1998). Raúl was aged 20, young, ingenuous, Catholic, obedient, idealistic and serious. The moment of real commitment to the cause came when in 1984 he was arrested and tortured.

Another example is Andrés, giving testimony to the CVR.[30] He narrates how around 1981 and 1982 red flags with the sickle and hammer appeared in trees and in the top of hills. Then, in the year 1983, terrorists arrived and began organizing his community, explaining the goals and objectives of their actions in different districts and inviting the population to come out of their houses, to abandon the community and hide in the mountains, arguing that the repression would kill them. The population, pressured by the *senderistas* and thinking that the police or the army would come after them, went to hide in the mountains taking their children, food, blankets and plastic sheets to make precarious tents. His mother did the same to save her life and those of her sons, leaving her house and her land.[31] They experienced many difficulties, running away from the army, the police and the *ronderos*.[32] In 1984, when Andrés was between 10 and 11 years old, his family was returning to their home to bring more food to the mountains. On the way back, his mother and sister-in-law were captured by the army and *ronderos*, beaten and taken to an abandoned house:

> I could hear the screams of many women ... they were around eighteen, all women, they concentrated them in a small house and I was watching; the soldiers entered the house and came out, and the next day, at 2 p.m., around forty soldiers shot them ... from then on, I

experienced a situation of trauma and had no one with me, just me and my little sister, we were together and slept together.[33]

In his resentment, blaming the *ronderos* and soldiers for his mother's death, Andrés joined Sendero. From that moment, he collaborated with the *senderistas,* carrying out tasks such as moving supplies to different places, vigilance and communication.

In this section we have shown how Sendero was not in itself an ethnic movement, but where it originated and had its initial huge success tells its own story. It originated, and had outstanding success in mobilizing indigenous people over nearly a decade, in the most indigenous and deeply unequal region of Peru. We have argued, based on the testimonies collected by the CVR, that Sendero was able to mobilize because of the vulnerability of indigenous people to its discourse, its promises and its mode of operation. We have argued that it was no coincidence that the appeal was felt most strongly where the traditional culture of dominance and dependence was still strong, despite the land reform, and where inequality, resentment and resulting conflict were high. In fact the national context of reform increased expectations, and in due course thereby the degree of frustration. The persistence of the traditional culture of domination left no room for the kind of grassroots organization which provided resistance to Sendero in other places. Sendero was able to use the need for a legitimate authority, a role never fully taken on by the state after the agrarian reform and the collapse of the old institutions. Guzmán demanded total submission, which we have seen attracted rather than repelled. Sendero also used need, as with the provision of a 'communal pot' in university dining rooms. They also, increasingly with time, used blackmail and coercion, as in the case of Armando quoted in Box 7.1. But the movement also of course appealed to people's sense of injustice. All these aspects of vulnerability relate to group inequality, though not exclusively – those suffering vertical inequality alone could also be vulnerable, and were.

But there is a further and crucial level to the analysis of the significance of HIs. We have seen that this also comes out tellingly in the testimonies. The nature of the state and police reaction, and Sendero's own behaviour, were *different* because of the reality of discrimination and prejudice. As we have shown, in the eyes of the members of the CVR, this was a characteristic of both sides, who are equally responsible for using indigenous people as 'cannon fodder'. An 'inferior' object may be more readily tortured, even killed, than one's equal. This is at the heart of the vicious circle: horizontal inequalities facilitated recruitment to violence, given the lack of alternatives and the degree of vulnerability they represented – and violence led to the worsening of HIs – in the worst cases, death.

The Impact of Political Violence and Recession on Group Inequalities

The spread of political violence also led to economic recession through its effect on investment, though the debt crisis and economic mismanagement were probably greater causes of recession. The significance of the growing economic chaos during the mid-1980s will become clear in the following chapter, which shows how economic chaos and political violence together produced a sense of 'lack of governability' and of 'demoralization' which formed the basis of the appeal of Fujimori's dictatorial and repressive policies, with profound effects on political space and certainly on political HIs. For now, we only need to observe how successive teams failed to deal with the long-term crisis in export supply, and how teams from either left or right ended up with 'short-termism', manipulating prices and restricting demand in a desperate attempt to restore equilibrium in the external accounts, once capital flows were reversed with the onset of the debt crisis in 1982. This reflected an inherited lack of state capacity. The government of Alan García (1985–9) rejected recession as a tool and focused on price freezes, producing hyperinflation by 1987.[34] In 1990 the new administration was handed a gravely distorted economy with inflation running at over 2,000 per cent.

Faced with a growing needy urban population, food aid was an obvious answer, and food aid under PL 480 played an important role, as part of the short-termism which characterized the decade.[35] However, such imports may have played a role in alleviating in the short term the situation of the urban areas, but at great cost to indigenous peasants, particularly in the Sierra. An important consequence of the manipulation of relative prices and the use of PL 480 was that real producer prices fluctuated wildly and declined over time (see Figure 7.1). The long-run stagnation of yields in the Sierra is suggested by Figure 7.2, which takes '*amilaceo*' maize as a Sierra proxy, and '*amarillo duro*' maize as a Coastal crop. The deterioration of yields was also affected by extreme drought. In 1983 Peru was hit by a disastrous *El Niño*, producing floods in the North of the country and terrible drought in the Southern Sierra.

Even with PL 480, however, the urban areas suffered gravely in the face of the recession. Indigenous migrants, above all in Lima, found themselves battling for survival in an increasingly hostile environment. As we explained in the previous chapter, by the 1960s migration was already

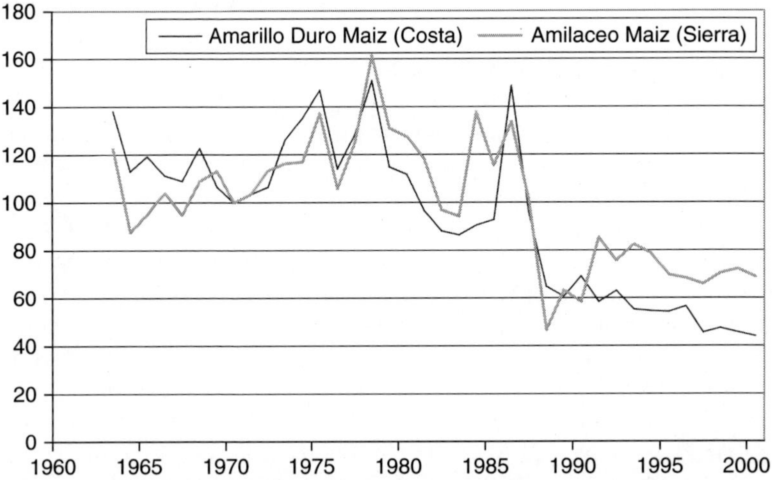

Figure 7.1 Index of real farm gate prices
Source: Ministry of Agriculture and OXLAD.

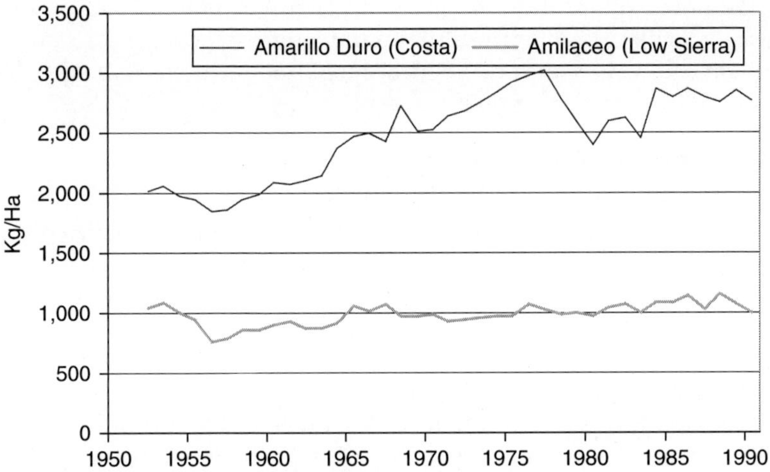

Figure 7.2 Costa Sierra productivity gap

a powerful 'mover and shaker'. Indigenous people arrived in urban centres, they learned Spanish, acquired some education and adapted to the dominant western-*creole* culture as a means of improving their socioeconomic situation, but typically resisted total acculturation.[36] They needed to rely on family or on patronage, and the old forms of patron–client relationships took on new life from necessity. The urban informal sector was the newcomers' main recourse for small economic opportunities, and informality grew at an amazing rate, with make-work jobs thriving on illegality and the many grey areas outside the formal sector. This was aided by the growth of the illegal economy: in the course of the 1980s the growth of the international trade in drugs sucked Peru into its centre, providing dollars but also contributing to the expansion of the informal/illegal economy. By the end of the decade, cocaine was Peru's largest export.

Futher, by the end of the 1980s, and above all as Sendero moved into Lima, investment and even day-to-day production were being seriously affected by growing violence. And violence had other impacts on socio-economic life as bread-winners were killed, herds and belongings were looted by both sides, and families were displaced. Discrimination in the labour market against Sierran migrants worsened as they became suspect as 'terrorist'. In the displacement process, too, within-group inequalities were exacerbated. Those migrants able to sell land or other property in their place of origin could make a new start more easily, with cumulative effects.

We now explore the impact of recession and political violence on urban mobilization, and use the example of the people's kitchens to explore the perversities of political mobilization interacting with the economy and the wider political scene.

The impact of recession and indigenous migrants' mobilization: an illustration from Lima

A vivid illustration of the impact of the deterioration we are describing comes from one of the most exceptional stories of grassroots vigour and organization that we encountered among migrants in Lima. We document in the following chapter instances of collective action in the 1990s and how they were affected by the closure of the system and by political violence, but one of these instances is already so clearly affected by the trends of the 1980s that we should anticipate the story briefly: the '*comedores populares*', CPs or people's kitchens, bringing together migrant indigenous and *chola* women living in the periphery of Lima. The first kitchens began in the late 1970s, centred in Lima but eventually spreading elsewhere.[37] These collective actions initially grew simply from working women aiding each other. The flavour is well given in the following description: Gloria Libia, a neighbourhood leader in El Agustino, a Lima *barrio*, recalls, 'At first, we were a sort of women's club. For example, we taught the señoras to read and write, we did literacy work. Then we saw the needs of our *barrios* [shantytowns] for example, myself and others left very early in the morning to work at La Parada [the market] ... We left our children at 5 am and only returned at 1pm to cook for them ... In one of our meetings, an idea was raised by one of our members who had seen a *comedor* in another neighbourhood. We thought, why don't we start one ourselves?' (Schönwälder 2002: 158). By 1986 there were 570 such people's kitchens in Lima (Huamán 1987, cited by Lora 1996). By the end of the decade the number was being put at around one thousand (Córdova and Gorriti 1989).

This rapidly became a serious instance of collective action and the building of a political identity based on migrant women's shared needs. A significant proportion of the kitchens evolved, as we show in the next chapter, from survival activity to more strategic levels of political analysis and political action. By the late 1980s, this 'autonomous' proportion of the total number of CPs is still put at 60 per cent by Carmen Lora, admittedly a vigorous defender of the CPs.[38]

At an early date the women of the people's kitchens realized that collective action was far more effective if the individual people's kitchens linked together.[39] Powerful federations developed in the different regions of Lima. By 1989 there were 42 '*centrales*', or groupings, with 15–40 kitchens belonging,[40] and in 1991 a formal Federation was formed (FECCPALC, Federation of Centrales of Self-managing People's Kitchens). The importance of this grouping is demonstrated in the efforts of successive governments to avoid the federation and deal directly with the kitchens. The increased level of coordination led to the gradual consolidation of a political agenda around a food programme which used nationally-produced ingredients, was linked to measures to support the small-scale agriculture producing these ingredients, and promoted indigenous ways of cooking healthy local ingredients. The documents contain a sophisticated analysis of the problem caused by food imports and the potential 'virtuous circles' implied by fostering consumption of Andean products.[41] What hit the headlines, however, was what was interpreted simply as a demand for 'subsidy', an emotive word given the multilateral-led fight against practices such as subsidies. In fact the key demand was for equal treatment with the Aprista kitchens, which were receiving free rations. The development of the agenda led to the first food march in 1988: the '*protesta con propuesta*', or protest with a proposal.

Various actors played key roles in supporting the people's kitchens to articulate and broaden their agenda and acquire new skills. These actors came from the political parties, many from the United Left (IU) and from the NGO sector. Particularly significant was the success of the IU in the municipal elections in Lima in the early 1980s. In various Lima slums the IU-led municipality launched local development efforts, notably in Villa El Salvador and El Agustino. Various municipalities gave the district committee of the people's kitchens an office in the municipality (e.g. San Martin de Porras – Lora 1996: 136).[42] Equally significant and drawing on the same constituency of committed middle-class progressives, various NGOs were generous with time and effort in helping the people's kitchens write the '*propuesta*', in promoting networking and education.[43]

However, there were serious obstacles faced in the form of the disempowering political context in which collective action was taking place. The magnificent '*protesta con propuesta*' was turned back with police violence used on women and children to prevent them reaching the Presidential palace. There was no reply other than that: the march was to be repeated year by year as a form of symbolic protest and was soon known as the '*protesta con propuesta sin respuesta*' – without reply.[44] So one aspect of the groups' lack of power is simply the lack of channels: the women with their constructive proposal had nowhere effective to take it.

Another example showing how the people's kitchens struggled in this chaotic context comes from Schönwälder's evocative description of the evolution of municipal politics in the 1980s (and 1990s) in San Agustino, a *barrio* of Lima: the story makes it abundantly clear how prone to divisiveness and suspicion local politics were (Schönwälder 2002). Lora (1996) has a nice description of how ordinary people's view of local politicians, and the politicians' view of such organizations as the people's kitchens (just interested in their own narrow sectoral claims), together created a 'subtle but consistent' wall between them (p.140). Migrant indigenous women faced the same serious obstacles that their counterparts in the countryside faced: they were immersed in a network of brokerage of political parties that was vertical and divisive.

Another point of vulnerability was poverty and the desperate need for food aid. From the early 1980s the self-help people's kitchens existed alongside 'party-political' kitchens, both Acción Popular and Aprista. Both with Belaúnde and then increasingly with García's government, food aid was an issue. The early autonomous kitchens did not receive food from the state. It would have required extraordinary far-sightedness to realize in the early 1980s that to fight for PL 480 supplies on the same terms as the Aprista people's kitchens was a dangerous path. Indeed, the culture of rights was much in the air in 1986–7: the fight for a Law giving equality of rights to food aid to all people's kitchens seemed an important battle.[45] A key analyst and participant in the process records that there was never any discussion of the problems and dangers of PL 480 imports.[46] In 1988 with increasing crisis, García decided to centralize all food aid distribution and the infighting intensified *'por la manguera'* – to access the gravy train. So the nature of the activity – survival – which we have argued did not make impossible a move to a more challenging agenda, did leave it terribly vulnerable to political forces and to pressures from competition and corruption. This would become tragically obvious in the 1990s.

But the worst form of vulnerability was to Sendero. Some of the worst events occurred early in the following decade, but they form an intrinsic part of the vulnerability we are analysing here. Sendero simply could not tolerate this example of constructive success, and was able to use these conditions of vulnerability and distrust to spread more discord. For Sendero, the women leaders were exactly the kind of people they needed to target: examples of constructive self-help, interfacing between the state and the poor. Sendero was able to use accusations of corruption to justify the terrible assassinations it began to carry out in 1989–91 in Lima. Of some hundred community leaders killed by Sendero in 1989–92, 24 were women.[47] The movement was savagely weakened in its leadership. The assassination of Elena María Moyano, a leader of the people's kitchens movement and Deputy Mayor of Villa El Salvador, became symbolic of this oppression.

The Collapse of Politics and Parties in the 1980s

Economic problems and the horrors of hyperinflation focused people's attention on survival activities, at the expense of more strategic political goals. But by the second half of the 1980s, the stronger effect on popular mobilization came from the impact of political violence that was now spreading into new areas. The war began to make it more difficult for indigenous people to organize across their communities for reasons other than self defence.[48]

The impact was larger in the central regions of the Sierra and the Amazon, and in Lima, than in the rest of the country. During the war, it was not only local authorities and social leaders who faced intimidation and repression, but also governing mayors, prefects, governors, lieutenants, local justices of the peace, and leaders of the zones which the armed conflict affected. According to the CVR (2003), approximately 2,267 people in authority were assassinated during the conflict, 70 per cent in only three departments, Ayacucho, Huánuco and Junín.

Of these, 1,680 were victims of Sendero. The elimination of such a large number of local officials – the majority of them members of the political parties that supported the new democratic regime in 1980 – constituted a severe breakdown of the capacity for political intermediation in the zones affected by the armed conflict.

In addition to the weak organizational infrastructure that indigenous peasants inherited from previous years, by the end of the 1980s they began to face the harassment of their leaders, a state of siege in the country and restrictions on free association. These different aspects came together to generate a situation in which the newly democratic institutions could not channel forces from below into the electoral arena, in contrast to what happened successfully in Bolivia and to some extent in Ecuador (Van Cott 2005). Paradoxically, the return to democracy proved to be a more hostile terrain for indigenous in Peru to mobilize than in previous years. We have explained how during the first half of the 1980s, indigenous peasants' organizations were absorbed into the vertical and divisive brokerage power of the Left. By the second part of the 1980s, political parties found it more difficult to provide any infrastructure at all to work through social organizations or on the basis of ideological sympathies. The radicalism of Sendero took leftwingers by surprise and finally forced leftist parties to enter into an ideological discussion over the means and ends of the 'political revolution', with mutual accusations of disloyalty to the 'real' cause (Tanaka 1998). Eventually, escalating distrust undermined the basis of their new and fragile unity, and by 1990, the project of a United Left in the country representing the demands of the popular sectors, including indigenous peasants, was at an end. The war also affected the ability of NGOs, and other organizations such as the church, to offer support. However, these organizations, principally the church, had built quite dense horizontal networks in the past, which were damaged but able to survive during the war. Such organizations provided the only means for indigenous peasants to make their views known in a context of increasing violence and human rights abuses.

But it was not only violence that was weakening the party system (Tanaka 1998). In political terms, we have argued that the vigorous upsurge of the Left fostered networking and alliances, but the culture of leftwing parties was authoritarian and ideological, so that where their influence was greatest there was little room for endogenous indigenous organization and mobilization around the issues that were central to indigenous interests. Clientelism remained the dominant culture, the more so as repression closed down associational space. The room for constructing an indigenous voice and political identity was steadily compressed.

Further, and perversely, the largest party, the APRA, was adversely affected in its effectiveness by the return to democracy, which signalled that the traditional reliance on union bases would be less important: the key was obtaining individual votes. This increased the already strong tradition of clientelism, as buying individual loyalties grew in importance – a paradoxical and pernicious consequence of the opening up of the political system.

In this section we have shown how political group inequalities – access and ability to use that access – were harshly affected by the violence and repression. We have shown how political violence led to the closing down of even the small signs of emerging networking and political activity among indigenous groups – by displacement of people, by the introduction of fear and distrust as leaders were assassinated. The insidious dimension was the sense of distrust and suspicion, nowhere better illustrated than in the account of the people's kitchens.

Conclusion

In this chapter we have explored how signs of hope and possibilities of change, observable by the 1960s, were frustrated over the next two decades. There was indeed growing political protest, especially over land issues, and this did indeed lead to one of the most radical land reforms of the time, carried out by the radical military government of Velasco. But we have shown in the first section above how the inherited lack of state capacity led to perverse outcomes, increasing conflict in many zones. In the region of most significance for its subsequent collapse into political violence, although many landlords had already abandoned or sold their estates, the state was unable to be present and extend rights to people. Instead, the reform allowed the better-off indigenous peasants to replicate deeply-rooted traditions of exploitation and clientelism, and new resentments and an increasing perception of lack of authority arose, allowing Sendero a fruitful entry.

A second sign of hope, as we showed next, was the emergence of class-based organizations among the indigenous peasants. The growth of political activism of the Left in the countryside and the increasing discontent with the manner in which the government of Velasco carried out the agrarian reform provoked a new phase of indigenous peasant mobilization that resulted in the building of more centralized and sophisticated forms of organizations. These new leftwing parties had a significant appeal for young urban-based activists, who had at this time their first radicalizing experience of the inequalities faced by indigenous people in the heartland of the Peruvian Sierra. We have traced the next perversity: the huge support to networking and brokering of interests occurred in the context of a deeply vertical ideology and practice. This vertical political culture helped mobilization over land claims, but left many peasants alienated and frustrated, especially by the parties' lack of sensitivity to the issues on the ground for struggling farmers. This was felt the more strongly since the context was one of opening up to democratic institutions and discourses, but the culture of those practising the 'new politics' did not change. We have illuminated the significance of this by contrasting the South, where the Left was most active, with the North, where the power of landlords and traditional institutions was much diminished already and where the Left played little part. Peasant organization in Cajamarca and other departments of the North flourished in a more autonomous and healthier form at the local level.

The significance of this became apparent as Sendero emerged. The movement could feed on the discontents of the Central Highlands, but made little or no headway in the North. The vulnerability to mobilization, we have shown, came also from the high degree of horizontal inequality: Sendero's techniques exploited need, frustration, a sense of injustice, and the degree of personal insecurity and need for new 'authority' and 'order'. But in a terrifying vicious circle, both Sendero's own techniques of recruitment became increasingly coercive, and the official response of police and army was itself violent, because of the inherited prejudice and discrimination. It was somehow more possible to kill someone seen as inferior. The violence from both sides served to aggravate HIs.

But the vicious circles did not stop there. As we have shown, violence affected investment and made coherent economic management and attention to long-run problems more difficult. Recession affected the marginal population particularly strongly, and migrants from the violence-affected areas found it harder than the rest to get jobs, always suspect as they were as 'terrorists'. The severity of recession sent people back into survival activity, while the emerging indigenous peasant organizations found their never-strong ability to network now even more restricted. We illustrate both the potential and the tragedy of these years with an account of the people's kitchens: an instance of constructive self-help by indigenous and *chola* women of an exceptionally encouraging form – yet ultimately it was much damaged by distrust, by the very need to survive and by terrorist violence. (The next chapter traces its fortunes under Fujimori.) Finally, we showed how recession and repression now closed up political space.

We see therefore that the political evolution and responses, direct and indirect, to the breakdown of the old hegemony resulted by diverse routes in a closing down of political space, which effectively stymied the potential of the return to democracy for giving new voice to indigenous people. Instead, the early policy response of land reform fed rural conflict, and Sendero was able to capitalize on this. The explosion of political violence produced repression with cumulative effects, and while the majority of Peruvians suffered a loss of political space and voice, and would do so more severely in the coming decade, indigenous people were particularly vulnerable, tarnished as they were as 'terrorists'.

In these interactions between inequality and political violence, we can capture much of the depth of the embedding of group inequality. We see first how political violence grew out of and reacted to group inequalities, though not exclusively – there were other forces. We see, second, how political violence, principally through the repression it induced, worsened horizontal inequalities, particularly political and socioeconomic. We see, third, how horizontal inequalities were also perpetuated and aggravated by the failure to construct healthier democratic politics, and in particular by the failure of the emerging left to facilitate participation, by the failure to resolve the economic crisis, and by its aggravation via hyperinflation.

Notes

1. Recognized since the 1920 constitutional reform as indigenous communities (Davies 1974).
2. It is always dangerous to talk about identities and often results in too clear-cut an adoption of one terminology, with all that implies in terms of assumptions and discourse. We seek to avoid this to the best of our ability, without losing sight of the real-life complexity. Rural indigenous men, women and children now moved as individuals and as groups. In the process, they built new identities, more fluid, more complex, sometimes internally contradictory – often, as they commonly said themselves, *en proceso*, still in process.
3. The incursion of the guerrilla movement and the army's response, as well as the implementation of an earlier agrarian reform in the area, contributed to their demobilization.
4. Mayer (2009), through a series of testimonies, narrates very vividly how indigenous people lived these conflicts.
5. Spaces in which civil and social rights are provided (but not necessarily political rights) within class-based forms of interest intermediation.
6. Interviews with political figures of the 1980s, Lima and Cusco (August 2008).
7. By the fourth congress of the CCP in May of 1974 the organization had a total of 336 delegates representing 144 base organizations – federations, unions, communities, cooperatives, and others – from 13 departments.

8. This group was founded in 1965 and had its roots in intellectual study circles and the university student movement. VR sought to correct the errors of earlier guerrilla groups by building a more substantial party organization and establishing links to social organizations in order to gain wider support for their revolutionary causes, developing significant political networks in the labour movement, particularly in the mining and fishing industries; in the early 1970s, the party worked energetically with peasants' organizations that were independent of Velasco's official organization, the CAN (Sinamos 1976).
9. Interview in Espinar, Cusco (August 2008).
10. For non-peasant allies what was going on was a struggle that would serve to create peasant organization to be used subsequently for other 'revolutionary' goals against the state. Among peasants and indigenous leaders this goal was not so clear. Montoya (1998) claims that the struggle for land was for peasants not only a material struggle for rights: it was the symbol of their historical deprivation as indians, of their exclusion from society, and the restoration of their culture and origins as a people. Further research needs to be done to better understand this important aspect of the struggle.
11. 'Tupak' is spelt with a 'k' in Aymara, with a 'c' in Quechua. In most of the region of Puno, Aymara is the indigenous language.
12. In 1979 they organized the first meeting of the Quechua and Aymara nationalities and the minorities of the Forest together with the Peasant Federation of the department of Cusco. The following year a 'congress of nationalities' was held, but it convoked fewer representatives than the first encounter. In 1981, the Tupak Katari federation was characterized as 'divisionist' by the CCP executive committee who held to a discourse of class throughout the 1980s and 1990s (Montoya 1989: 65).
13. Interviews in Cusco (August 2008).
14. We describe them more fully in the next chapter. They rapidly developed additional community functions including communal justice.
15. Réñique (2004) describes how the central organization provided a Bulletin which circulated among a selected cadre. See Paredes (2009).
16. In our interviews we heard how the *ronderos* in Cajamarca feel no commonality with the indigenous populations of the South. In Cajamarca, peasants have passed through a deeper process of racial and cultural *mestizaje*. They do not speak an indigenous language or live according to the principles of communal land property, but they retain several communal Andean characteristics in the reproduction of their everyday life, such as the logic of reciprocity, communal links, institutions and values for marriage, labour, production and communal work (Yrigoyen 2002).
17. Mobilization in Piura started in 1972 in the Valley of Chira and by 1974 extended to the Highlands in Morropon and Huancabamba. In Cajamarca the peasant federation, FEDECC, was founded with the support of the FENCAP with an APRA orientation, but from the beginning of the 1970s, the Left acquired more influence, and in 1973 the FEDECC was affiliated to the CCP. Between 1973 and 1974, the FEDECC led clashes with the agrarian reform officers and police in several places, such as Huacataz, Pomobamba, the zone of Tual-Negritos-Manzanas, Chota. By the mid-1970s, land mobilization in the Northern Highlands had already decreased (García-Sayán 1982).
18. This paragraph relies on Degregori (1990: 41–6).

19. Counterfactuals are difficult, but it is at least worth contemplating that had dictatorship continued, Peru would have seen a more Central American type of guerrilla warfare, less extremist and more widely based (we exclude Guatemala from this comparison). The key consequence of the timing of the emergence of violence may be that the government's concern with the threat of terrorism prevented a deal with the army, which might have removed them more fully from the scene. The army remained strong, with consequences that we will trace below.
20. Henry Pease, former Senator and leading political figure on the Left, put emphasis on this point in interview (Lima, August 2008).
21. 1980 speech of Abimael Guzmán to the First Military School of Sendero, cited in Starn *et al.* (1995) (our modification of the translation).
22. This and the following paragraphs draw extensively on Portugal (2008), working paper no. 57, prepared for the project and available on the CRISE web site, where much supporting detail may be found.
23. CVR (2003, Vol.V: 581).
24. '... cuando ya ingresé a la Universidad, el materialismo dialéctico, el materialismo histórico te abre los ojos ... Comprendí más el proceso, el proceso de la lucha, que el pueblo siempre ha luchado y luchará y esa lucha misma sirve para transformar. Se estudió la revolución francesa, que ha sido sangrienta, que ha habido excesos, que ha sido violenta, sí, pero eso de que sirvió, de transformar a la sociedad y eso es lo que pesa y ahora y pues, si no se hubiera dado esa situación, ¿cuántos años más hubieran pasado para que pueda devenir todo lo que es el capitalismo ahora? Hubiera demorado más; ellos han tenido trescientos años para tomar el poder y consolidarse en el poder' (CVR 2003 Vol. V: 615: student 1985–90, militant of Sendero, imprisoned in the prison Santa Mónica in Lima).
25. 'Entre los años 1977, 1978 y 1979 es bastante notorio que [los militantes del Sendero] viajaban específicamente a las provincias de Víctor Fajardo y Cangallo a formar escuelas populares y captar estudiantes; al mismo tiempo que trabajaban en estas zonas, seguían consiguiendo militantes en la Universidad' (CVR 2003, Vol.V: 587. Presentations of the Workshop "Universidad y violencia política").
26. Degregori (1990) shows how where traditional power structures were disrupted, nothing in the way of democratic forms replaced them, and the culture of domination was so strong that richer peasants could take advantage of the disruption to create new forms. The resulting conflicts favoured the penetration of Sendero.
27. CVR, Testimony 700041. Female born in Ayacucho in 1963, independent worker, member of Sendero, imprisoned at the *Penitenciaría de Máxima Seguridad de Mujeres* in Chorrillos.
28. 'Matan 60 personas y a lo mejor ahí hay 3 *senderistas* ... y seguramente la policía dirá que los 60 eran *senderistas* ... creo que sería la peor alternativa ...' (Interview in *Que Hacer* 1983, quoted by CVR 2003 Vol II: 256).
29. The CVR (2003) analysis is that *both* sides used indigenous people as 'cannon fodder', and that it was less problematic to torture and assassinate if the object was seen as inferior (Vol. 8: 114–5).
30. CVR, Testimony 720036. Male, born in 1973 in Ayacucho, Chief of Security of the Sendero, imprisoned at the *Penal de Yanamilla* in Ayacucho.

31. 'Aproximadamente en el año 1981 a 1982, en los árboles y en la cima de los cerros aparecían izadas, banderas rojas con la hoz y el martillo ... el año 1983, llegaron los subversivos y empezaron a organizar mi pueblo, explicándoles los fines y objetivos de sus acciones en las diversas circunscripciones del territorio nacional, e invitaron a toda la población a salir de sus casas, abandonar el pueblo y refugiarse en los montes y quebradas, argumentando que la represión vendría por ellos y les daría muerte ... la población, al verse presionados a salir por los *senderistas* y creyendo que vendrían los policías o militares a darle muerte, fueron a los montes y quebradas llevando consigo a sus pequeños hijos, sus víveres, frazadas y plásticos para confeccionar carpas y pasar la noche ... Mi madre también hizo lo mismo, quien por preservar la salud y vida de sus hijos, abandonando su casa, sus chacras, fue a los montes.' CVR, Testimony 720036. Male, born in 1973 in Ayacucho, Chief of Security of the Sendero, imprisoned at the *Penal de Yanamilla* in Ayacucho.
32. The *ronderos* were peasants from the communities that followed, at least in name, the model that emerged in the North as a defence against robbers. In complete contrast to the *ronderos* of the North, most of the *rondas* were controlled by the army and did not have the self-help characteristics of the original model.
33. '...pude escuchar fuertes gritos y pedidos de piedad de muchas mujeres ... como 18 personas eran, todas mujeres, allí concentraron en una casita, y yo estaba mirando del frente; los militares entraban y salían de esa casa y al día siguiente, metieron una ráfaga del patio; eran casi 40 soldados ... Desde ese momento, atravecé una situación crítica y no tuvé a nadie a mi lado, pues con mi hermana chiquita, juntos andábamos y dormíamos juntos'. CVR, Testimony 720036. Male, born in 1973 in Ayacucho, Chief of Security of the Sendero, imprisoned at the *Penal de Yanamilla* in Ayacucho, p.3.
34. This was an extreme version of the common result of so-called 'heterodox' stabilization experiments which tried to restrict inflation by price freezes in situations where economic management and monitoring mechanisms were not very sophisticated. Demand/supply imbalances became greater and relative price movements were very exaggerated. In Peru the result was hyperinflation because of the lack of restraint on the demand side coupled with limited instruments to control prices.
35. PL 480 is the controversial US law allowing the 'gift' of surplus food from the US to countries in need.
36. These indigenous migrants constructed, and/or had constructed a new identity for them, a new '*cholo*' identity. This process occurred in a society that had not yet overcome its prejudice, and often, in an effort to avoid discrimination, they reproduced racism and discriminatory practices against those less literate and less urban than themselves.
37. Sara-Lafosse (1984) locates the first initiatives in Comas and El Agustino in 1978 (starting with children's breakfasts and progressing to the full idea of a *comedor* by 1979).
38. Lora (1996). See also Blondet in Molyneux and Razavi (2002); Cueva and Millán (2000: 47).
39. All observing the early people's kitchens were impressed by their capacity for networking and organization. Violeta Sara-Lafosse, interview, Lima.

40. See Lora (1996: 39). On p.40 she gives a reference to an evaluation of the people's kitchens, documenting the effectiveness of this move to a more centralized structure.
41. See Lora (1996: 50 and Appendix 2).
42. See also Schönwälder (2002: 160ff).
43. Alternatíva, FOVIDA and SEA are the most frequently mentioned.
44. The story of this movement is well told by Lora (1996, Chapter 6).
45. Interview with Carmen Lora (27 November 2007).
46. Cecilia Blondet, interview Lima (3 December 2007). Blondet played a leading role in NGO support to the people's kitchens movement, and attempted to work for six months with the Toledo government as Minister for Women.
47. Burt reports an interview from 1994 in San Juan de Lurigancho, where a member of the movement claims to see Sendero's assassination of a local *comedor* leader as justified as she was involved in corruption (Burt 1997: 303).
48. The fierce competition of Sendero and the armed forces to control community spaces forced people to leave their villages and towns. The degree of displacement in these years is one of the fundamental elements to understand the destruction of community organization. Nevertheless, those who stayed rapidly felt the need to organize to defend their communities. '*Rondas campesinas*' (peasant watchdog groups) were formed and organized during the Fujimori Government with the support of the military.

8

The Fujimori Years: The Remaking of Political and Economic Exclusion

The last chapter ended with a state of total crisis in both the economy and polity at the end of the 1980s, with negative institutional consequences: overwhelming political fragmentation and anomie, and a sense of ungovernability as inflation and terrorism took off to terrifying heights. This chapter now explores the resolution of crisis. We analyse the institutional consequences both in the economy and the polity, and the results for structures of exclusion, above all for indigenous and *cholo* people. While in some ways state capacities are increased, there are new elements of exclusion and top-down characteristics to policy, and damage to incentives to organize and participate.

The events of 1990 are well known. As the elections approached, it was perhaps inevitable, with the weakness and even discrediting of party politics, that a complete outsider without party would capture the public's imagination. Alberto Fujimori went from complete unknown to top of the polls in just three weeks, and eventually won in the second round, ironically with huge support based precisely in his lack of party and his Japanese ethnicity, which made him an outsider and therefore one of the 'marginals' in the eyes of the indigenous and *cholo* population. For a time it appeared that he was thinking of alternative and more inclusive economic policies, but it eventually emerged that he had two teams working in ignorance of each other, one on orthodox neo-liberal lines (based in Miami) and the other in Lima, looking at inclusive alternatives. His first trip abroad to talk to donors convinced him that he had to go with the Miami option.

Severe adjustment policies followed, and it is one among many painful ironies that privatization brought capital inflows, while mineral prices recovered, in time to stimulate growth and prevent the worst negative feedbacks that typically characterize such policies. Meanwhile the intelligence forces' capture of Guzmán and a large proportion of the Sendero leadership in 1992 produced a dramatic effect on violence, which ended practically overnight. The huge political appeal of the restoration of order on both economic and political fronts gave Fujimori backing for the continuation of repressive policies. Congress was closed; 'elections' were held in a climate and manner which made them a mockery. Meanwhile the economy relapsed into 'old-style' primary-product-led growth, but in its worst incarnation from the point of view of equality: a mining boom.

In the first section below we trace out the story of neo-liberal policies and the mining boom and the consequences for group inequalities when combined with increasingly extreme neo-liberal policies and top-down social policies. Next, we show how the fragmentation and discrediting of party politics, and particularly of the Left, was completed through these years. This collapse provided a space for the use of ethnic politics, but the institutional legacies accumulated by this point made ethnic political dynamics extremely perverse and unable to provide indigenous people with proper channels of political representation. We then explore through community level studies how the closing of the political system and the nature of institutions and policy management deepened the embedding of inequality by their effect on collective action among indigenous and *cholo* populations, and thereby the likelihood of successful grass roots promotion of change. The Final section concludes.

Neo-Liberal Policies, Top-Down Social Policies and the Return to Mining

Various laws were passed in the first two years of Fujimori's regime as the underpinning of the new 'free' market.[1] Labour and land markets were liberalized.[2] Privatizations were accelerated to generate fiscal revenue, to signal commitment to the market model, and to attract foreign capital. Regulating bodies began to be put in place. The liberalization of trade and the abolition of all incentives to non-traditional exports were clear signs that the model was to be based initially on traditional exports, while 'pure' competitive pressures were expected to generate new opportunities with time. Important laws implementing the new commitment to the primary sector included Decree Law 662, which gave incentives to foreign investment; Decree Law 674, which promoted privatization; and Decree Law 818 (1996), which provided the framework for large-scale investments in natural resources.[3]

The need for institutional development has been a recurring theme of this book. It is important to note that Fujimori did implement significant institutional development, but that his reforms in support of his economic model focused on the need for finance and for political control, to the neglect of the micro side. The reforms involved a massive body of legislation in the first few years. Reforms of specific organizations focused on revenue collection, with a deep and initially very well-managed reform of the tax administration system (SUNAT) as well as a reform of the customs agency (SUNAD)[4]. The reforms however were not backed by the required reforms of the judiciary or the tax system itself: it is important to administer tax collection better but if taxes are not well designed or at the required levels, and evasion is not appropriately and effectively sanctioned, the impact of better administration is limited. But at least tax revenue as a per cent of GDP rose from its disastrously low level in the first half of 1990 (4.9 per cent of GDP) to 13.4 per cent by 1995.[5]

With time, as shown in the next section below, the political strategy became increasingly one of control with little attempt to create a political base, except in so far as patronage could do this. By mid-term, social spending policies were subsumed in a policy of patronage through the Ministry of the Presidency, notably in the spending programmes of FONCODES and PRONAA.[6] Policies of control blended into corruption, as the 'vladivideos' were subsequently to reveal.[7] The use of patronage and corruption as political tools made it impossible that reform of the judiciary should have featured. The creation of INDECOPI, the government's agency for protection of intellectual property and competition, appears to have been more a response to external prompting and conventional wisdom than an integral element of institution building (though it went on to achieve good results). The other institutional surprise – the Office of the Ombudsman – was rather similar in its birth. It was made surprisingly vigorous by the appointment of Jorge Santistevan to lead it. A lawyer who had been working outside Peru for some years, he courageously created an organization with teeth and integrity which did what it could to stem the tide of corruption and abuse of rights. However, in the later years of the regime, even the key institutional success – SUNAT – was itself in some measure subverted for purposes of political control, which as time went on required increasing elements of manipulation of information.[8]

Elements such as supply-side support to restructuring arising from tariff cuts were simply not part of a model which was seen as needing to be ultra-committed to the market to ensure continued flows of capital. All instruments of intervention and/or potential support were disbanded in the first few years. The PYME sector (small and medium enterprises) is very important in Peru;[9] apart from government, the other kind of supply-side support, especially for this sector, can come from the technical, managerial and other advice provided by civil society agents such as NGOs. The latter were hardly the regime's favourite category of social actor.[10]

Where progress was made was in rural infrastructure. Roads, schools, clinics, sewerage, electrification and small-scale irrigation schemes all expanded (Escobal and Ponce 2002). However, the availability of credit was a problem, especially in the rural sector. The abolition of the Banco Agrario, whatever its faults, did nothing to improve the availability of credit to small rural producers. Such credit depended on banks, big firms, a few NGOs and the rural and municipal savings banks. While the municipal banks in particular were able to make a contribution,[11] the system was (and still is) totally inadequate.[12]

An important difference with previous bonanzas was the overlap of the mining boom with increasingly strong neo-liberal policies. In the past the disincentive to other sectors had principally been the natural result of an export bonanza, which led entrepreneurs and resources to move to the booming sector as a result of market incentives – the standard result of Dutch Disease. In the 1990s, *apertura* and the consequent increase in international competitive pressure formed a deliberately sought strategy to repair the perceived damage of previous protectionist policies. In the first boom of the twentieth century, reduced protection had been a pure consequence of the profitability of primary export sectors and the effect of that on the exchange rate. In the second boom, the government of Odría neglected industry and by removing the import controls that had been a major source of unrest certainly helped to give a disincentive to industry. But it was not a principal policy goal to open the industrial sector to competition (Thorp and Bertram 1978, Chapter 13, Section 2). In the 1990s, by contrast, *apertura* was the major instrument to modernize and shake up the economy, and indeed to take the strategy beyond the exporting of primary products. The maximum tariff was reduced in two steps in 1990–91 from 84 per cent to 25 per cent and the average tariff by March 1991 was 17 per cent. Rojas cites an effective rate of protection of 123 per cent in July 1990 and 41 per cent in December 1990.[13] The consequence was that increased competition was a central characteristic of the model. As we shall see, de-industrialization over this period was far more pronounced, given the lack of supply-side measures to support a response to competitive pressures.

An illustrative example of the difficulty of achieving results against a weak institutional background, with consequences for group inequalities, comes from the liberalization of the market for milk and the reduction of tariffs on imports of powdered milk. Under García there was a single farm-gate price independent of location or quality. In practice, this provided a subsidy to remote small producers. This restriction was ended in 1990. Initially this actually favoured relatively small indigenous producers in the Sierra, since the new grading of prices was by fat content, which was high for such producers. However as more sophisticated systems were introduced, paying for quality based on bacterial count, proximity and quantity, small remote producers such as those of the Sierra of Arequipa found themselves in dire straits. The model had its intended effect of forcing a change in mentality, but the appropriate support in terms of reliable market information, explanation of the importance of standards and so forth, was not available. The alternative small niche markets for products such as oregano and paprika are volatile and fragile, and pose collective action problems. There existed no producer associations capable of resolving such problems.[14]

Another difference with previous booms was the increase in social spending which occurred, a typical development throughout Latin America at this time. We have described, however, how these social programmes were used for patronage. The two key programmes, FONCODES and PRONAA, have been extensively evaluated: although by no means not without welfare effects, the quality of spending left much to be desired and their use for co-option meant that even if they improved socioeconomic HIs in the short term, they did not empower indigenous groups (Tanaka and Trivelli 2002, Vásquez and Riesco 2000).

Another difference with previous booms was the potential offered by the new popularity of privatization policies, particularly because state ownership had expanded significantly, above all under Velasco. This provided opportunities to attract foreign capital above and beyond that attracted to the export sector, which helped to cement the allegiance to this policy option.[15]

The immediate significant achievement of the 1990 *ajuste* was price stabilization. Inflation fell from the hyperinflation levels of 1989–90 (7,650 per cent in 1990) to 74 per cent by 1992 and 24 per cent by 1994. Thereafter it continued to decline, approaching price stability by the end of the decade. The second major achievement, significant for its effect on confidence and investment besides its political impact, was the 1992 capture of Guzmán and the arrest of a significant proportion of the leadership of Sendero Luminoso.

The initial recovery mechanism was the return of normality, with modest growth resuming in consumption and investment in 1991–3. Imports rose rapidly with the liberalization measures of 1990–1 and an initial balance in the external accounts was secured by inflows of short-term capital and debt refinancing.

Between 1994 and 1997, the economy entered into its export-led phase, responding to buoyant mineral prices and to privatization initiatives with large investment projects and the beginning of the gold boom above all. It was long-term foreign capital inflows which dominated and provided solvency, allowing reserves to rise strongly.

However, as mineral prices and a renewed surge of foreign investment 'solved' the economic side of the structural crisis, the new-old path of trusting to primary exports and foreign investment continued new-old elements of great significance for the issue of group inequalities and potential conflict. Over one third of indigenous community land in the 1990s was the site of mineral claims, while over half of the 6,000 communities were living in zones affected by mining.[16] All new mineral exploration now occurring involved the 'acquiring' of community land: this was not a new phenomenon, but new in its extent. By the end of the 1990s there were some forty 'hot spots' of actual or imminent conflict over land, with violent aspects, all concerning indigenous populations. The institutional mechanisms and formal or informal norms to resolve such issues were almost non-existent.[17] The most interesting and possibly most important institutional innovation of the 1990s, the *Defensoría del Pueblo*,[18] was reluctant to become involved: it was beginning to develop a role only by the middle of the next decade – notably in the dispute over the Río Blanco copper project in Piura. Again, only in 2002 did the Ministry of Energy and Mines create a department of social affairs, and this lost importance in the Ministry as the importance of getting foreign investors committed took over.

Environmental issues associated with these investments were key issues, with a huge incidence in ethnic inequality, since the prime threat was to indigenous communities and their surrounding urban and rural populations – a threat to water supplies, to the food supplies depending on that, to clean water and sometimes to their way of life.[19] Important legislation was passed in the 1990s, on for example the rules governing a company's responsibility for an environmental plan, but the problem remained one of implementation. This is a typical example of how the embedding of inequalities over time can make the problem almost imperceptible: given the history of centralization on Lima, it seemed 'natural' to hold public hearings on, say, a company's proposed environmental plan, in Lima. Yet this was to ignore the real costs and resulting lack of voice suffered by indigenous populations because of transport costs, opportunity costs and lack of information.[20]

Further aspects of natural resource policy of extreme interest to the indigenous-*cholo* population of the provinces – provincial towns as much as rural areas – were how far tax revenues are distributed to local governments and how far local linkage effects can be incentivated and supported. On the tax front, while initially in the 1990s the government was busy giving all kinds of incentives to foreign capital and not looking to negotiate benefits for the local area or the national economy, gradually more significant sums were being passed through under the 'canon'.[21] But spending this money was only too often the problem. In many cases, unspent balances accumulated. The failure to spend was a product of several factors, all of them important for the reinforcement of horizontal inequality.

First, the demand side of linkage effects from large-scale mining was increasingly limited. By the 1990s, mining technology had taken a step up in scale and complexity compared with the previous boom, with new methods of open cast mining and extraction on site (Kuramoto 1999: 27). Only the increasing prevalence of 'just-in-time' management was working in the opposite direction, generating a new interest in local suppliers of inputs to facilitate low inventories. The sector also continued to bear the brunt of the bias toward international suppliers inherent in the whole system of international financing and feasibility studies. Most large projects require significant external funding, which, if linked to official sources, often brings with it requirements to purchase from the suppliers of the country providing the funding. The feasibility studies of foreign investors effectively excluded local firms by the requirements set and by pre-existing relations with suppliers.[22] The import bill of the mining sector in the late 1990s amounted to 12 per cent of GDP; if only a small part of this could have been sourced locally it would have had significant linkage and multiplier effects.

In regard to the supply side of linkage, the key sector for local response is light engineering. Sadly, in Peru light engineering had already been pushed into crisis by the stagnation of mining in the 1980s.[23] The liberalization of imports in the 1990s further increased pressure on this sector.

But the story is not exclusively about local supply. Local government matters too, and national and regional level government efforts and initiatives are needed to provide supportive infrastructure – financial, physical and technical – and probably a 'vision' for the region. Instead the local level suffered because of severe restrictions of capacity. Further, it faced restrictive bureaucracy imposed from the Centre – the '*SNIP*' system for monitoring public investment.[24] Instead of bureaucratic obstacles, what was needed was national and regional level cooperation in infrastructure and the provision of market opportunities. In the next section below we discuss a poignant example of the difficulty of local development spending, in the context of the Tintaya mine. Another example is the case of the Yanacocha gold mine in Cajamarca, the largest in Latin America. Even once the company recognized the political value of local purchases, which took some considerable time, its efforts to encourage a local group to organize an earth-moving company (CONGECASA) ended in disaster. Local capacities for organization, entrepreneurship and levels of experience were not adequate to take advantage of the situation, with the result that even food tended to be brought in from outside. The mine needed to purchase in bulk for economic reasons. It would have required a very systematic, coherent and supportive development policy on the government side, to produce an adequate supply response.[25]

An additional aspect hindering such local development was the way the neo-liberal policies espoused from 1990 interacted with the continuing centralization of the economy and polity on Lima. Such centralism increased with Fujimori, and was only briefly and in limited fashion reversed after 2000.[26] The combination of trade policies and centralization on Lima significantly reduced the chances of spread effects from mining – or indeed other stimuli to local developments benefiting provincial urban *cholo*-indigenous populations.[27]

Thus while in principle it would seem that a regionally-based primary export-led model combined with trade liberalization attacking a previously rather centralized industrial structure would benefit the provincial *cholo*-indigenous population while the Lima *cholo*-indigenous population suffered relatively, it is not clear that this happened. The centralizing forces meant benefits to Lima in commerce and even processing, relative to the provinces, and the problems with linkages severely limited multiplier effects from export projects in the Highlands. (Coastal export agriculture was possibly more open to such processes.) But perhaps of most relevance to us is that once again there was a widening of the perceived interests of different subgroups in the indigenous and *cholo* populations. The old days, when striking miners would be supported by fellow unionists in Lima, were long gone for many reasons, to be replaced by a great fragmentation.

The Closing Down of Politics

Alberto Fujimori – the son of Japanese migrants and an 'outsider' from the party system – brought the traditional party structure to an end. He closed the Congress in 1992 with massive popular support and became an emblematic case of a new political phenomenon in Latin America, the 'democradura': a democratic dictatorship as set out by Levitsky (1999). By the end of 1993, Congress had been restored with a composition in which Fujimori had a large majority, a new Constitution had been approved, and several new competing groups calling themselves 'independent' and 'apolitical' replaced the 'traditional' parties with a pragmatic rather than ideological strategy. Alberto Fujimori was also looking to gather other forms of electoral support: he was the first major presidential candidate in Peru to make significant appeals on an ethnic basis to the public (Madrid forthcoming). (Since then, ethnicity has been used even more widely by Alejandro Toledo and, most recently, by Ollanta Humala in a new context.) The new Congress and Constitution gave Fujimori great freedom of authority to end the internal war at any cost and to reorganize the economy radically, as we have seen in the previous section.[28] In 1995, Fujimori was re-elected with almost two-thirds of the vote in an election accepted by both the national and international community. His second period was less well received and the dangers for the democratic system rapidly became obvious: the armed forces acted through shady agreements with Fujimori's prime adviser, Vladimiro Montesinos; free thinking journalists and opposition leaders were subject to fierce harassment; and there were systematic human rights abuses. Fujimori attempted to win a third term of office, but he no longer enjoyed popular support, and doubt was cast on the fairness of the elections. Clear charges of corruption and mobilization on the streets brought Fujimori's third period to an end. In November 2000, he resigned, by fax from Malaysia, on his way to Japan. After the collapse of Fujimori's regime, Peru's fragile but persistent democracy has ensured a succession of genuinely competitive elections, each producing a peaceful transfer of power, all in the context of an economic bonanza led by high mineral prices.[29]

We have shown how by the end of the 1980s, the collapse of the party system was clear, and the project of a leftwing party channelling the demands of the population, including indigenous peasants, had failed badly (Tanaka 1998). What followed in 1990 with the election of Alberto Fujimori was a model of electoral organization in which new independent parties were little more than labels or 'candidate-centred' vehicles for politicians of all ideological colours who left their established parties to join so-called 'de-ideologized' and 'pragmatic' projects (Cameron and Levitsky 2003). The result was the further fragmentation of politics at all levels. At the national level, the relationship to the media and the development of a national public image became essential for presidential and congressional elections (Conaghan 2002, Tanaka 1998). At municipal levels the new electoral model together with the heavily fragmented political organization of the country (195 provincial and 1,833 district municipalities) made politics in Peru extremely disjointed, particularly in those areas where indigenous people live.

Table 8.1 shows how the predominance of these fragmented local parties is larger in those regions with a stronger indigenous character. Figure 8.1 shows the increase of local political organizations in the peripheral Central and Southern Highlands, the areas more affected by the internal war and where the indigenous population is most concentrated. The 1995 peak reflected the reduction in the climate of fear once the war ended, and also the increasing demands for local autonomy as a reaction to Fujimori's attempt to gain control over the countryside and poor urban neighbourhoods after the close results obtained in the referendum in 1993.[30] Local mayors contested the centralized way in which the Ministry of the Presidency was implementing an ambitious plan of social expenditure. In order to weaken this wave of opposition at municipal level, Fujimori created a municipal political organization in 1996 that participated in the elections of 1998, *Vamos Vecino* (Let's Go Neighbour). In the 1998 elections, *Vamos Vecino* succeeded with strong support from the government, but in 2000 its popularity collapsed and local parties again proliferated.

Table 8.1 Electoral results in provincial municipalities, 1980–93 (per cent of votes cast)

	1980	1983	1986	1989	1993
Izquierda Unida (IU)	23	29	31	18	4
Acción Popular (AP)	36	17			13
APRA	22	33	47	20	12
Partido Popular Cristiano (PPC)	11	14	14		5
Others (independents)	8	7	4	30	66
Fredemo (right-wing coalition)[a]				32	
	100	100	100	100	100

[a] Acción Popular and Partido Popular Cristiano contested the 1989 election as part of the Fredemo right-wing coalition.
Source: Tuesta (1994).

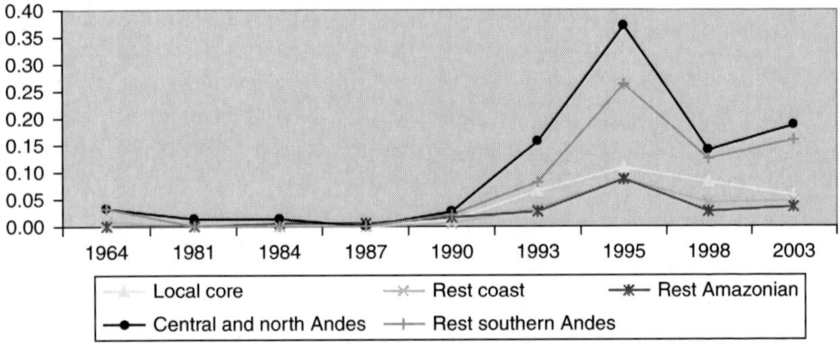

Figure 8.1 Percentage of provincial municipalities run by local political organizations
Source: Paredes (2008).

In this pragmatic political culture and a context of high fragmentation, presidential candidates have made more use of ethnic politics. We have mentioned how after Fujimori, other candidates like Toledo and Humala have employed a variety of ethnic elements in their campaigns, and by doing so have politicized ethnic politics in a form that was new in Peru. They have used indigenous clothing, used indigenous sayings and languages, and invoked indigenous cultural symbols. They have called attention to their own ethnicity and they have contrasted their backgrounds with those of their competitors.[31] Most importantly, they have recruited numerous indigenous and *cholo* candidates to their campaigns, as we reported in Chapter 3 of this book. The new electoral institutions are enhancing these political practices with the aim of expanding representation, but the outcomes are bounded by the institutional legacies that have emerged. In a context of political fragmentation and state harassment of social leaders and organizations, ethnic electoral politics is not likely to broaden indigenous political representation. Politicians have been able to use ethnic discourses to build linkages with voters and have brought a small number of indigenous leaders into the political arena with them, but these efforts have not been backed by more institutionalized forms of organization of collective action, and therefore have failed to establish enduring ties to the indigenous population and provide accountable responses to their demands.

This has happened in a similar manner at the local level. From 1995 on we find political parties with names in an indigenous language or making specific reference to their peasant identity. This was a new political phenomenon at the provincial level, since up to that point the 'quechua' or 'peasant' identity had been largely a phenomenon of intra-communal affairs, an even more local space than the district one. There were three of these groups in 1995, seven in 1998 and 15 in 2001. All of them had victories in provinces in the Highland periphery. Of these 25 groups, 20 were in the Southern Highlands, three in Cajamarca and one in Piura (Huancabamba). In 2003, the Frente Popular Llapanchik had three mayors in Apurimac and the MINCAP and INTI in Huancavelica won two municipalities. With the exception of the Movimiento Campesino Atusparia which won the municipality of Sihuas three times in a row, up to 2003 none of these groups had been re-elected under the same name.

Political fragmentation based on localized and fragile organizations was the outcome of 15 years of internal war and a national politics that tried to control local politics instead of opening channels to provide popular access. The municipal elections in 2002 revealed the largest levels of political fragmentation ever. Eighty-three per cent of the groups competing for provincial municipalities were local organizations, 13 per cent regional organizations and only 4 per cent were connected to national political parties. This fragmentation was most severe in those provinces where most of the indigenous live, particularly in the Central and South Highlands (JNE 2007). In 2006, the situation in regard to fragmentation improved, leading to expectations of association at regional level. In that year, 43 per cent of the groups competing for provincial municipalities were associated with a regional movement, 41 per cent remained as local organizations and 16 per cent were associated with a national party, whether by membership or electoral alliance.[32]

In conclusion, after the 1990s, the new electoral model that emerged made indigenous participation even more difficult. Indigenous people, and indeed all Peruvians, faced a political system that was problematic to manage outside their own local spaces. As we will explain in the next section, reaching national and regional politics required economic resources, connections with the political and media establishment and engagement in clientelistic relations with those who had already achieved political popularity. In this context, candidates use indigenous people's grievances to build electoral support during national campaigns, but these practices do not build accountable forms of representation. The next section explains how this resulted in disillusion and scepticism as to the possibility of democracy, and the current party model.

Community Action and its Context after 1990

To explore further the difficulty of indigenous and *cholo* people themselves achieving effective voice in this political context after 1990, we carried out a number of community-level studies of collective action or its absence.[33] We have presented the results fully elsewhere[34]: here we summarize our main observations. We show first the tragic results in terms of distrust and fear, from the legacy of political violence and the manner of its repression, and from the divisiveness which we have documented in the political system. As a result, we show how the system at the local level was impenetrable to efforts at change, in ways which caused promising community-level activism to run into the sand. And second, we show how the lack of management and administrative capacity at the local level and the lack of effective links in policy-making structures between the local and the national, led to frustration and discontent even where initial results looked promising.

For the interpretation of our findings, we need to set out briefly the context of our different cases and the nature of the collective action we were observing. We have indicated already how the regional dynamics of political mobilization varied in the important decades from 1960 to the 1980s. We have seen the impact of the Velasco reforms, which created economic and social openings for communities previously dominated by landlords and freed them from semi-feudal working conditions. However, land distribution and accompanying policies regulating community organizations[35] affected people differently across regions. The peasant federations of the Southern Highlands and the *rondas* of the North represented specific and different reactions to the contradictory policies of the corporatist state and its continuation through the 1980s. The evolution of the poorest part of the Central Highlands – in particular Ayacucho – is however a negative story of lack of mobilization, and part of another process, the emergence of Sendero.

To explore the significance of this regional diversity in the new context of the 1990s, we took examples from three regions of the Sierra, and a diversity of experiences of indigenous/*cholo* populations in Lima. The three Sierra cases were all medium-sized towns and their surrounding countryside, and represented different trajectories of political mobilization as well as different experiences of political violence.

Our first case was an obvious choice, at least in terms of type – there are many like it. We wanted a case to exemplify the Southern Highlands, with significant activity in terms of the peasant federation and the presence of political parties. We also wanted an area of indigenous communities much affected by the presence of mining, to reflect the fact that some 80 per cent of Highland communities own land with mineral deposits. We took Espinar, at a height of 4,000 metres and a population of some 57,000, in the high Sierra of the department of Cusco, with a large mine, Tintaya, nationalized under Velasco and subsequently re-sold to the private sector. Espinar has the most homogeneous population of our cases, ethnically indigenous and Quechua-speaking, one of the most important basis of the National Peasant Confederation and very poor.

Our second Sierra case was chosen to exemplify the Northern Highlands, with its somewhat greater prosperity and lesser role of national political actors: Bambamarca in Cajamarca, at a height of 2,700 metres and population of some 76,000, also a mining area and an area of dairy and livestock farming. Here the population is relatively homogeneous, not Quechua-speaking, of indigenous origin but lighter-skinned than in the South. The division of large estates occurred as it were 'naturally' in this area, as large estates were sold or divided. Since the land was being divided in any case, communities did not need to mobilize immediately, and enjoyed allies who were less vertical, coercive or dominant than those of communities in the South. They were able to build autonomous spheres in which actors could create new groups not based in a class discourse, and were able to organize themselves in defence of their rights as part of culturally-formed groups, the *rondas*.[36] These are community organiations which had their beginnings in patrols against cattle thieves. These *rondas* evolved gradually into a source of identity and commitment: if asked how they identified themselves, the fieldworkers and farmers with whom we spoke would say with unanimity "somos *ronderos*" – we are *ronderos*.

For our third case, it was essential to take a case from Ayacucho, the 'cradle' of the worst political violence Peru has known, and the area of least political mobilization at the meso level. We have stressed how conflictual was the impact of the agrarian reform. We have seen the very limited development of peasant organizations, and the degree of internal differentiation. We took Huanta, a city of some 65,000 inhabitants, a place deeply drawn into the violence with ten thousand killed between 1980 and 1992. The city is at almost 3,000 metres. Its surrounding Sierra is high, and cultivated land goes from 2,500 to 3,500 metres. We have already reported in Chapter 2 on our interview material on internal differentiation and prejudice, particularly the townspeople's severely negative view of '*chutos*': according to many Huantinos, ignorant pig-like uncivilized people who live in the Highlands.

In addition, to capture more fully the urban dynamics of indigenous migrants' collective action or its lack, we included a Lima migrant district, San Juan de Lurigancho, and specifically within that, two settlements largely formed by people displaced by violence from Huanta in Ayacucho: Huanta Uno, largely middle class and *mestizo*, and Huanta Dos, poor indigenous/*cholo*. This fourth case, Huantinos in Lima, reflects the differentiated structure of Huanta, but in Lima the differentiation takes the form of two physically separate settlements, which nevertheless have a degree of differentiation within them, as we shall see.

We also studied a collective action phenomenon encountered in all urban areas in Peru, though our interviewing was Lima-based: the communal kitchens, known as *'comedores populares'*, or people's kitchens, a remarkable instance of collective action and collective self-help which began at the end of the 1970s among indigenous/*chola* women in two of Lima's *barriadas*, and which spread to become a national phenomenon (we have introduced this case already in Chapter 7).[37] We chose this because of the strength of the movement's initial promise and impact, and because our initial studies of collective action in the Sierra produced little or no evidence of indigenous women in leadership roles. It seemed important to reflect on at least one instance where indigenous and *chola* women took the lead. In terms of the issue considered above, the degree of differentiation, the movement was initially rather homogeneous but became more differentiated with time, as we explain below.

The Southern Highlands: Espinar

The instance of collective action we focused on was community action targeting the large copper and gold mine of Tintaya. The typical catalysts of collective action have been perceived injustice and material need, and usually there is some external agent which plays some role. Thus, in Espinar, collective action targeting the mine was facilitated by a local grassroots organization and by NGOs. The mine was nationalized during the Velasco regime. The state company followed a policy of expropriation of the land of peasant communities, with inadequate compensation and poor alternative provision.[38]

21 May 1990 is the day remembered in the recent history of the province (and celebrated every year). Our interviewees told us how between 20,000 and 30,000 people mobilized against the mine, led by FUCAE, the local branch of the peasant federation whose growth in the 1980s we have described above, and by the *Frente Unico de Defensa de los Intereses de Espinar*, a civic organization created to defend Espinar in the face of issues such as the mine. Firebombs were thrown, fire started inside the mine, mine personnel were threatened and three people were taken hostage. No deaths occurred. The attention of the Central Government was successfully drawn to their problem, and one positive outcome was the electrification of the city of Espinar. However there was no progress on the rural community's problems, such as land access and water contamination.

In the 1990s, the mine was privatized, and eventually sold to BHP Billiton, its owners until 2006, when it was bought by Xstrata, the present owners. In this period the rural communities affected began to organize themselves more effectively, and in 1999 created CORECAMI-Cusco (Regional Coordinator of Communities Affected by Mining). CONACAMI, the national organization of communities affected by mining, came in to give support. NGOs, both local and international, began to get involved. At the international level, Community Aid Abroad (CAA), the Australian member of Oxfam International, began to work with the parent company, BHP Billiton, on corporate social responsibility.[39] A particularly interesting initiative of CAA was to take a group of top executives on a field trip to India to see the environmental and social consequences of a big mining project at first hand through the eyes of the affected population. The Managing Director of Tintaya at the time went on the visit and describes it as a turning point both for him personally and for the company.[40]

We shall see later that the final outcome has not been so good, but the intermediate outcome was startling: over the three years 2000–2002, against all expectations, dialogue made significant progress. A '*Mesa de Dialogo*' or Forum for Dialogue was established, and the company eventually made two agreements, one to make a payment of US $1.5 million annually to the Municipality for local development. The second agreement with the rural communities proposed the distribution of 2,368 hectares of land, the consultation of communities in future explorations, and a fund of US $300,000 annually, for three years in the first instance, for the community's projects.

The Northern Highlands: Bambamarca

In Bambamarca, the impulse to collective action came from poverty, vulnerability and from a different form of state failure, centred in this case on the failures of the police and the justice system. The generalized state of disorder and banditry led in the 1970s to the formation of an exceptional phenomenon: the *rondas*. We described above how these community groups evolved gradually into a source of identity and commitment. This identity is focused on a pride in being effective, and on the recognition of their important role in the community. A number of *ronderos* who were interviewed said that they were proud that the *ronda* effectively sorted out problems of rustling, boundary disputes and even domestic conflicts, rapidly and with almost no additional costs: 'we go directly to the place in question, with the actors involved in boundary disputes and in one afternoon we sort out the problem and pass a judgement that is respected ... legal processes only waste time and money, and maybe even lives because sometimes the litigants assault each other'.[41]

Thus in many places the *rondas* have evolved into institutions that administer justice within the community on a variety of issues and function as a source of education, self-esteem and respect, and as a training in social responsibility and awareness within their communities. They are also important as a factor explaining absence of violent conflict and have increasingly taken up issues such as how to confront a mine owner whose mine is causing contamination. This type of problem has led the *rondas* to work hand in hand with the assembly of the community and the irrigation committee and with other communities and *rondas* that face the same problem. The most notable case has been the long-running conflict over contamination and damage to fish stocks in the Llaucano River, by the Yanacocha mining company. This culminated in a huge demonstration organized in 2001 by the *rondas* of Bambamarca, protesting the death of fish from contamination. This seems a genuine case of evolution to a deeper understanding of the necessary agenda – from practical to strategic interest,[42] but ultimately it produced little real progress on the issue in question.

What made *ronderos* a particularly significant movement is that they were able to go from near invisibility to significant political prominence, and all that in the middle of violent internal conflict in the country.[43] As argued in the previous chapter, they created a significant political regional actor, whose recognition has pressed the state into a more culturally rooted and heterogeneous notion of citizenship and into giving space at the same time to autonomous spheres of political rights and customary governance.[44]

Huanta

Our third Sierra case study is our key instance of *absence* of collective action: Huanta. The need for collective action from necessity was more severe in Ayacucho than in our two previous cases. However, there was no tradition of collective action of a constructive nature, in a society where traditions of domination, hierarchy and passivity were pre-eminent. Land reform was carried out but the conflictual institution of the SAIS was not created, probably because there were no important *haciendas* by the time of the reform. Levels of conflict among communities were very high but tended to be small scale and personal. The networking that might have moved people from personal discontent to a wider agenda was non-existent. Individuals and families opted for migration as a solution to economic problems and then to violence, further weakening the social fabric since the more capable typically left first. As a result, almost no collective movement emerged to confront the armed conflict that ravaged the department, producing 10,000 victims, above all indigenous people. As we have argued in the previous chapter, we consider that the explanation lies in the fact that the emergence of Sendero coincided with a gradual but fairly advanced process of loss of regional identity and population.

Collective action in Lima

Our final set of case studies concern areas of indigenous settlement in Lima, by migrants from the Sierra. We took an interesting double case of migrants from Huanta. This provided an unusual laboratory to analyse further the way collective action varies with prior endowments of capabilities, for the migrants naturally formed two settlements: Huanta Uno which comprises the middle-class former 'nobles' in the valley, who often also had family and property in Huanta itself and already typically self-identified as *mestizo*, and Huanta Dos, Highlanders, indigenous people, peasants who fled from severe experiences of violence to sanctuary, initially with relatives somewhere in Lima. Then we looked at the 'people's kitchens', as an instance of women leading collective action, largely *mestizo* women mobilizing indigenous women.

Turning first to the Huanta migrants, the two settlements came about in 1984 from the initiative of Dr Venegas, Mayor of San Juan de Lurigancho and a Huantino himself. The population of Huanta Uno, some 300 families, was constituted by professionals, with a large representation of teachers: 86 according to one of our informants. People owned property in the city of Huanta which they were able to sell to fund their establishment in Lima. Huanta Dos, originally some 360 families, comprised smallholders or *comuneros*, some cultivators of coca from the Ceja de Selva, and people who had come from a much more traumatic experience of violence, with family members dead or missing, livestock destroyed and land abandoned.

The initial impulse to collective action was parallel in the two groups: the need to establish themselves with housing, basic services and living conditions, in a situation where all faced discrimination as possible terrorists because of being *ayacuchano*. All informants talked of how difficult it was – and is even today – to find employment for that reason. In all the Lima instances studied, the role of external actors was less important than in our Sierra cases. In San Juan de Lurigancho, from the beginning the collective action was meso of its nature – initiatives to get basic services, and subsequently in Huanta Uno also improved education and quality of urban life. Here no external agents played a role: these were determined and independent agents.

Given the poor record of constructive collective action over the years in Huanta, it was a surprise to find how vigorously both communities organized themselves in the first year or so, to get the '*junta directiva*' registered, to develop elections and statutes, and to move to get water, sanitation and electricity. Both groups succeeded. It was clear from our interviews that the essential quality of the collective goods drove the community, who were also united by their sense of menace from a hostile world.

However, the difference between Huanta Uno and Huanta Dos in the ability to form an agenda and move on from immediate practical needs was marked, and part of the explanation for the different outcomes: Huanta Dos was less successful and had to struggle far more for what they were able to achieve.

As is well known, in our second case, the early people's kitchens were also autonomously generated, though often supported by parishes and increasingly by NGOs. It is important to make clear that there is great variety under the label of *comedor*: as the early independent kitchens proved themselves, political parties began to see their value in political terms, and created their own. These were anything but independent. We have seen that in the 1980s there were Acción Popular and Aprista kitchens. In the 1990s Fujimori jumped on the band wagon. Here we are interested in studying the genuinely autonomous instances: as we mentioned above, by the late 1980s this 'autonomous' proportion of the total population of CPs is still put at 60 per cent by Carmen Lora (Lora 1996).

Such autonomous people's kitchens grew quickly into a wider agenda and even into strategic interests. First, women who began collective action because they could see the value in pooling resources and effort (taking turns cooking, buying in bulk) rapidly found they needed skills to manage money, purchasing, diets, etc. Classes in literacy and various skills were in great demand. From this grew the consciousness-raising discussions on family issues, domestic violence, and topics such as small business management.

Secondly, as conditions became harsh with the collapse of García's effort to grow out of inflation in 1986–7, so women realized they had to understand the world at whose mercy they so evidently were. So new elements were added to the classes and debates.

Thirdly, as we showed in the previous chapter, the separate kitchens began to recognize the power of the collectivity and Federations were formed. In 1991 a formal Federation was formed (FECCPALC, *Federation of Centrales of Self-managing People's Kitchens*). The story of the *'Protesta con Propuesta sin Respuesta'* was told in Chapter 6. The quality and significance of the level of organizational capacity was attested to in a poll of views about women as political actors in 1997, cited by Blondet as demonstrating that 'the experience these women gained in social and political organisations and trade unions over the last fifteen years was vital in building a self-image of efficiency, developing self esteem and gaining confidence in their ability – and that of other women – to assume positions of public responsibility.'[45]

These Limeño stories strengthen the evidence from the Sierra: with the single, and very important, exception of Ayacucho, and even in the deteriorating climate of the Fujimori years we do not find evidence that problems of collective action of the Olsonian kind are part of the explanation of the embedding of inequality. People did organize, they built on previous experience, and they did collaborate, and the sense of shared identity, need and threat brought them successfully together. Yet the processes of scaling up, of linking unconnected sites, of creating larger identities and finally of penetrating formal politics in Peru seem to be almost impossible, and a ready cause of disillusion.

The analysis of the cases

The general story throughout our cases is of little or no final success in outcomes, often not even within their own contexts, but also it is notable that they were never able to link their actions with others and achieve a wider impact. There might be 'intermediate' success: learning by doing, the acquiring of skills and the ability to move from a short-term practical agenda to a more strategic agenda. But because they were not able to make links and alliances, they failed in their efforts to change the extent of group inequality. We analyse the causes as the result of the complex, divisive and perverse nature of the political system as it is today interacting with the legacy of violence. In two cases, this weakness was the result of the lack of the necessary brokerage, in organization or sometimes just in understanding policy needs, between the local level and the national level. As political parties weakened or collapsed together with early forms of grassroots organization, these forms were quickly replaced by a narrow, personalistic and clientele-based system, and the result was a lack of positive and effective intermediation.

While we found evidence in most of our cases of the tragic effect of the divisiveness of local politics and of the political violence which was the context up to 1992 and left a legacy which coloured all the nineties, the strongest impact of political violence on collective action was obviously Huanta. There were thousands of deaths in the province through this period. Sendero issued threats against the authorities and people went missing because of the actions of both sides. The level of violence was a serious block to collective action, above all in the political sphere. Moreover, the armed forces controlled how the population organized itself, principally through self defence committees (CVR 2003). These played an important role in the confrontation with Sendero, especially among the communities of the high Andes if they survived the initial onslaughts of Sendero and the army. Other groups learned techniques of surviving between the two fires, giving lip-service to both.

From the mid-1990s the situation changed, with the ending of the armed conflict. Peasant communities today fiercely resent Sendero for its role in initiating the violence.[46] In the urban centre of Huanta, political life has restarted – but without any evident fresh effort at solving the problem of lack of capacity for public life. So public administration is weak and the population continues to be alienated from political life. Meanwhile, the communities from the Highlands remain isolated with little opportunity to participate in public decisions affecting them, and struggle constantly not to be under the thumb of communities at lower altitude. An example is Huayllay which we visited in the course of our fieldwork in Ayacucho in 2005.

While the armed conflict was raging, the only organizations in evidence were the self-defence committees. Today these are less evident and many other organizations have more dynamism, such as '*clubes de madres*', '*comités del vaso de leche*', and also producers' associations. But collective action remains weak: people find others are 'egoists', not willing to put time into organizing communal affairs. The president of the fruit growers association of the valley of Huanta told us: 'Farmers do not participate; there is apathy and lack of interest. They think that working alone can make them advance but that is impossible. There is too much egoism and envy; my house has been robbed and my possessions taken. Farmers do not have any specific association they belong to. What exists is distrust, probably as a consequence of the social problems here.'[47] The Truth and Reconciliation Commission has met with approval – but it is notable that no collective action has emerged to pressure the state to implement recommendations which would benefit Huanta.

Violence thus interacted with the overlapping ethnic and class differentiation of Huanta to have a bearing on the weakness of collective action, so sustaining the embedding of inequality. The conflicts that differentiation gave rise to allowed the entry of Sendero, and the resulting huge escalation of violence almost totally inhibited subsequent peaceful collective action. In that subsequent weakness, the continuing and accentuated differentiation was an element in its own right making for suspicion and distrust.

As we see here, the legacy of violence was to sharpen distrust and divisiveness. This was very much in evidence also in Huanta Dos, and made collective action difficult. This was evidenced by descriptions of the discords over the nursery and the communal kitchen, as members of the group recounted them. But as they told the stories, it was clear in the account that, as in our other cases, much of the divisiveness was a product of other factors in addition to the legacy of violence: above all the way state agencies enter the picture as a result of the weakness/fragility of institutions, e.g. property rights.

The inhabitants of Huanta Dos found the system impenetrable. In our discussions, it seemed as if the inhabitants of Huanta Dos *only* had marches as a strategy.[48] The world of '*trámites*', or official paperwork, they found very difficult, frustrating and obscure. The secretary general recounted how there was always something missing from the paperwork, always another day wasted. The world in which they have to function is alien, unfriendly, and they have no good strategies to deal with it. This sense of helplessness was aggravated by the fact that they felt abandoned by their initial sponsor, Dr Venegas – though his version is that they were impossible to work with. They wanted more land, and attempted to make the case for acquiring their neighbours', the settlement of Jose Carlos Mariátegui. The mayor claims they made an obviously false case. When they staged a protest march, they were easily outwitted.[49]

The contrast with Huanta Uno is enlightening: in the latter we found many instances of capacity to manage both the system and internal divisions. This is in part a consequence of the fact that at higher levels of income, they were able to handle their relations with public officials in ways that were less divisive than in Huanta Dos. This was partly a matter of level of education: the higher level in Huanta Uno allowed them to manage the institutional incoherence. Although by no means well off in terms of Lima, Huanta Uno has a huge concentration of professionals. In interviews, people revealed a whole strategy about how to make friends with influential people. They dealt with bureaucrats by inviting them to the community, showing them Ayacuchan hospitality, food, music. They know the importance of stamina and perseverance in pushing for their goals.

However, the divisions of Huanta Uno, although less marked, still had their costs. They arose from the seemingly inevitable incursion into politics, which brought discord and so led to the collapse of significant external aid, according to Venegas.[50]

The impenetrability of the system emerged in all the cases where collective action was to be found, but with particular force in Bambamarca. Despite highly successful collective action at the community level in the form of the *rondas* and the recognition of their customary rights, the results of their attempts at greater meso and macro influence, both on the political and economic side, are not clear (in contrast to their success at the micro level, in reducing cost and risks, protecting peasant assets from robbery). The most notable case has been the conflict over contamination and damage to fish stocks in the Llaucano River, by the Yanacocha mining company, a conflict which has run since 2001 and produced no real result – perhaps surprising given the strength of the *rondero* movement.[51] What our analysis concludes is that at the heart of the problem is the negative role that political parties have played in the *rondas* due to the sort of party divisions we have been describing. The negative role was increased by the lack of any previous positive role, in contrast with the Southern Highland story. The efforts of political parties such as APRA and Patria Roja to control the *rondas* at this late stage, and impose their political discourse, are much criticized by the *ronderos*. In interviews people described the acute divisiveness of the electoral campaigns as a result of the competition between the APRA, Patria Roja, and AP. The *ronderos'* efforts to get their own candidate elected as Mayor of Bambamarca led to reduced prestige of the *ronda*, as a consequence of the divisions and personal resentments which resulted. An unusual success was that the *ronderos* of the province of Hualgayoc, in a display of unity, managed to form a single 'Front' uniting different political groupings, which has lasted from 1990 until the present day. But our correspondents were all deeply aware of the danger of party divisions and competition and the damage these could do.[52] A frequent view was that things would go sour if they ventured 'into politics' – which invariably turned out to mean signing up with some particular party and becoming drawn into the petty world of party competition.[53] Thus this unusual success at the regional level still never managed to make alliances beyond its region.

Yet without those links, influence and ideas remain limited. We were struck by the lack of awareness people showed of the relation between their problems as farmers and the national issue of powdered milk imports, a topic that has appeared frequently in our historical account. Real progress in the obvious comparative advantage of Cajamarca – the milk industry – lies in modifying the impact of a mining boom on agriculture at the national level. It is interesting and probably very important that people seemed often completely unaware of this need for action at a 'higher' level. It seems that it is not always easy to see the national picture when immersed in the local without the adequate trans-communal structures that can be used as vehicles to disseminate and process information and ideas from the micro to the macro and vice versa. This reflects again the lack of intermediaries or networks that could make such links.

Impenetrability, divisiveness and distrust were also key themes in the case of Espinar and the deal with the mining company. Despite the apparent triumph of the agreement with the company, the true gains have proved fragile and limited. The same date as in 1990 – 21 May – provided the occasion in 2005 for a mass demonstration, this time of 2,000 people and again with firebombs and threats. When the Mayor tried to intervene he was taken hostage.

What went wrong? Over years of patient negotiation, communities have built up a level of confidence, ability to negotiate and a sense of their own worth which are real 'goods'. However, as yet, the benefits are not significant enough to give confidence that frustrations can be managed, while the increasingly divisive role of the new multinational actor, the mining company, is interacting with the clientelism of party politics, despite the earlier good beginning. In this, our analysis of Espinar parallels directly our conclusions from Bambamarca, in which the nature of the local political system and the communities' lack of confidence in it are responsible for lack of success. Initially, the role of the political system had been positive, as we have seen, in the shape of the Mink'a mayor. Local organizations had also contributed, such as FUCAE and the Frente. But with time, familiar characteristics of the Peruvian system won out, helped by the role of the multinational. The Mink'a mayor is seen by some as having lost the next election 'because the people of the city didn't like him working so hard for the people of the countryside'. The next Mayor was from the Aprista party and did not generate confidence. The view that emerged in many interviews was: 'leaders from political parties make promises during elections but then forget communities'.[54] Also, the municipality has argued that the community has the company money and does not need the municipality – a fallacious argument in the sense that there are coordination, infrastructure and planning needs that need the public sector.[55] The communities feel they do not have a say in the fund established via the Municipality, and the company that today owns the mine, Xstrata, is widely viewed as having the Mayor in its pocket and conducting a vigorous propaganda through the radio and through bribes.[56] The FUCAE, the local branch of the already-discredited CCP, was further weakened by its failure to stand up to the company after its initial vigorous stand.[57] Specific projects to be funded from the company grant require contributions in kind from the community: with the boom in mineral prices the sense that the company 'has plenty of resources' feeds resistance to collaboration, and trust has not been fostered by reduced levels of interaction.[58] Thus money remains unspent for lack of consensus and proper fulfilment of the conditions imposed for its disbursement.

However, a further important point became apparent to us in the course of our interviews. Such local development also needs the *national* government and this it conspicuously did not have. The carefully-controlled violence is indeed judged to bring the attention of National Government to a greatly neglected area.[59] Both in 1990 and in 2005, Ministers flew in and the national spotlight of the media was certainly turned on Espinar. However, and this is of the greatest importance, at no time was there serious support forthcoming from the national level to work on increasing absorptive capacity, nor was any national programme of works carried out to support new ventures.

In the case of the people's kitchens, the story is equally full of lights and shadows, violence, suspicion and distrust. The first impact of the new government was the Fujishock: as a result, there was a massive expansion in the numbers of people's kitchens that occurred in response to extreme need. By the end of 1991 figures as high as 7,000 people's kitchens were being given for Lima alone. It was impossible for the NGOs working in building capacities and support to do more than touch the edge of this need. As a result, many were left with no institutional support, in a frightening context. As a careful observer and participant says of this expansion, 'It was impossible to provide, on the scale required, spaces for reflection, for formation of a critical awareness, awareness of the importance of bonds of friendship … and to forge ways of behaving based in solidarity and mutual support, as had been done for the first generation of kitchens' (Lora 1996: 31).

As a result, as the movement grew, so did the degree of differentiation and with this the susceptibility to distrust. This interacted with the nature of local politics. The very few educated *chola*/indigenous women formed the leadership; the bulk of the membership had very little education. If they saw their leaders consorting with another world, they became readily distrustful, lacking comprehension and fearing the worst. The centrality of food distribution in the collective action did not help: it readily exposed leaders to accusations of misappropriation, and left them vulnerable to downturns in the supply of food – unable to provide for their members.

In addition, another aspect of the wider system came into play. Part of the political deterioration under Fujimori was his need to use strategies of cooptation, given his lack of a political base. Cooptation characterized in a damaging way his relations with the people's kitchens. He created a Ministry for Women, but gave it 'a maternalist discourse' based on 'the role that women played are playing and should play as "natural" mothers and care-takers of the family and the community' (Boesten 2003: 117). He asked people to stand in the 'elections' that followed his closure of Congress, with 'bargains': implicit promises of aid for political support.[60] 'Foodstuffs came with aprons and cooking hats in orange, the colour of Fujimori's movement, and with the PRONAA logo, and there was the obligation to paint the kitchen with state-issued orange paint and put PRONAA on the kitchen's façade. A large picture of the hero of the nation, Alberto Fujimori, had to be hung on the façade of the building as well .... loyalty to the government was enforced by the threat ... of the withdrawal of alimentary support' (Boesten 2003: 118). It is hardly surprising that by the mid-1990s a once-vital self-help movement appeared weak and exploited.

Added to this, a further weakening was occurring because with the crisis, more women were seeking work, and with increasing education levels, at least in Lima, increasing differentiation was occurring, and with this increased potential for division. The increasing number of second generation migrants probably assisted the shift in values. As some women became busier they started to subcontract their turn at working in the *comedor* for money. So '*socias pasivas*' and '*socias activas*' developed. PRONAA, the government's food distribution agency, deliberately targeted the so-called 'active' members and encouraged them to get themselves elected.[61] As Lora describes it, the passive members gradually became distanced and the active were more subject to PRONAA. The whole culture shifted and became more orientated to securing food. Complaints to the ombudsman about the behaviour of PRONAA brought no response.[62]

Most important of all, Sendero could not tolerate this example of constructive success, and was able to use the conditions of vulnerability and distrust to spread more discord. As noted in Chapter 7, for Sendero, the leaders were exactly the kind of people they needed to target: examples of constructive self-help, interfacing between the state and the poor. Sendero implemented a systematic policy of assassinations, as we have described, with major consequences for the movement and for the NGOs supporting it. Maria Elena Moreno and others paid with their lives. Other dedicated women had to think of the safety of their families and reduce their activity.

As a result of all these factors, the years 1994–6 were disastrous: an important actor and witness of the process thinks that all of the people's kitchens were seduced in those years.[63] The techniques were simple: 'when the bus came to take you to a demonstration, you had to get on or you didn't get supplies'.[64] After 1996 came the fight back and work to raise awareness. 'You don't lose your identity for a sack of potatoes or a bag of rice.'[65] But then in 1998 came a new opportunity and threat: the '*Ley de Cuotas*' which said that in municipal elections 25 per cent of the candidates on a list had to be women. Fujimori asked people to stand in the 'elections' that followed his closure of Congress, with 'bargains': implicit promises of aid for political support.[66] Quite a number of the older leaders now moved into politics, some with much heart searching, given that the 'elections' were widely felt to be a façade for a very non-democratic regime.[67]

We thus see how a combination of a climate of fear and violence, economic pressures and political strategies of cooptation and bribery served to weaken the culture of mutual help and shared responsibility, which, together with the imperative of survival, reinforced vulnerability to manipulation and division. A further element weakening the movement was the failure or shakiness of many efforts to introduce productive activity to the people's kitchens – micro enterprises. This often did not work well. The two logics of solidarity and the market, while they can be made to fit together, do not do so without considerable care.[68]

The surprising fact is that even under severe attack from both Sendero and the clientelistic political system, and also exposed to the contradictions of the interface with the market, a significant number of the autonomous people's kitchens survived, and still survive today.

Conclusion

This chapter has shown how the crisis of governability and the economic crisis were both 'resolved' in the early years of the Fujimori government, in that 'order' was restored and growth resumed. But the routes to both outcomes interacted in various ways to reinforce exclusion and the degree of both vertical and horizontal inequality.

Fierce adjustment at the beginning weakened social movements such as the people's kitchens. The combination of rising mineral prices and an over-arching commitment to neo-liberal policies meant huge new mining projects with international technology and ownership, needing fine-tuned micro-level policies and support at just the moment when this was given no attention within the policy-logic. Increasing frustration led to repeated violent conflict, a state of affairs which lasted into the next decade, with cases such as Yanacocha and Tintaya. Efforts at necessary institutional reform focused on revenue raising, with initiatives on the environmental side that lacked the implementation and fine-tuning necessary for impact. As Fujimori closed down politics with the closure of Congress, any minimal remaining chance of corrective feedbacks was gone. Fujimori's lack of an institutional political base increased his dependence on Montesinos and his underground manipulation, and the web of clientelism and corruption grew stronger, further damaging social movements, as the people's kitchens case showed. The type of ethnic politics that emerged in this period has been shaped by the way institutional legacies interact with indigenous people's hostile terrain for collective action.

As these interactions became more deadly, those on the margin suffered most. The indigenous and *cholo* inhabitants of Huanta Dos lost out compared to their neighbours in Huanta Uno. The protests over company behaviour achieved little, since injections of cash, from the canon or from companies trying to acquire good will, met limited and ineffective spending capacity. Accusations of environmental contamination or other harm lingered on unresolved in the face of communities' limited negotiating ability and weight. We have argued that the suffering catalysed vigorous and often constructive protest – but the efforts to penetrate and change the system met the barriers of clientelistic and often corrupt meso levels of politics. Intermediaries and networks that might have built links were lacking. Groups *became* divided, fearful and suspicious as they tried to make their way in local politics. And the outcome of violence was everywhere. Even with the victory over Sendero, the legacy of violence and repression remained, to weaken further social movements and all levels of politics, through distrust, fear and suspicion.

Notes

1. Jiménez, Aguilar and Kapsoli (1999) and Rojas (1996) give a detailed description.
2. For instance, the 1992 new labour laws gave the government free rein to break up strikes, insisted that strikes be approved by secret and notarized ballots of union members, and made unions active in essential public services ensure these services continued to run during any strike activity (*Andean Report* 30 July 1992). In 1991, laws were passed that relaxed rules on job

stability – allowing employers to offer temporary contracts, minimal hours of employment and making dismissals easier (*Perú Económico*, Enero, vol. XIV no. 1, 1991).

3. As of early 2000, privatization receipts totalled $9.75bn and additional investment pledges were $7 bn as of 1999, according to Copri (*Andean Report* 2 March 1999).
4. SUNAT*: Superintendencia Nacional de Administración Tributaria*. SUNAD: *Superintendencia Nacional de Aduanas*.
5. The increase was partly due to the reduction of inflation, which we describe below. Inflation erodes tax revenues by its effect on 'bracket creep' and by the incentive to delay payments. See Durand and Thorp in Crabtree (1999).
6. FONCODES: Community Development Fund. PRONAA: food programme. See Tanaka and Trivelli (2002) for a helpful account.
7. Remarkable secret films apparently made by Montesinos, of numerous private conversations in which bribes were clearly offered and accepted.
8. Francisco Durand, interview, Lima (2 June 2001). INDECOPI was suffering a similar attack for similar reasons just as the Fujimori regime collapsed (interview, Armando Cáceres, Lima, May 2001).
9. In 1995, according to PEMTEC (*Pequeña Empresa, Tecnologia y Sociedad*), 59 per cent of the labour force was employed by small and medium enterprises (5–19 employees) and this sector produced 31 per cent of GDP (*Perú Económico*, Sept, vol. XIII, no. 9, 1990).
10. Non-governmental organizations had come under pressure from Sendero Luminoso until 1992. The government now in turn found them suspect and subjected them to new processes of registration and monitoring.
11. The development of the municipal finance system for micro enterprises has been one of the most impressive success stories of the 1990s. Set up with strong technical support from German aid agencies, and closely monitored by these for the initial period, they have developed an excellent capacity to reach and support micro entrepreneurs, with impressively low rates of default. Some have been subject to political interference, but the record in general has been good.
12. Figueroa (2001) substantiates this conclusion with reports in Chapter 8 on fieldwork interviewing credit agencies in three regions of Peru. These interviews confirmed that the rural *cajas* have not been as successful as the *cajas municipales*. The former were created with the specific inducement that the owners could lend to themselves, and this has led to significant abuse. (Interview with directors of the Caja Municipal of Arequipa.)
13. Rojas (1996: 252), citing Central Bank figures; Jiménez, Aguilar and Kapsoli (1999: 30).
14. An example comes from oregano production. For a quality product, the oregano needs to be sun-dried, then only the large leaves sent in. A small producer described how he put in the small ones as well, because people didn't notice and paid anyway. He had no perception of the long-run damage to markets this does (interview reported by Alipio Montes Urday, Arequipa June 2001).
15. Note that the largest share of foreign capital that came into Peru from 1990 to 1998 went to telecommunications (27 per cent of foreign investment or $2,060m). Finance received a sizeable 10.5 per cent of the total – $791.6m

(*Comisión Nacional de Inversiones y Tecnologías Extranjeras*, cited in *Perú: Inversiones y Programas*, available at www.cideiber.com/infopaises/Peru/Peru-09-01.html, quoted in Thorp and Zevallos 2002).

16. Data supplied by *Cooperacción*, Lima.
17. See Crabtree and Thomas (1998) for an account of institutional reform and its limits in this period. For an illuminating analysis of why some reforms are so hard to achieve, see Kaufman and Nelson (2004). First, while some needed institutional reforms were introduced, such as a law providing a framework for foreign capital, the creation of an ombudsman and reforms of the tax administration and customs, other crucial reforms were missing. Important absences for our purpose were any reform of the judiciary or the tax system itself, essential if the poor are to benefit from better tax administration, and the many measures needed on the micro side if a strong policy of opening up to the international economy was to be anything but disastrous.
18. The Office of the Ombudsman was unexpectedly effective under the leadership of a lawyer, Jorge Santistevan. Possibly against the expectations of the regime, he courageously created an organization with teeth and integrity. His office worked creatively on issues of access to public services and to public spaces for indigenous people but could not stem the tide of corruption and abuse of rights. See Pegram (2006).
19. An example is the project to exploit the Quilish mountain at the Yanacocha site. This is a sacred mountain for local populations, so the threat went beyond water supplies.
20. NGOs' campaigning gradually began to remove this invisibility. The Tambogrande project was a good example of an instance where the public hearings were not adequately communicated or the presence of those most affected facilitated.
21. The 'canon' is the tax on revenues from natural resources, which is redistributed from the central government to sub-national level according to an agreed formula.
22. An interesting exception to the general failure is FIMA S.A. But, significantly, it is Lima-based. This firm has become a successful supplier of inputs to the mining sector through its strategic alliances and diversification (Kuramoto 1999). However, its managers testify to the major impact of tied financing on their market. They estimate that Peru's Gran Minería buys locally only 10 per cent of what it could buy were it not for tied financing agreements. (Interview with Eduardo Carrero and Wilfredo Cáceres, Lima, 26 June 2001.)
23. Though some firms rescued themselves by moving to supply the fishmeal sector (interview with Eduardo Carrero and Wilfredo Cáceres, FIMA S.A.). This firm took the lead in innovating to be able to supply the fishmeal sector.
24. The *SNIP* is the *Sistema Nacional de Inversión Pública*, the system introduced and managed by the Ministry of Finance to manage public investment.
25. That this is not impossible can be seen from a Chilean case study. In Rancagua a group of small firms, supported by SERCOTEC, the national agency for technical support, formed an association, AEMET, 'to (politely) attack CODELCO'. They have succeeded, and the effort has transformed their way of working. Now they are finding other customers (Angell,

Lowden and Thorp 2001). On CONGECASA see Thorp and Zevallos (2002).

26. See previous chapters. Fundamental sources on this issue are Cotler (1994); González de Olarte (1982, 1992, 2000); Iguíñiz (1984).
27. The kind of process we mean is the way in which with liberalization, firms have tended to switch their sourcing to Lima or abroad and local firms have been driven to close or move as a result. A classic example is the Gloria evaporated milk plant in Arequipa. For years, it had tolerated the 'double transport cost' of bringing sheet metal from Lima and returning the tins filled. When faced both with domestic competition for the first time in many years and with lower cost imports of powdered milk, the economic logic became overwhelming: in 1999, the plant was closed and a new plant opened in Lima.
28. On political reform, an extensive report has been developed by the Truth and Reconciliation Commission (CVR 2003).
29. After a short period of transition under the leadership of Valentín Paniagua, who took office in November 2000, Alejandro Toledo was elected in 2001 and Alan García in 2006.
30. Municipalities were significantly revitalized during the last two thirds of the 1990s despite the interest of Fujimori in controlling them. They became the state institutions in which citizens had more trust. The *'Asociacion de Municipalidades del Peru'* (AMPE), during these years and up to 1998, was clearly the most important opposition to the Fujimori government.
31. See the forthcoming book by Raúl Madrid, *The Rise of Ethnic Politics in Latin America*.
32. One thousand four hundred organizations that competed in regional elections in 2002 did not participate in the elections of 2006. Five hundred and twenty-two new organizations participated in 2006 and only 38 organizations continued to participate after 2002.
33. These studies were carried out in collaboration with Ismael Muñoz from the Catholic University of Peru.
34. The reader is referred to the paper we are here drawing on for a fuller account (Muñoz, Paredes and Thorp 2007).
35. Such as codes introduced at the beginning of the 1970s regulating cooperatives and communities, which stipulated, for example, who could benefit from credit schemes.
36. These community organizations had their beginnings in patrols against cattle thieves. As we described in the previous chapter, the *rondas* now became a community institution, the first of the new style being founded in 1976 in Cuyumalca in the province of Chota. During the following three years, hundreds of other communities in Chota and the neighbouring provinces of Hualgayoc and Cutervo formed their own *rondas*, as they spread towards the zones of the Sierra of the neighbouring departments of Amazonas, La Libertad, Lambayeque and Piura. One of the oldest comuneros of the *ronda* in Bambamarca told us that before 1978, when the *rondas* did not exist, due to *campesinos'* isolation they were unable to confront bandits who, for example, threatened to target their houses if they discovered that one of their neighbours was being robbed. For that reason, the authorities of various communities and young catechists like him at that time, called

the community to form a *ronda* like that which had been created in Chota (interview, Neptali Vasquez, April 2005).

37. This draws on Thorp (2010).
38. The community of Tintaya Marquiri, for example, lost all its lands. The collective memory is that they 'took us out of our houses and destroyed them.' Interview with Aquilino Ccapa and Eduardo Cutimerma, leaders from Tintaya Marquiri (4 August 2005).
39. CAA created a 'mining ombudsman', a staff member whose full-time job was to work with all sides in attempting reconciliation in such conflicts. She spent many months on the Tintaya case.
40. Interview with Lucio Rios, General Manager of Tintaya mine at the time (4 September 2005).
41. Interview with Jesús Llamoctanta from El Tambo in Bambamarca (4 March 2005).
42. We find very useful the distinction between practical and strategic interest made by Molyneux (1985).
43. The huge violence precipitated by Sendero Luminoso, the Maoist-inspired movement which arose in the early 1980s, did not mobilize vast sectors of the indigenous who rapidly rejected Sendero's authoritarian discourse, though ethnicity was key in the way violence unfolded with 75 per cent of those killed of indigenous origin.
44. The *ronderos* in Cajamarca felt no commonality with the indigenous populations of the South. In Cajamarca, peasants have passed through a deeper process of racial and cultural *mestizaje*. They do not speak an indigenous language or live according to the principles of communal land property, but they retain several communal Andean characteristics in the reproduction of their everyday life, such as the logic of reciprocity, communal links, institutions and values for marriage, labour, production and communal work (Yrigoyen 2002).
45. In Molyneux and Razavi (2002: 283 and fn8).
46. There is some evidence at the time of writing of a renewed presence of and recruitment by Sendero, however, with a new and ominous link to the drugs activity.
47. Interview with Héctor Merino Gutiérrez, President of the Fruit Growers Association of the Valley of Huanta (13 May 2005).
48. Though they were good at this. One of the members of the group we interviewed gave us a brilliant description of the events of International Women's day 1985, when they had to force themselves on the attention of the Municipality of Lima, since Venegas was refusing them recognition. They took advantage of the big meeting in Lima to celebrate the day, smuggling themselves in small groups into the municipality, secretly clutching food supplies to be able to settle down to a hunger strike, carefully placing women and children on the edge of the group. By 8pm that evening they had their recognition (group interview with the community of Huanta Dos, 8 November 2005).
49. Dr Venegas tells how once the march was launched, the inhabitants of Mariátegui, alerted by his staff, moved quickly to flatten the whole settlement of Huanta Dos. When the march arrived at his office and he told them Huanta Dos was no more, they turned around in panic to get back to defend what was left (interview with Oscar Venegas, 18 August 2005).

50. He tells how he was on the point of closing a deal with the Dutch Royal family when an unpleasant incident occurred during the visit of their representative, and the deal collapsed (interview with Oscar Venegas, 18 August 2005).
51. In 2001, *ronderos* from Bambamarca, Chota y Chugur demonstrated in the central plaza of Cajamarca to protest over the death of trout in the Llaucano River caused by Yanacocha's acid mine drainage. They blocked the highway to the mine and eventually set on fire the office of Yanacocha. A Forum for Dialogue (*Mesa de Dialogo*) was created, but no results were achieved. In 2002, the *rondas* again took the central Plaza of Cajamarca and blocked the highway to the mine for 4 days. In this case, they were protesting because the government's report on the Llaucano River case insisted that the death of the trout was caused by asphyxia, not contamination. Another dialogue forum was built to mitigate the tension but no outcome was reached. Finally, in 2004, the *rondas* were key in the mobilizations against the exploration of a new mining site in Cajamarca. The protest lasted for two weeks and as a consequence Yanacocha stopped its exploration permit. However, the conflict is still ongoing.
52. According to Zarzar (1991), at the beginning of the 1990s four regional confederations claimed to represent the *rondas* of Bambamarca, two connected to APRA and two to factions to the left. Although the *ronderos* reached unification, the new elected president (from the left) was kidnapped and tortured by a committee of *ronderos* who were dissatisfied with the unification.
53. According to Starn (1999) and Gitlizt and Rojas (1983) the *rondas* have a significant consensus at community level but confront each other at regional level. The centre of these conflicts often is party competition (APRA, Patria Roja, Accion Popular) for regional offices and to achieve the prevalence of their discourse.
54. Interview with Aquilino Ccapa from Tintaya Marquiri (4 October 2005).
55. Interview, president of the Assembly of Tintaya Marquiri, Marta Chirme, Espinar (13 August 2008).
56. Interview with members of the Frente, David Alvarez and Alberto Chani Chani, Espinar (11 August 2008).
57. Interview, Oscar Mollehuanca, former Mayor of Espinar, Espinar (11 August 2008).
58. The former director in charge of community relations used to spend time 'on the ground' listening to views of community members. The management of Xstrata has not seen the importance of building trust in this manner.
59. Our interviewees explained how violence needed to be nicely judged: enough to get attention at the national level, but not enough to risk repression.
60. See Blondet in Molyneux and Razavi (2002: 303) for a detailed account.
61. Carmen Lora, interview, Lima (27 November 2007).
62. Pina Huaman, interview, Lima (30 November 2007).
63. Benedicta Serrano, interview, Lima (29 November 2007). She finished her term as president of the *Junta Directiva* of the Federation of People's Kitchens in 1994.
64. Maruja Barrig, interview, Lima (27 November 2007).
65. Benedicta Serrano, interview, Lima (29 November 2007).

66. See Blondet in Molyneux and Razavi (2002).
67. Benedicta Serrano described her heart-searching eloquently in interview. She finally decided that the view of a wise personal adviser was correct: "politics happens on the inside. Go in but don't allow yourself to be contaminated" (the Spanish was '*manchada*' – stained).
68. Virginia Vargas, interview, Lima (3 December 2007).

9
Conclusion

The newly elected National Congress in Peru opened its first session in July 2006 with controversy when two congresswomen, María Sumire and Hilaria Supa, insisted on using their original language – Quechua – to take their oaths of office. When Sumire pronounced the vows in Quechua, the president of the ceremony interrupted her twice, and asked her three times over to repeat the vows. Some congress members expressed dissatisfaction: 'If I were in Machu Picchu and did not understand Quechua, I would have to conform; but in the Congress, the official language is Spanish.'[1] According to article No. 48 of the Constitution of Peru, indigenous languages are official in territories where these languages predominate. Although in the Congress the majority of members speak Spanish, Sumire and Supe argued that they represented Peru's large numbers of indigenous and Quechua speakers. Some newspapers covered the news for a couple of days, but for the most part the controversy remained at the level of anecdote.

María Sumire and Hilaria Supa, elected in 2006 – together with Paulina Arpasi, elected in 2001 – are atypical characters in the Peruvian Congress. Their demands to speak in their indigenous languages, their indigenous dress and their proposals are typically seen by their colleagues in the Congress and the national media as a colourful irrelevance. Their solitude is emblematic of the weakness of indigenous politics in Peru, and of the limited presence of an indigenous voice in mainstream politics. It is also somehow emblematic of how difficult the fight has been to reshape fundamental group inequalities in Peru: in the twenty-first century indigenous demands become 'irrelevance'. Only in 2009 have natural resource conflicts begun to make a part of the agenda seem to some dangerously relevant and with the potential for a strong negative outcome.

This book has argued that we can only understand this state of affairs in the light of history and the deep embedding of inequality between groups which occurs as socioeconomic events interact with social attitudes, geography and political violence. The embedding occurs through the creation and reproduction of institutions. In this concluding chapter, we summarize our analysis of the growth and embedding of horizontal inequalities in the first section. Part of the embedding process is the failure of forces for change to coalesce and penetrate the political system in spite of the new characteristics of political 'openness'. We reflect on the failure to develop indigenous politics and on why collective action seems so limited in its impact. In the second section, we turn back to the more conceptual contribution of our analysis: the value of the HI perspective, the importance of searching out the interactions of economic, political, social and geographic factors, and the need to keep both structure and agency in a healthy tension. We end on perspectives for change: is the glass half empty or half full?

Long-Standing Group Inequalities in Peru

The growth path and the embedding of group inequalities

The embedding of group inequalities in Peru cannot be analysed separately from the growth path of the economy and society, for it is the interaction of economic, geographical, social and political factors with institutions that does the embedding, as we saw in the way the centring of the economy and polity together on the Coast, and specifically on Lima, led to policies and institutions that shaped and reshaped discrimination both against the Sierra, with a culture of the unimportance and limited possibilities of the Sierra, and within the Sierra, against indigenous people.

We have seen how the evolution of the colonial period was extremely unfavourable to the group equity we are interested in. The pattern of economic growth which emerged, out of resource endowments and the interests of the colonizers, made the overt use of discrimination, prejudice and exploitation in an ethnic form entirely rational and profitable, which cemented a social system to support the economic. The mode of interaction of society and economy meant that the need for labour created a need for control, which led to the disruption of identity elements through *reducciones*, the use of religion to maintain control, and the cultivation of ambiguity in the position of *mestizo*s. All these elements meant that the chance of successful political forces emerging to change the situation was infinitesimal. When uprisings occurred in the

18th century in Cusco, the actors lacked strength and resources, and the reaction left indigenous people in a worse situation. Repression led to the elimination of indigenous leaders. Peru was not going to see indigenous political demands for negotiation with the Colonial system.

With Independence, the confirming of Lima as the capital (rather than a Highland city), and the political dominance of white Coastal elites, reinforced a path of economic growth and a sequence of export products which never needed the Sierra or its indigenous population to be productive – just to provide cheap labour. By the twentieth century the gradual elimination of profitable export crops produced in the Sierra and Selva, such as rubber, wool and coca, which declined because of weakening international markets, further embedded the Sierra in its role as the supplier of cheap labour to the Coast. Mining remained rooted in the Sierra, but with time used progressively less labour in its operations, and increasingly purchased inputs abroad or from Lima. It was rational for Coastal elites to import food, but disastrous for the Sierra. The role of foreign capital in the economy compounded the tendency to seek integration with the international system in ways undermining to the Sierra. Multinational purchasing policies cemented the damage being done by price controls and openness to imports, as imported powdered milk and fine wheat flour provided short-term solutions to supply difficulties.

The very shift of political focus to the Coast and the lack of interest of Coastal elites in the Sierra allowed the continued dominance and renewal of the region's traditional power brokers. So '*gamonalismo*' emerged and embedded itself – the 'satraps' of the Sierra, *mestizo*s between two worlds but holding the local monopoly of power. The working out of power relations involved a forceful method of cooptation, sucking in individuals who then saw the route to their own advancement as possible through the displacement of their countrymen. Thus a 'double group inequality' emerged based in regional and ethnic hierarchies. In this new context formal and informal norms diverged, as formal policies and discourse became those of market freedoms and equality of all, while informally the norms of the colonial society persisted and won out. Now a strong shift in the political and economic structure and functioning of Peru occurred, with the emergence of Lima as pre-eminent, a shift that would shape the evolution of organizations and institutions, as well as policies. The political and economic dynamics of the first century and a half of independence constructed a huge gulf between Coast and Sierra-Selva, between white-*mestizo* and indigenous. We have seen how in the nineteenth century there were still profitable opportunities for some Sierra products – but the evolution of power relations left indigenous peoples benefiting relatively little. This was nowhere more vivid than in the wool boom of the South at the close of the century.

The war with Chile in 1879–83 formed a discontinuity in the evolution of institutions: the shock for the elite of realizing that 'the indian not the Chilean was the true threat' confirmed attitudes of discrimination and prejudice, but also created a new 'norm': political 'inclusion' and 'integration', but through education and hygiene. Assimilation was necessary to civilize the threat, in a deeply paternalistic and prejudiced context. So the education system is revealed as part of the problem as well as part of the solution, reinforcing norms and actual differences, particularly for indian women, a situation which persists into the contemporary period. The view that school is likely to be a place where indigenous girls are abused has died out very slowly, and the education system still does not do enough to imbue indigenous pupils with skills and self-esteem to match their white or *mestizo* counterparts.

As the prosperity of the Sierra suffered, so people opted to migrate. The *mestizo* elites, who might have lobbied for better infrastructure and services, increasingly based themselves in Lima. The more educated and entrepreneurial of the indigenous population moved, first to small Sierra towns and then by the 1940s in great numbers to the Coast and Lima. The damage to indigenous leadership done by the Colony and by Independence was thus compounded by the dynamics of economic growth after Independence, and more strongly as the decades passed. The interaction of economics and politics meant that indigenous people saw the route to prosperity as one of migration, to seek education and Coastal jobs, so weakening endogenous forces for change that might have fought for a stronger autonomous role of the Sierra. This process fragmented the indigenous population over time. A new and crucial gap developed within the indigenous-origin population itself, between the Andean peasant and the urban *cholo*. An important aspect of the embedding of norms is that prejudice and discrimination are characteristics within the group as well as between groups, and overlap with emerging divergent material interests, a phenomenon enhanced as the twentieth century progressed, and sharpened even more when the last and greatest primary export boom of the century took over, beginning in the final decade but gathering force in the first decade of the next century.

Through all these years a particularly perverse interaction went on in the way foreign capital interacted with local elites, providing them opportunities, and carrying out many of the functions elsewhere provided by the state. Local elites developed a symbiotic relation with foreign firms which was profitable and supportive; the resulting need for the state was for order, prudent economic management and exchange rates favouring exports – not for a developmental state as in Chile to diversify the economy and foster opportunities elsewhere. This had long-run consequences for the politics shaping state formation and learning by doing, and was responsible for a lack of adequate state response to the developmental challenges of the Sierra, even when there was political will. Elites with good will perceived a problem in group inequalities, and pushed education as the solution, but failed to understand that education superimposed on inequality and discrimination, in many ways reinforces them and so becomes part of the problem. But the myth of education as the solution persisted for a century – supported by international thinking and advice and money – so enabling people of good will to think they were on the way to solving the issue of group inequalities.

In the last third of the twentieth century dramatic changes occurred with what might seem some opening up of possibilities. The discontinuity represented by the Velasco regime in itself, and the economic and political stalemate to which it was responding, opened up a time of change and radical action, which might have reshaped HIs. But we have shown how policies interacted with economic and social characteristics to produce perverse results. The most significant new policy of the 1970s was a radical land reform, which perversely increased conflicts and resentments and allowed Sendero an entry point, above all in Ayacucho and the surrounding departments. Although Sendero never used an ethnic discourse, its tactics and message exploited the vulnerability of indigenous people. A vulnerability rooted in previous exploitation and domination. The culture of discrimination and prejudice allowed both political violence and its repression 'legitimately' to inflict disproportionate suffering on indigenous people. The old norms of discrimination and prejudice were reinforced by the association of 'Andean indigenous' with 'terrorist'. Over the same period, the emergence of a serious legal leftwing movement was itself disrupted over the issue of recourse to arms and what view to take of Sendero: this came on top of the Left's prior failure to mobilize successfully in rural areas. In spite of its significant support for networking and organization, unfortunately the work of the Left in the South helped to build a vertical and ideological structure, rather than a forum for indigenous awareness and organization.

Meanwhile, the legacy of an ineffective state which, as we have seen, developed out of the nature of the export economy, now compounded international shocks and natural disasters, and by the late 1980s hyperinflation was added to terrorist violence, creating escalating urban poverty and unstable and generally unfavourable prices for rural producers. The combination of economic recession and political violence weakened democratic structures and the party system through these years. While these were 'bads' for all Peruvians, the failure to find viable alternatives for the Sierra and to create an effective state presence in the Highlands and job opportunities throughout the economy, all contributed to trap indigenous and *cholo* people ever more firmly in their situation of inequality.

The 'Fujishock' brought abrupt stabilization and a sharp swing to neo-liberal policies, fostered by a mining boom, plus a political closing down. Each element in that spelt an increase in HIs, as forced migration swelled the urban informal sector, indigenous communities found themselves displaced by mining companies, and any residual political voice or constructive self-help activity was repressed or co-opted. The only compensating factor – though not enough – was significant building of infrastructure in the Sierra. The swing back to an economy of extractives drew indigenous communities into new forms of conflict and instances of state failure, while the inherited institutions of the past tended to reproduce and consolidate inequality. Even what seemed initially a success often subsequently failed. A good example, as we have seen, was the agreement in Espinar over the Tintaya mine. Initial good outcomes providing generous payments to affected communities then struggled given the inherited macro–micro structures and lack of local capacities, in addition to inherited 'negative' norms such as suspicion and distrust.

Indigenous collective action and the impenetrability of the political system

The previous section has described the historical 'layering' which has resulted in the contemporary economic and political terrain for the collective action, by indigenous people and others, that might have changed the situation of enduring inequality. One early hypothesis of this study was that the weakness of indigenous political organization might have its origin in an absence of collective action at the micro and meso level, but we have learned that this is not the case. On the contrary: we certainly cannot conclude that any fundamental weakness in the propensity for collective action among indigenous people explains the durability of HIs. We have found impressive instances of vigorous and well-organized collective action, a product of leadership, immediate need and a strong sense of community, aided where it existed by low levels of differentiation. Catalysts tended to be important in the provincial experiences though less so in Lima. The strong group identities of the *ronderos*, and the strength of the perceived communal wrong in the case of Espinar, were helped by the relatively low level of differentiation. In Bambamarca, as with the people's kitchens, there were positive roles played by the progressive wing of the Church and by NGOs. In the Southern Highlands case of Espinar, an early positive role of the political parties in creating networks and supporting the peasant federation, weakened with time and eventually became negative.

Felt need and learning by doing also enabled a group to deepen its agenda beyond immediate practical issues such as security or food for one's children. Thus the women of the *comedores* found out on the job what skills they needed, and set about acquiring them. The very context of 'the group' in the *comedor* led naturally to group reflection – aided sometimes by watchful NGOs. The *ronderos* too went through similar experiences, seeing and gradually understanding different levels of injustice. Accumulated experience over time, and a place and opportunity for discussion helped (for them the framework of the community assembly, or *asamblea*).

Nonetheless, when collective action attempted to go from the micro to the next level it typically failed, as a result of the institutional context and the nature of politics. The principal reason for this, emerging from these cases, is that community level action needs to interact with an intermediate level to achieve change successfully. If the intermediate level is controlled by political parties that are fragmented, corrupt, and prone to personalism and favouritism, then the connections go sour and trans-communal structures are difficult to build. The growing *cholo* population on the Coast could have redefined the face of politics and brought strength to indigenous collective action, but this was not to be – or not yet. We have explained how the mainstream political model, centrist and based in Lima, was always clientelist and personalist. But at least by the post-World-War-Two period there were significant political parties with a following. But as the economic model ran into crisis, so the political system was seen as failing to deliver a solution. From the military coup of Velasco, the traditional party system came under threat and was increasingly discredited. The coincidence of the return to democracy and to the market paradoxically further weakened the most prominent party, the APRA.

We have seen how the democratic state of the early 1980s in fact related to indigenous organizations through the paternalistic and vertical brokerage of the political parties. This perverse brokerage, particularly by the parties of the Left, was possible because of the organizational and symbolic resources that these parties had accumulated. We have explained how Velasco's policies on land and the suppression of party politics spurred a foundational association between the Left and indigenous people's organizations, with strong consequences in the highly ideological class-based orientation of indigenous political identities and the verticality of their organizations. The consequences of the democratic period of the 1980s are many, but two are central to the embedding of inequality: weak autonomous structures and disillusion with political collective action. After the collapse of the parties, just when most needed, structures were so weak that other clientelistic forms developed and were accepted. These forms were fragmented, immediate, short-term and pragmatic. Meanwhile disillusion was evident: leaders or entrepreneurs, like Crecencio Merma, did not feel motivated to take the risk of new loyalties, and did not want to be distrusted in a context where all politics is labelled 'dirty'. The way that the state relates to indigenous people, rejects, dismisses and patronizes their organizations, creates an arena of mobilization where the main characteristic is polarization, and eventually may be violence. Without accountable representation, ethnic politics and conflict in the way it emerges are only likely to feed the embedding of inequality, rather than to open the door for a new path.

Thus at the grassroots, incipient or regionally confined political protest was fragmented and divided. While some of the groups were able to overcome much of the damage resulting from the divisiveness of the Velasco agrarian reform, and provide signs of potential national mobilization, the required brokerage was not available. Moreover, the early associations made with the Left inhibited the construction of an autonomous brokerage. The alternative of a healthy leftwing party ran into the morass of excess dogmatism and ideology, and became in its turn not only deeply divided and incapable of opening new spaces of indigenous leadership, as we have seen, but also incapable of elaborating pragmatic solutions that touched the needs of the marginal populations (in town or country) for economic opportunities.

The legacy of political violence and the repression it generated now interacted with the fragmentation of social movements and the nature of politics itself. The fear of organizing, under the threat of reprisal or repression, accentuated the role of clientelistic relations. The suspicion and divisiveness resulting from the war weakened organization. When democracy returned, there were few options. Parties and candidates came and went. Support for *Fujimorismo* remained strong, above all in rural areas, because he had brought order and built schools and clinics. Progressive leftwing candidates got minuscule support in the elections of the new century. Ollanta Humala garnered votes to the point of terrifying the Lima middle class in the 2006 elections, but then his party split and has since been out of sight.

Contributions to the Analysis of Inequality

The relevance of group – or horizontal – inequality

Through all of the above, we can trace the relevance of groups, and in that the relevance also of their relative political, socioeconomic and cultural position. We therefore conclude that if inequality is to be shifted, we need to measure and monitor group inequalities, and understand as far as possible the dynamics of group interactions.

Politics, of course, is based on groups. Political group inequalities matter in themselves, but also, if a group is unable to represent its interests, then the chance of the inequities of all sorts suffered by that group being remedied is much reduced. We have seen the importance of the cumulative absence of an indigenous politics or an indigenous political voice in the Peruvian system. A history which built a culture of discrimination, clientelism and verticality stacked the odds against group challenges to that system – unless by violence. We have seen how when that came to be perceived by certain groups as the only escape route, the result was terrible repression, made worse by group inequalities and the culture of prejudice in which they were embedded. Such violence and violent repression had feedbacks on prejudice and discrimination and severely weakened social movements.

A second aspect of the importance of groups that has emerged as crucial in the embedding of inequality is where group inequalities overlap. Suffering political, socioeconomic and cultural inequality together makes it harder to break out, the incidence of frustration greater and the possibility of violence as a result higher (this is a CRISE finding; see Stewart 2008). But also, belonging to overlapping and discriminated groups can produce an even deeper embedding. For example, ethnicity and class inequalities overlap to a large extent in Peru, as we have often observed. Sendero used a rhetoric of class to mobilize. The fact of overlap meant that those who responded to the rhetoric in the key regions where Sendero operated were predominantly indigenous, and as such vulnerable to Sendero's techniques of recruitment because of their situation, as we have shown. Their ethnicity then meant that their treatment, both at the hands of the army and police and of Sendero itself, was peculiarly vicious – a deep and nasty vicious circle emanating from the overlap of inequalities and from the depth of discrimination and prejudice in Peruvian society.

A further example of overlap, and increased significance because of that, is the connection we have made between regional inequality and ethnic inequality. Through a number of crucial decades, the Sierra has been discriminated against in national policy making and in the attitudes of the white/*mestizo* Coastal elite – but the indigenous living in the Sierra have been doubly discriminated and unequal, suffering also the burden of *gamonalismo*, subordinate and lacking in respect, often abused and exploited.

Another example of such overlap is that of ethnicity and gender. Indigenous women have lower levels of education and fewer opportunities than their male counterparts. As indigenous men found jobs in town, the women remained to manage the land. Low levels of education and limited Spanish exposed the *comedores* to internal division and distrust. Family attitudes limited daughters' roles and expectations. Indigenous girls today are faring better than their mothers in years of education, but the education levels of young adult indigenous women still show the effect of history. Indigenous girls may still not go to school – remember the woman whose own abuse as a child in school led to her keeping her daughters at home. And the culture embedded through the school may even today still fail to empower.

A further aspect of the need for group-based analysis is the importance of discrimination and prejudice: always a matter of groups. You may *dislike* an individual and treat him or her unfairly: if you *discriminate* it is because of group characteristics. We have seen how discrimination and prejudice have been key to the impotence of education to change the balance of capabilities and power. We have shown how a situation of inequality, overlapping HIs and discrimination eroded the power of education. There was eventually significant progress in education – long the prized instrument of the development agencies and multilaterals. Indigenous men are now close to their white/*mestizo* counterparts in years of secondary and primary education – and even progressing at the tertiary level. Yet so far this is not reflected as might have been expected in economic opportunities or presence in professional and public sector roles.

Discrimination can consolidate an economic model in a 'convenient' way: this was true of the colonial system but it can also be true today.

We have seen how steep-sided the pyramid of employment opportunities has become with time: jobs need to be rationed and there is some evidence of direct discrimination in the labour market on ethnic grounds (Ñopo *et al.* 2004). More pervasive is the indirect effect of support to a system which delivers unequal capacity-building and supports the 'inferiority' of the products of indigenous agriculture, preferring products such as fine wheat flour. We have seen how migrants themselves absorb and reproduce discrimination, as the motor mechanic of Chapter 2 did when his fellow countrymen wanted to buy a car. Precious economic opportunities need to be conserved.

The importance of timing

Political and social structures, interacting with the economic structure along the course of the historical experience of societies, have shaped the institutions and norms that have reproduced group inequalities and also have inhibited the creation of those institutions which could have protected the interests of the excluded or the partially included. Over time, there has been change. However, each period of change has made group inequalities different, more complex, often more hidden – but has not removed them. We have seen the power of actors attempting education in the early 20th century, the ending of the landlords and the achieving of land reform in the 1970s, and the achievement of the indigenous vote in the 1980s. Yet, education policies were undermined by *gamonalismo*, land reform by the lack of state capacity to bring new forms of opportunity and authority to the Sierra, the vote by the verticality of the brokerage. Actors have attempted and brought change, both intentionally and unintentionally. But institutional legacies from each previous period, interacting with the structures of economy and geography, with the institutions, with the dynamics of culture and actors, have not avoided change, but directed it in a perverse path.

Thus it is over time that agents have interacted with structures and have both shaped and been shaped by them. To understand how to think about policies that might support equity-building change given such a powerful set of structural forces, we have argued that we need a full understanding of the historical legacies and how they have shaped and conditioned actors and their responses over time. This is the task we have tried to undertake in this book. Nonetheless, we have also emphasized the need to balance in a healthy tension the elements of structure and agency. Thus our understanding is fundamentally institutional and structural, but we do see genuine space for the role of strong actors who could have changed the path. It is the interaction of structure, institutions and agency which has shaped life, decade by decade, in a direction where many potential agents of constructive change have been disempowered.

Is the Glass Half Empty or Half Full?

Finally, are there grounds for hope? We have seen the weight of the negative story – more than a half-empty glass, it seems. Yet there are signs of change. We began the book with the account of the café closed by INDECOPI: such actions have continued and the Defensoría is now monitoring points of tension around mining in order to pre-empt HIs exploding into conflict. Conflict has indeed exploded in the area outside this book: the Selva, over oil, and the political ripples from the resulting violence continue at the time of writing. Fujimori went on trial and has been convicted of corruption and human rights violations, and an early poll showed 55 per cent of the population approving of the trial. The Truth and Reconciliation Commission was set up and successfully reported in 2003 with 8,000 pages of extraordinary testimonies and analysis. Grassroots' contestation of mining companies over damage to livelihoods is vigorous in many places. María Sumire, Hilaria Supa and Paulina Arpasi made it to the Congress as indigenous women. Self-help literacy programmes are producing a new form of engagement and empowerment among indigenous communities. Gaston Acurio is leading a culture shift to value traditional Peruvian ingredients in the kitchen – not a minor matter when we recall the importance of food import policies over the decades to our vicious circles. We regard such important acts and actors as phenomena that could, if given leadership, change the face of Peru.

But significant reduction of inequality will not come about unless the depth of the embedding of group inequalities is faced. The interactions of the economic model, the geographical structure of the country, the modus operandi of institutions and their legacies shaped in a specific history, and the inherited weakness of politics, particularly of the capacity of the system to give voice to the marginal groups, all continue today and reinforce each other. International forces as well as history continue to make it difficult to modify mining dependence or spread its benefits more widely across groups. Multiple discriminations still impede the democratic flourishing we would all like to see. And two central difficult aspects remain: the need for a development strategy which provides more economic opportunities for the marginalized groups, and the need to revive party organization and life in a way that provides political opportunities.

Note

1. Martha Hildebrandt, a member of the National Congress, vice-president of the Commission of Ethics in the National Congress and Permanent Secretary of the Peruvian Academy of Language.

Bibliography

Ainsworth, M. P. (1920). 'Indian Legislation in Peru', *The Hispanic American Historical Review,* vol. 3(4 (Nov.)): 509–34.

Alberti, G. and Sánchez, R. (1974). *Poder y Conflicto Social en el Valle del Mantaro, 1900–1974,* Lima: Instituto de Estudios Peruanos.

Aljovín de Losada, C. and López, S. (2005). *Historia de las Elecciones en el Perú. Estudios Sobre el Gobierno Representativo,* Lima: Instituto de Estudios Peruanos.

Allport G. (1954). *The Nature of Prejudice,* Cambridge, Mass: Addison-Wesley Pub.

Alvarado, J. (1989). 'Instrumentos de Política en la Reforma Agraria'. *Debate Agrario,* vol. 7: 33–61, Lima: Cepes.

Andean Report (1999) March, vol. 2, London: Latin American Monthly Newsletters.

Andean Report (1992) July, vol. 30, London: Latin American Monthly Newsletters.

Anderson, B. (1983). *Imagined Communities. Reflections on the Origin and Spread of Nationalism,* London: Verso.

Angell, A., Lowden, P. and Thorp, R. (2001). *Decentralizing Development: The Political Economy of Institutional Change in Colombia and Chile,* New York; Oxford: Oxford University Press.

Ansión, J. (2006). *Education in Peru: Builder of Democracy or Reproducer of Inequalities?,* conference paper for the Latin America Workshop, Santa Cruz de la Sierra, September 18–20, CRISE, University of Oxford, available at http://www.crise.ox.ac.uk/workshops.shtml#latam.

Apel, K. (1957). *De la Hacienda a la Comunidad: La Sierra de Piura 1934–1990,* Lima, Instituto de Estudios Peruanos/Instituto Francés de Estudios Andinos.

Arce, E. (1985). 'Comunidades Campesinas y Políticas del Estado: Década del 70'. *Socialismo y Participación,* vol. 12: 81–91, Lima: Cedep.

Ares, B. and Gruzinski, S. (1997). *Entre dos Mundos: Fronteras Culturales y Agentes Mediadores,* Sevilla: Escuela de Estudios Hispanoamericanos.

Assadourian, C. (1994). *Transiciones hacia el Sistema Colonial Andino.* México, D.F.: Colegio de México, Fideicomiso Historia de las Américas; Lima: Instituto de Estudios Peruanos.

Balibar E. (1991). 'Is there a Neo-Racism?', in E. Balibar *et al.* (eds), *Race, Nation, Class. Ambiguous Identities,* London; New York: Verso, pp. 17–18.

Barrón, M. (2008). *Gender and Ethnic Inequalities in Latin America: a Multidimensional Comparison of Bolivia, Guatemala and Peru,* working paper no. 32, CRISE, University of Oxford, available at http://www.crise.ox.ac.uk/pubs.shtml.

Barth, F. (1969). *Ethnic Groups and Boundaries. The Social Organization of Culture Difference,* Bergen: Universitetsforlaget; London: Allen & Unwin.

Basadre, J. and Yepes, E. (2003). *Memoria y Destino del Perú: Textos Esenciales,* Lima: Fondo Editorial del Congreso del Perú.

Basadre, J. (1980). *Elecciones y Centralismo en el Perú: Apuntes para un Esquema Histórico,* Lima: Centro de Investigación de la Universidad del Pacífico.

Bates, R. (1971). *Unions, Parties and Political Development. A Study of Mineworkers in Zambia,* New Haven: Yale University Press.

Bates, R., De Fígueiredo, R. and Weingast, B. (1998). 'The Politics of Interpretation: Rationality, Culture and Transition', *Politics and Society,* vol. 26(4): 603–42.

Bedford, R. and Snow, D. (2000). 'Framing Processes and Social Movements and Assessment', *Annual Review of Sociology,* vol. 26: 611–39.

Blondet, C. (2002). 'The Devil's Deal: Women's Political Participation and Authoritarianism in Peru', in M. Molyneux *et al.* (eds), *Gender Justice, Development and Rights*, New York; Oxford: Oxford University Press, pp. 277–305.

Boesten, J. (2003). 'Poor Women in Peru: Reproducers of Poverty and Poverty Relievers', *Women's Studies Quarterly*, Fall 2003.31, 3/4 pp.113–128.

Bourque, S. and Palmer, D. (1975). 'Transforming the Rural Sector: Government Policy and Peasant Response', in A. Lowenthal (ed.), *The Peruvian Experiment: Continuity and Change under Military Rule,* Princeton, NJ: Princeton University Press, pp. 179–219.

Bourricaud, F. (1970). *Power and Society in Contemporary Peru,* Translated by Paul Stevenson, London: Faber.

Brass, P. (1997). *Theft of an Idol: Text and Context in the Representation of Collective Violence,* Princeton, NJ: Princeton University Press.

Brodsky, J and Oser, J. (1968). 'Land Tenure in Peru: A CIDA study', *American Journal of Economics and Sociology,* vol. 27 (4): 405–21.

Brown, K. (2008). 'La Transformación de la Real Hacienda Peruana bajo los Borbones: El Caso de Arequipa', in A. Espinoza *et al.* (eds), *Arequipa a Través del Tiempo. Política, Cultura y Sociedad,* Arequipa: Centro de Estudios Arequipeños/ Universidad Nacional de San Agustín.

Brubaker, R., Loveman, M. and Stamatov, P. (2004). 'Ethnicity as Cognition', *Theory and Society,* vol. 33 (1): 31–64.

Burga, M. and Flores Galindo, A. (1979). *Apogeo y Crisis de la República Aristocrática: Oligarquía, Aprismo y Comunismo, 1895–1931,* Lima: Ediciones Rikchay.

Burt, J. M. (1997) 'Political Violence and the Grassroots in Lima, Peru', in D. Chalmers *et al.* (eds), *The New Politics of Inequality in Latin America: Rethinking Participation and Representation,* Oxford; New York: Oxford University Press, pp. 281–309.

Caballero, J. M. (1981). *Economía Agraria de la Sierra Peruana Antes de la Reforma Agraria de 1969,* Lima, Instituto de Estudios Peruanos.

Cameron, M. and Levitsky, S. (2003). 'Democracy Without Parties? Political Parties and Regime Change in Fujimori's Peru', *Latin American Politics and Society,* vol. 45(3): 1–33.

Cánepa, G. (2008). *The Fluidity of Ethnic Identities in Peru,* working paper no. 46, CRISE, University of Oxford, available at: www.crise.ox.ac.uk/pubs.shtml

___ (1998). *Máscara, Transformación e Identidad en los Andes: La Fiesta de la Virgen del Carmen Paucartambo.* Cuzco; Lima: Pontificia Universidad Católica del Perú.

Caravedo, B. (1978). *Desarrollo Desigual y Lucha Política en el Perú, 1948–1956: La Burguesía Arequipeña y el Estado Peruano,* Lima: Instituto de Estudios Peruanos.

___ (1976). *Burguesía e Industria en el Perú, 1933–1945.* Lima: Instituto de Estudios Peruanos.

Carrión, J. and Zárate, P. (2006). *La Cultura Política de la Democracia en el Perú: 2006,* Lima: Universidad de Vanderbilt/Instituto de Estudios Peruanos.

Cohen, J. L. (1985). 'Strategy or Identity: New Theoretical Paradigms and Contemporary Social Movements', *Social Research,* vol. 52 (4 (winter)): 663–716.

Comisión de la Verdad y Reconciliación (2003) *Final Report,* Available at: www.cverdad.org.pe.

Conaghan, C. (2002). 'Cashing in on Authoritarianism: Media Collusion in Fujimori's Peru', *Harvard International Journal of Press/Politics,* vol. 7 (1 (winter)): 115–25.

Congreso Nacional del Perú, Lista de Congresistas de la República, 1992–2011, Dirección General Parlamentaria, available at http://www.congreso.gob.pe/organizacion/pleno.asp?mode=Pleno.

Confederación Campesina del Perú-CCP. (1974). 'Selección de las Conclusiones del IV Congreso de la Confederación Campesina del Perú', reprinted in H. Pease (ed.), *Material de Trabajo del Curso Realidad Social Peruana,* Lima: Pontificia Universidad Católica del Perú, pp. 32–43.

___ (1975). *Informes y Mociones del II Congreso Extraordinario Nacional Campesino,* July, 18–20, Querecotillo, Piura: CCP.

Consejo Nacional de la Magistratura. (2004) *Informe de Consejeros Nombrados 1995–2004,* data base acceded in 2007 at http://www.cnm.gob.pe/cnm/.

Contreras, C. and Cueto, M. (1999). *Historia del Perú Contemporáneo,* Lima: Instituto de Estudios Peruanos/ Red para el Desarrollo de Estudios Peruanos.

Contreras, C. (1996). *Maestros, Mistis and Campesinos en el Perú Rural del Siglo XX,* documento de Trabajo no. 80, Serie Historia 16, Lima: Instituto de Estudios Peruanos.

___ (1996a) 'La Descentralización Fiscal en el Perú después de la Guerra con Chile 1886–1895', *Relaciones. Estudios de Historia y Sociedad,* vol. 67/68, pp. 203–231.

___ (1988). 'Estado Republicano y Tributo Indígena en la Sierra Central en la Post Independencia', *Revista de Indias,* vol. 48 (182/183): 517–50.

Contreras, M. (2000) 'Bolivia, 1900–39: Mining, Railways and Education', in E. Cardenas *et al.* (eds), *An Economic History of Twentieth-Century Latin America, Volume 1: The Export Age: The Latin American Economies in the Late Nineteenth and Early Twentieth Centuries,* London: Palgrave McMillan, pp. 188–216.

Cook, N. (1981). *Demographic Collapse: Indian Peru, 1520–1620,* Cambridge: Cambridge University Press.

Córdova, P. and Gorriti, C. L. (1989). *Apuntes para una Interpretación del Movimiento de Mujeres: los Comedores Comunales y los Comités del Vaso de Leche en Lima,* Lima: SUMBI.

Cotlear, D. (1989). *Desarrollo Campesino en los Andes: Cambio Tecnológico y Transformación Social en las Comunidades de la Sierra del Perú,* Lima: Instituto de Estudios Peruanos.

Cotler, J. (1995). 'Political Parties and the Problems of Democratic Consolidation', in S. Mainwaring *et al.* (eds), *Building Democratic Institutions: Party Systems in Latin America,* Stanford, CA: Stanford University Press, pp. 323–53.

___ (1994). *Política y Sociedad en el Perú: Cambios y Continuidades,* Lima: Instituto de Estudios Peruanos.

___ and Portocarrero, F. (1976). 'Organizaciones Campesinas en el Perú', in J. Matos Mar (ed.), *Hacienda, Comunidad y Campesinado en el Perú,* Lima: Instituto de Estudios Peruanos, pp. 267–310.

___ (1970). 'La Mecánica de la Dominación Interna y del Cambio Social en el Perú', in J. Matos Mar *et al* (eds), *El Perú Actual, Sociedad y Política*, Mexico DF: Instituto de Investigaciones Sociales de la Universidad Autónoma de México, pp. 47–87.

Crabtree, J., and Thomas, J. (1998). *Fujimori's Peru: The Political Economy*, London: Institute of Latin American Studies.

Craig, W. (1969). 'Peru: The Peasant Movement of La Convención', in H. A. Landsberger (ed.), *Latin American Peasant Movements*, Ithaca, NY: Cornell University Press, pp. 274–96.

Cueto, M. (1997). *El Regreso de las Epidemias: Salud y Sociedad en el Perú del Siglo XX*, Lima: Instituto de Estudios Peruanos.

Cueto, S., Jacoby, E. and Pollitt, E. (1997). 'Time on Task and Educational Activities in Rural Schools in Peru', *Revista Latinoamericana de Estudios Educativos*, vol. 27 (3), pp. 105–120.

Cueva, H. and Millán, A. (2000). *The Women's Food Organizations and their Relationship with the Government*, report for the Comparative Regional Project, Civil Society and Democratic Governability in the Andes and the Southern Cone, Lima: Ford Foundation/Pontificia Universidad Católica del Perú.

Davies, T. M. (1974). *Indian Integration in Peru. A Half Century of Experience, 1900–1948*, Lincoln: University of Nebraska Press.

De la Cadena, M. (2000). *Indigenous Mestizos: The Politics of Race and Culture in Cuzco, Peru, 1919–1991*, Durham: Duke University Press.

Deere, C. D. (1990). *Household and Class Relations: Peasants and Landlords in Northern Peru*, Berkeley, CA: University of California Press.

Degregori C. I. (1992). 'Campesinado Andino y Violencia, Balance de una Década de Estudios en Perú' in C. I. Degregori *et al.* (eds), *El Problema Agrario en Debate, SEPIA* IV, Lima: SEPIA, pp. 413–39.

___ (1990). *El Surgimiento de Sendero Luminoso: Ayacucho, 1969–1979*, Lima: Instituto de Estudios Peruanos.

___ , Blondet, C. and Lynch, N. (1986). *Conquistadores de un Nuevo Mundo: de Invasores a Ciudadanos en San Martín de Porres*, Lima: Instituto de Estudios Peruanos.

Del Mastro, M. (1979). *El Movimiento Campesino Cusqueño: 1968–1978*, dissertation, Sociología, Pontificia Universidad Católica del Perú, Lima.

Dew, E. M. (1969). *Politics in the Altiplano: the Dynamics of Change in Rural Peru*, Austin: Institute of Latin American Studies/University of Texas Press.

Dirección Nacional de Estadística y Censos del Perú. (1969) *Anuario Estadístico del Perú. 1966*, Lima: Dirección Nacional de Estadística y Censos, etc.

___ (1966). *Resultados de los Censos Nacionales de Población, Vivienda y Agropecuario de 1961*, Lima: Dirección Nacional de Estadística y Censos, etc.

___ (1965). *Primer Censo Nacional Agropecuario de 1961*, Lima: Dirección Nacional de Estadística y Censos, etc.

___ (1945). *Extracto Estadístico, Resultados de 1943*, Lima, Dirección Nacional de Estadística y Censos, etc.

Drake, P. W. (1989). *The Money Doctor in the Andes: the Kemmerer Missions 1923–1933*, Durham, N. C.: Duke University Press.

Durand, F. and Thorp, R. (1999). 'La Reforma Tributaria: Análisis del Experimento SUNAT', in *El Perú de Fujimori*, J. Crabtree *et al.* (eds), Lima: Universidad del Pacífico/Instituto de Estudios Peruanos.

Elster, J. (1999). *Alchemies of the Mind: Rationality and the Emotions*, Cambridge: Cambridge University Press.

Escobal, J. and Ponce, C. (2002). *The Benefits of Rural Roads: Enhancing Income Opportunities for the Rural Poor,* documento de trabajo no. 40, Lima: Grade.

Ewig, C. (2004). 'Piecemeal but Innovative: Health Sector Reform in Peru', in R. Kaufman *et al.* (eds), *Crucial Needs, Weak Incentives: Social Sector Reform, Democratization, and Globalization in Latin America,* Baltimore: Johns Hopkins University Press/Woodrow Wilson Centre.

Figueroa, A. (2008). *Education, Labour Markets and Inequality in Peru,* working paper no. 48, CRISE, University of Oxford, available at: www.crise.ox.ac.uk/pubs.shtml.

___ and Barrón, M. (2005). *Inequality, Ethnicity and Social Disorder in Peru,* working paper no. 8, CRISE, University of Oxford, available at: www.crise.ox.ac.uk/pubs.shtml.

___ (2001). *Reformas en Sociedades Desiguales: la Experiencia Peruana.* Lima: Pontificia Universidad Católica del Perú.

___ (2001a). 'Social Exclusion as a Distribution Theory' in E. Gacitua *et al.* (eds), *Social Exclusion and Poverty Reduction in Latin* America, Washington, DC: The World Bank.

___ (1973). *El Impacto de las Reformas Actuales sobre la Distribución de Ingresos en el Perú,* conference paper, Seminario Internacional Distribución del Ingreso y Desarrollo, Marzo 12–16, Lima: CISEPA.

Fisher, J. R. (1977). *Silver Mines and Silver Miners in Colonial Peru, 1776–1824,* Liverpool: Centre for Latin-American Studies/University of Liverpool.

Flores Galindo, A. (1986). *Buscando un Inca: Identidad y Utopia en los Andes: Ensayo,* Ciudad de La Habana: Ediciones Casa de las Américas.

___ (1976). *Túpac Amaru II-1780. Sociedad Colonial y Sublevaciones Populares,* Lima: Retablo de Papel Ediciones.

Franco, C. (1991). *Imágenes de la Sociedad Peruana: La Otra Modernidad,* Lima: Cedep.

Frost, M., Forste, R. and Hass, D. (2005). 'Maternal Education and Child Nutritional Status in Bolivia: Finding the links', *Social Science and Medicine,* vol. 60 (2): 395–40.

Gamson, W. A. (1992). *Talking politics,* Cambridge: Cambridge University Press.

García, M. E. (2005). *Making Indigenous Citizens: Identities, Education, and Multicultural Development in Peru,* Stanford, CAl.: Stanford University Press.

___ (2003). 'The Politics of Community: Education, Indigenous Rights, and Ethnic Mobilization in Peru', *Latin American Perspectives,* vol. 30 (70): 70–95.

García-Sayán, D. (1982). *Tomas de Tierras en el Perú,* Lima: Cepes.

Geertz, C. (1973). *The Interpretation of Cultures; Selected Essays,* New York: Basic Books.

Gellner, E. (1983). *Nations and Nationalism,* Oxford: Blackwell.

Gitlitz, J. (1998). 'Decadencia y Supervivencia de las Rondas Campesinas del Norte del Perú'. *Debate Agrario,* vol. 20: 23–53, Lima: Cepes.

___ and Rojas, T. (1983). 'Peasant Vigilante Committees in Northern Peru', *Journal of Latin American Studies,* vol. 15(1): 163–97.

Glave, L. M (1992). Vida, Símbolos y Batallas: Creación y Recreación de la Comunidad Indígena, *Cusco, siglos XVI–XX,* Lima: FCE.

Golte, J., and Adams, N. (1990). *Los Caballos de Troya de los Invasores. Estrategias Campesinas en la Conquista de la Gran Lima,* Lima: Instituto de Estudios Peruanos.

Gonzales, M. J. (1980). *Cayaltí. The Formation of a Rural Proletariat on a Peruvian Sugar Cane Plantation, 1875–1933*, doctoral dissertation, University of California at Berkeley.

Gonzáles de Olarte, E. (2000). *Neocentralismo y Neoliberalismo en el Perú*, Lima: Instituto de Estudios Peruanos.

___ (1992). *La Economía Regional de Lima: Crecimiento, Urbanización y Clases Populares*, Lima: Instituto de Estudios Peruanos.

___ (1982). *Economías Regionales del Perú*, Lima: Instituto de Estudios Peruanos.

Gootenberg, P. (1999). *Cocaine: Global Histories*, London: Routledge.

___ (1991). *Between Silver and Guano: Commercial Policy and the State in Post Independence Peru*, Princeton, N.J.: Princeton University Press.

Green, D. and R., Seher (2003). 'What Role does Prejudice Play in Ethnic Conflict?', *Annu. Rev. Polit. Sci.*, vol. 6: 509–31.

Guzmán, V. and Vargas, V. (1981). *El Campesinado en la Historia: Cronología de los Movimientos Campesinos, 1956–1964*, Lima: Ideas.

Hall, G. and Patrinos, H.A. (2006). *Indigenous Peoples, Poverty and Human Development in Latin America*, New York, NY: Palgrave Macmillan.

Hall P., and Taylor C., 'Political Science and the Three Institutionalisms', IMIFG Scientific Advisory Board Discussion Paper 96/6.

Hamilton D. and Sherman, J. (1994). 'Steoreotypes', in T. R. Srull *et al.* (eds), *Handbook of Social Cognition*, Hillsdale, NJ: L. Erlbaum Associates, pp. 1–68.

Hobsbawm, E. (1969). 'A Case of Neo-Feudalism: La Convención, Peru', *Journal of Latin American Studies*, vol. 1 (1): 31–50.

Hogg M. and McGarty C. (1990). 'Self-Categorization and Social Identity', in D. Abrams *et al.* (eds), *Social Identity Theory: Constructive and Critical Advances*, Hemel Hempstead: Harvester Wheatsheaf.

___ and Abrams, D. (1988). *Social Identifications: A Social Psychology of Intergroup Relations and Group Processes*, London: Routledge.

Huaman, J. (1987). 'Economía y Organización en los Comedores', in N. Galer *et al.* (eds), *Mujer y Comedores Populares*, Lima: SEPADC.

Hunt, S. (1977). *Real Wages and Economic Growth in Peru 1900–1940*, discussion paper no 25, Centre for Latin American Development Studies, Boston University.

___ (1974). *Direct Foreign Investment in Peru: New Rules for an Old Game*, discussion paper no.44, Woodrow Wilson School Research Program in Economic Development, Princeton University.

___ (1973). *Growth and Guano in Nineteenth Century Peru*, discussion paper no.34, Woodrow Wilson School Research Program in Economic Development, Princeton University.

Ibarra, H. (2002). 'Gamonalismo y dominación en los Andes', *Iconos Revista de Ciencias Sociales*, vol. 14: 137–147, Flacso, Quito.

Iguíñiz, J. (1984). 'Ciclos Económicos y Región en el Perú: 1971–1981' *Allpanchis Phuturinqa*, vol. 23.

Instituto Nacional de Estadística e Informática (2003). *Resultados de la Encuesta Nacional de Hogares (EHAHO), Condiciones de Vida en el Perú*, available at http://www.inei.gob.pe/.

___ (2002). *Encuesta Nacional de Hogares (ENAHO)*, available at: www.inei.gob.pe.

___ (2001). *Encuesta Nacional de Hogares (ENAHO)*, available at: www.inei.gob.pe.

INEI (Instituto Nacional de Estadísticas e Información), *Censo Nacional 1961*.

Isaacs, H. (1975). *Basic Group Identity: The Idols of the Tribe*, in *Ethnicity: Theory and Experience,* N. Glazer *et al* (eds), Cambridge, Mass.: Harvard University Press.

Jacobsen, N. (2002). 'Pensamiento Económico y Políticas Económicas en el Perú, 1885–1899: Los Límites de la Ortodoxia Liberal', in C. Contreras *et al.* (eds), *Estado y Mercado en la Formación de la Economía Peruana,* Lima: Pontificia Universidad Católica del Perú.

___ (1997). 'Liberalism and Indian Communities in Peru, 1821–1920', in R. H. Jackson (ed.), *Liberals, the Church, and Indian Peasants: Corporate Lands and the Challenge of Reform in Nineteenth-Century Spanish America,* New Mexico: University of New Mexico Press.

Jiménez, F., Aguilar, G. and Kapsoli, J. (1999). *De la Industrialización Proteccionista a la Desindustrialización Neoliberal,* Lima: CIES.

Jurado Nacional de Elecciones. (2007). *Elecciones Municipales 2006,* Lima: JNE.

___ (2003). Direcciones y Teléfonos de Alcaldes Provinciales a nivel Nacional (2002–06). Original Data from Consejo Nacional de Descentralizacion, Lima.

___ (2006). Resultados de las Elecciones Regionales y Municipales del 2006, Lima.

Kapsoli, W. (1987). *Los Movimientos Campesinos en el Perú,* Lima: Ediciones Atusparia.

Kaufman, S. (2001). *Modern Hatreds: The Symbolic Politics of Ethnic War,* Ithaca, NY; London: Cornell University Press.

Kaufman, R., and Nelson, J. (2004). *Crucial Needs, Weak Incentives: Social Sector Reform, Democratization and Globalisation in Latin America,* Washington, DC: Woodrow Wilson Center Press and Johns Hopkins University Press.

Klaren, P. F. (2000). *Peru: Society and Nationhood in the Andes,* New York; Oxford: Oxford University Press.

___ (1976). *Formación de las Haciendas Azucareras y Orígenes del APRA,* Lima: Instituto de Estudios Peruanos.

Knight, P. T. (1975). 'New Forms of Economic Organization in Peru: Towards Workers' Self-Management', in A. Lowenthal (ed.), *The Peruvian Experiment: Continuity and Change under Military Rule,* Princeton, NJ : Princeton University Press.

Kuramoto, J. (1999). *Las aglomeraciones productivas alrededor de la minería: El caso de la Minera Yanacocha S.A.*, documento de trabajo no. 27, Lima: Grade.

Laitin, D. (1986). *Hegemony and Culture: Politics and Religious Change among the Yoruba,* Chicago: University of Chicago Press.

Lajo, M. (1983). *Alternativa Agraria y Alimentaria: Diagnostico y propuesta para el Perú,* Piura: CIPCA.

Larson, B. (2004). *Trials of Nation Making: Liberalism, Race, and Ethnicity in the Andes, 1810–1910,* Cambridge: Cambridge University Press.

Lavallé, B. (2004). *Les Autorités Indigenes entre Deux Mondes: Solidarité Ethnique et Compromission Coloniales,* París: CRAEC Université de la Sorbonne Nouvelle.

Levitsky, S. (1999). 'Fujimori and Post-Party Politics in Peru', *Journal of Democracy,* vol. 10(3): 78–92.

López, S. (1997). *Ciudadanos Reales e Imaginarios: Concepciones, Desarrollo y Mapas de la Ciudadanía en el Perú,* Lima: Instituto de Diálogo y Propuestas.

Long, N. and Roberts, B. (1978). *Peasant Cooperation and Capitalist Expansion in Central Peru* Austin, TX : Institute of Latin American Studies/University of Texas Press.

Lora, C. (1996). *Creciendo en Dignidad: Movimiento de Comedores Autogestionarios*, Lima: Bartolomé de las Casas.

Lovell, P. A. (1999) 'Development and the Persistence of Racial Inequality in Brazil: 1950–1991', *The Journal of Developing Areas*, vol. 33(3(spring)): 395–418.

Low, A. (1976). *The Effect of Foreign Capital on Peruvian Entrepreneurship*, Doctoral dissertation, University of Oxford.

Lowenthal, A. F. (1975). *The Peruvian Experiment: Continuity and Change under Military Rule*, Princeton, N.J.: Princeton University Press.

Madrid, R. [Forthcoming]. *The Rise of Ethnic Politics in Latin America*, New York: Cambridge University Press.

Mallon, F. (1995). *Peasant and Nation: the Making of Postcolonial Mexico and Peru*. Berkeley, CA: University of California Press.

___ (1992). 'Indian Communities, Political Cultures, and the State in Latin America, 1780–1990', *Journal of Latin American Studies*, vol. 24 (Quincentenary Supplement.): 35–53.

___ (1987). 'Nationalist and Anti-State Coalitions in the War of the Pacific: Junín 1870–1902', in S. Stern (ed.), *Resistance, Rebellion and Consciousness in the Andean Peasant World, 18th–20th Century*, Madison: University of Wisconsin Press, pp. 232–79.

___ (1983). *The Defence of Community in Peru's Central Highland: Peasant Struggle and Capitalist Transition, 1860–1940*, Princeton, NJ: Princeton University Press.

Manrique, N. (2002). *El tiempo del miedo: La violencia política en el Perú, 1980–1996*, Lima: Fondo Editorial del Congreso del Perú.

___ (1988). *Yawar Mayu: Sociedades Terratenientes Serranas, 1879–1910*, Lima: Instituto Francés de Estudios Andinos/DESCO.

___ (1987). *Mercado Interno y Región: La Sierra Central, 1820–1930*, Lima: Centro de Estudios y Promoción del Desarrollo.

___ (1981). *Las Guerrillas Indígenas en la Guerra con Chile*, Lima: Centro de Investigación y Capacitación/Editora Ital Perú.

Matos Mar, J. and. Mejía, J. M. (1980). *Reforma Agraria: Logros y Contradicciones, 1969–1979*, Lima: Instituto de Estudios Peruanos.

Martínez, P. (2004). *La Libertad Femenina de dar Lugar a Dios. Discursos Religiosos del Poder y Formas de Libertad Religiosa desde la Baja Edad Media hasta el Perú Colonial*, Lima: UNMSM/Movimiento Manuela Ramos.

Martínez-Alier, J. (1977). *Haciendas, Plantations, and Collective Farms: Agrarian Class Societies, Cuba and Peru*, London: Frank Cass.

Mayer, E. (2009). *Ugly Stories of the Peruvian Agrarian Reform*, Durham: Duke University Press.

McAdam, D., Tarrow, S. and Tilly, C. (2001). *Dynamics of Contention. Cambridge Studies in Contentious Politics*, Cambridge; New York: Cambridge University Press.

McEvoy, C. (1999). *Forjando la Nación. Ensayos de Historia Republicana*, Lima: Pontificia Universidad Católica del Perú; Sewanee: University of the South.

Mendez M. (1996). 'Incas, Si; Indios, No: Notes on Peruvian Creole Nationalism and its Contemporary Crises', *Journal of Latin American Studies*, vol. 8(1):197–225.

Ministerio de Educación del Perú (2007). 'Factores Asociados al Rendimiento Estudiantil. Resultados de la Evaluación Nacional 2004', mimeo, Lima: Unidad de Medición de la Calidad Educativa.

Molyneux, M. (1985). 'Mobilisation without Emancipation? Women's Interests, the State and Revolution in Nicaragua', reprinted in M. Molyneux (ed.), *Women's Movements in International Perspective: Latin America and Beyond,* London: Palgrave/Institute of Latin American Studies, London University.

Molyneux, M. and Razavi, S. (2002). *Gender Justice, Development and Rights,* Oxford: Oxford University Press.

Montoya, R. (1998). *Multiculturalidad y Política: Derechos Indígenas, Ciudadanos y Humanos,* Lima: SUR, Casa de Estudios del Socialismo.

___ (1992). *Al Borde del Naufragio: Democracia, Violencia y Problema Étnico en el Perú,* Lima: SUR.

___ (1989). *Lucha por la Tierra, Reformas Agrarias y Capitalismo en el Perú del Siglo XX,* Lima: Mosca Azul Editores.

Morner, M. (1980). *Estratificación Social Hispanoamericana durante el Periodo Colonial,* research paper, Stockholm: Institute for Latin American Studies.

Muñoz, I., Paredes, M. and.Thorp, R. (2007). 'Group Inequalities and the Nature and Power of Collective Action: Case Studies from Peru', *World Development,* vol. 35 (11): 1929–1946.

___ and Paredes, M., and Thorp, R. (2006). *Collective Action, Conflict and Ethnicity in Peru,* working paper, no. 24, CRISE, University of Oxford.

Ñopo, H., Saavedra, J. and Torero, M. (2004). 'Ethnicity and Earnings in Urban Peru', discussion paper no. 980, IZA, Bonn: Institute for the Study of Labour.

North, D. C. (1990). *Institutions, Institutional Change, and Economic Performance,* Cambridge; New York: Cambridge University Press.

Nugent, G. (1992). *El Laberinto de la Choledad,* Lima: Fundación Friedrich Ebert.

O'Donnell, G. (1999). 'Delegative Democracy', in O'Donnell, G. (ed.), *Counterpoints: Selected Essays on Authoritarianism and Democratization,* Notre Dame, IN: University of Notre Dame Press.

Oficina Nacional de Procesos Electorales (1998). *Padrón Electoral,* available at: www.onpe.gob.pe.

___ (2001). *Padrón Electoral,* available at: www.onpe.gob.pe.

O'Phelan, S. (1985). *Rebellions and Revolts in Eighteenth Century Peru and Upper Peru,* Köln: Böhlau.

Paredes, M. (2009). *The Making of Weak Indigenous Movements: Peru 1970–1990,* working paper no. forthcoming, CRISE, University of Oxford, available at: www.crise.ox.ac.uk/pubs.shtml.

___ (2007). *Fluid Identities: Exploring Ethnicity in Peru,* working paper no. 40, CRISE, University of Oxford, available at: www.crise.ox.ac.uk/pubs.shtml.

Pegram, T. (2006). *Accounting for the Strength and Survival of the Ombudsman: The Case of the Peruvian 'Defensoría del Pueblo', 1996–2001.* M. Phil dissertation, University of Oxford.

Physicians for Human Rights – PHR (2007). *Deadly Delays: Maternal Mortality in Peru. A rights based approach to safe motherhood,* Washington: PHR.

Pierson, P. (2004). *Politics in Time: History, Institutions, and Social Analysis,* Princeton, NJ: Princeton University Press.

Planas, M. and Valdivia, N. (2007). *Qualitative Report,* unpublished report prepared as part of the project Raising Awareness on the Connections between Race/Ethnicity, Discrimination, Poverty and Health Inequalities in Perú, GRADE/ FASPA and the *Alianza para la Equidad en Salud* (AES), Lima.

Platt, T. (1982). *Estado Boliviano y Ayllu Andino: Tierra y Tributo en el Norte de Potosí*, Lima: Instituto de Estudios Peruanos.

Portocarrero, G. M. (2004). *Rostros Criollos del Mal: Cultura y Transgresión en la Sociedad Peruana*, Lima: Red para el Desarrollo de las Ciencias Sociales en el Perú.

___ (1998) *Razones de Sangre: Aproximaciones a la Violencia Política*, Lima: Pontificia Universidad Católica del Perú.

___ (1993). *Racismo y Mestizaje*, Lima, SUR.

___ (1983). *De Bustamante a Odria. El Fracaso del Frente Democrático Nacional 1945–1950*, Lima: Mosca Azul Editores.

Portocarrero, F. (2006) *Wealth and Philanthropy: The Economic Elite in Peru, 1916–1960*, doctoral dissertation, University of Oxford.

Portugal, A. (2008). *Voices from the War: Exploring the Motivation of Sendero Luminoso Militants*, working paper no. 57, CRISE, University of Oxford, available at: www.crise.ox.ac.uk/pubs.shtml.

Portugal, E. (2004). *Tiempos Nuevos para la Alfabetización en el Perú*, Lima, ITDG/ ODEINS/ CARE-Perú.

Quijano, A. (1980). *Dominación y Cultura: Lo Cholo y el Conflicto Cultural en el Perú*, Lima: Mosca Azul Editores.

Réñique, J. L. (2004). *La Batalla por Puno: Conflicto Agrario y Nación en los Andes Peruanos 1866–1995*, Lima: IEP/SUR/CEPES.

Rivera, I. (1979). *Los Determinantes de la Calidad de la Educación en el Perú. Un Estudio ECIEL*, documento de trabajo no. 44, CISEPA, Departamento de Economía, Pontificia Universidad Católica del Perú.

Roberts, K. (1992). *In Search of a New Identity: Dictatorship, Democracy and the Evolution of the Left in Chile and Peru*, doctoral dissertation, Stanford University.

Rojas, J. (1996). *Las Políticas Comerciales y Cambiarias en el Perú, 1960–1995*, Lima: PUCP.

Rostworowski, M. (1993). *Ensayos de Historia Andina: Élites, Etnías, Recursos*, Lima: IEP/BCRP.

Sala i Vila, N. (1996). *Y Se Armó el Tole Tole. Tributo Indígena y Movimientos Sociales en el Virreinato del Perú, 1784–1814*, Ayacucho: Instituto de Estudios Regionales José María Arguedas.

Samañiego, C. G. (1974). *Local Social and Economic Differentiation and Peasant Movements in the Central Sierra of Peru*, doctoral dissertation, University of Manchester.

Sanborn, C. (1991). *The Democratic Left and the Persistence of Populism in Peru: 1975–1990*, doctoral dissertation, Harvard University.

Sánchez-Albornoz, N. (1974) *The Population in Latin America: A History*, Berkeley, CA: University of California Press.

Santos-Granero, F. and Barclay, F. (2002). *La Frontera Domesticada: Historia Económica y Social de Loreto, 1850–2000*, Lima: Pontificia Universidad Católica del Perú.

Sara-Lafosse, V. (1984). *Los Comedores y la Promoción de la Mujer*, Lima: SUMBI.

Schmidt, G. (1984). *State, Society, and the Policy Process: Planning, Decentralization, and Public Investment in Peru, 1956–1980*, doctoral dissertation, Cornell University.

Schönwälder, G. (2002). *Linking Civil Society and the State: Urban Popular Movements, the Left, and Local Government in Peru, 1980–1992*, University Park, PA: Pennsylvania State University Press.

Searle, J. (1995). *The Construction of Social Reality,* New York: The Free Press.

Sen, A. (2006). *Identity and Violence: The Illusion of Destiny,* New York: W.W. Norton and Co.

Serulnikov, S. (2006). *Conflictos Sociales e Insurrección en el Mundo Andino. El Norte de Potosí en el siglo XVIII,* Buenos Aires: Fondo de Cultura Económica.

Silva N.V. (1992). *Racial Discrimination in Income,* conference paper presented at the International Seminar 'Labor Market Roots of Poverty and Inequality', Aug 12–14, Rio de Janeiro.

Silverblatt, I. (1987). *Moon, Sun, and Witches: Gender Ideologies and Class in Inca and Colonial Peru,* Princeton, NJ: Princeton University Press.

Sinamos (1976). *Vanguardia Revolucionaria. Reseña Histórica, Concepciones Políticas y Lineamientos Estratégicos de VR, VR-proletario y PCR,* Lima, Sinamos.

Spalding, K. (1984). *Huarochiri: An Andean Society under Inca and Spanish Rule,* Stanford: Stanford University Press.

Starn, O. (1999). 'I dreamed of Foxes and Hawks: Reflections on Peasant Protests, New Social Movements and the Rondas Campesinas of Northern Peru', in Escobar, A. and Alvarez, S.(eds), *The Making of Social Movements in Latin America: Identity, Strategy and Democracy,* Boulder, CO: Westview Press

Starn, O., Degregori, C. and Kirk, R. (1995). *The Peru Reader: History, Culture, Politics,* Durham, NC: Duke University Press.

Stavig, W. (1999). *The World of Tupac Amaru. Conflicts, Community and Identity in Colonial Peru,* Lincoln: University of Nebraska Press.

Stein, W. (1988). *Levantamiento de Atusparia: El Movimiento Popular Ancashino de 1885: Un Estudio de Documentos.* Translated by Jessica McLauchlan, Lima: Mosca Azul Editores.

Stern, S. J. (1998). *Shining and Other Paths: War and Society in Peru, 1980–1995,* Durham, NC: Duke University Press.

___ (1993). *Peru's Indian Peoples and the Challenge of Spanish Conquest: Huamanga to 1640,* Madison,WI: University of Wisconsin Press.

___ (1987). *Resistance, Rebellion, and Consciousness in the Andean Peasant World, 18th to 20th Centuries,* Madison, WI.: University of Wisconsin.

Stewart, F. (2008). *Horizontal Inequalities and Conflict: Understanding Group Violence in Multiethnic Societies,* Basingstoke; New York: Palgrave Macmillan.

Sulmont, D. (2010) 'Race, ethnicity, and political action in Peru', unpublished, forthcoming as working paper on CRISE web site.

Sulmont, D. (2006). *Race, Ethnicity and Political Action in Peru: An Analysis of the 2005 CRISE Perceptions Survey in Peru,* conference Paper, Latin America Workshop, CRISE, Oxford University, Santa Cruz de la Sierra, September 18–20, available at: www.crise.ox.ac.uk/workshops.shtml#latam.

Szeminski, J. (1987). 'Why Kill the Spaniards? New Perspectives on Andean Insurrectionary Ideology in the 18th Century', in S. Stern (ed.), *Resistance, Rebellion and Consciousness in the Andean Peasant World, 18th to 20th Centuries,* Madison, WI: University of Wisconsin Press.

Tamayo, G. and Francke P. (1997). *Análisis del Gasto Público en Salud,* conference paper, Seminario de Modernización del Sistema de Financiamiento de Salud. Lima: Ministerio de Salud del Perú.

Tanaka, M. and Trivelli. C. (2002). *Focalización y la Participación. Pobreza y Políticas Sociales en el Perú durante la Década de Fujimori,* documento de trabajo no. 121, Serie de Sociología y Política 35, Lima: Instituto de Estudios Peruanos.

Tanaka, M. (1998). *Espejismos de la Democracia. El Colapso del Sistema de Partidos en el Perú en Perspectiva Comparada, 1980–1995,* Lima: Instituto de Estudios Peruanos.

Tandeter, E. (1992). *Coacción y Mercado. La Minería de la Plata en el Potosí Colonial, 1692–1826,* Cuzco: Bartolomé de Las Casas.

Tarrow, S. (1994). *Power in Movement: Social Movements, Collective Action, and Politics,* Cambridge [England]; New York: Cambridge University Press.

___ (1983). *Struggling to Reform: Social Movements and Policy Change during Cycles of Protest,* Ithaca, NY: Center for International Studies, Cornell University.

Thelen, K. (2003). 'How Institutions Evolve: Insights from Comparative Historical Analysis', in J. Mahoney *et al.* (eds), *Comparative Historical Analysis in the Social Sciences,* New York: Cambridge University Press. pp. 208–40.

Thomson, S. (2002). *We Alone Will Rule: Native Andean Politics in the Age of Insurgency,* Madison; London: University of Wisconsin Press.

Thorp, R. (2010). 'Acción colectiva y exclusiones sobrepuestas en un mundo Sigma', in Jiménez,F. (ed.), *Teoría Económica y Desarrollo Social: Exclusión, desigualdad y democraia, Homenaje a Adolfo Figueroa,* Lima, Fondo Editorial, Pontificia Universidad Católica del Perú.

Thorp, R. (2000). *Has the Coffee Federation become Redundant: Collective Action and the Market in Colombian Development,* Helsinki: UNU/World Institute for Development Economics Research.

___ (1998) *Progress, Poverty and Exclusion: An Economic History of Latin America in the 20th Century,* Johns Hopkins, Inter-American Development Bank and the European Union, Washington and Baltimore.

___ (1991) *Economic Management and Economic Development in Peru and Colombia,* London: Macmillan.

___ and Bertram, G. (1978). *Peru, 1890–1977: Growth and Policy in an Open Economy,* London: Macmillan.

Thorp, R. and Zevallos, G. (2002). 'The Economic Policies of The Fujimori Years: A Return To The Past?', working paper no. 83, Queen Elizabeth House, University of Oxford.

Thurner, M. (1997). *From Two Republics to One Divided: Contradictions of Postcolonial Nation making in Andean Peru,* Durham, NC; London: Duke University Press.

Trivelli, C. (2005). *Los Hogares Indígenas y la Pobreza en el Perú . Una Mirada a Partir de la Información Cuantitativa,* documento de trabajo n° 141, Serie de Economía 41, Lima: Instituto de Estudios Peruanos.

Tuesta, F. (1994). *Perú Político en Cifras: 1821–2001,* Lima: Fundación Friedrich Ebert.

Tullis, F. L. (1970). *Lord and Peasant in Peru: a Paradigm of Political and Social Change,* Cambridge Mass.: Harvard University Press.

UNDP-Perú. (2005). *La Democracia en el Perú,* Vol. 1, report available at: www.pnud.org.pe/frmPubDetail.aspx?id=41.

Van Cott, D. L. (2005). *From Movements to Parties in Latin America: The Evolution of Ethnic politics,* New York; Cambridge: Cambridge University Press.

___ (2000). *The Friendly Liquidation of the Past: The Politics of Diversity in Latin America,* Pittsburgh, PA: University of Pittsburgh Press.

___ (1994). *Indigenous Peoples and Democracy in Latin America,* New York: St Martin's Press in association with the Inter-American Dialogue.

Van de Berghe, P. (1981). *The Ethnic Phenomenon,* New York: Elsevier.

Vargas Llosa, M. (1990). *Question of Conquest. What Columbus Wrought, and What He Did Not*, Harper's Magazine.

Vasquez, E. and Riesco, E. (2000). 'Los programas sociales que 'alimentan' a medio Perú', in F. Portocarrero (ed.), *Políticas Sociales en el Perú, nuevos aportes*, Lima: CIUP/*Red para el Desarrollo de las Ciencias Sociales en el Perú*, pp. 89–152.

Walker, C. H. (1999). *Smoldering Ashes. Cuzco and the Creation of Republican Peru 1780–1840*, Durham, NC: Duke University Press.

Webb, R. (1974). *Government Policy and the Distribution of Income in Peru 1963–1973*, doctoral dissertation, Harvard University.

___ and Figueroa, A. (1975). *Distribución del Ingreso en el Perú*, Lima: Instituto de Estudios Peruanos.

Yashar, D. (2005). *Contesting Citizenship in Latin America. The Rise of Indigenous Movements and the Post Liberal Challenge*, New York: Cambridge University Press.

Yrigoyen, R. (2002). 'Rondas Campesinas y Pluralismo Legal: Necesidad de Reconocimiento Constitucional y Desarrollo Legislativo hacia una Ley de Rondas Campesinas', in *Defensoría del Pueblo*: *Hacia una ley de Rondas Campesinas*, Lima: Defensoría del Pueblo.

Zarzar, A. (1991). 'Las Rondas Campesinas de Cajamarca: de la autodefensa al autogobierno?', in Pasara, L. (ed.), *La Otra Cara de la Luna: Nuevos Actores Sociales en el Perú*. Buenos Aires, CEDYS.

Index